Islamic Law in Saudi Arabia

Studies in Islamic Law and Society

VOLUME 56

The titles published in this series are listed at *brill.com/sils*

Islamic Law in Saudi Arabia

By

Dominik Krell

BRILL

LEIDEN | BOSTON

Open Access funding provided by Max Planck Society.

Library of Congress Cataloging-in-Publication Data

Names: Krell, Dominik, author.
Title: Islamic law in Saudi Arabia / by Dominik Krell.
Description: Leiden ; Boston : Brill, 2025. | Series: Studies in islamic law and society, 1384-1130 ; volume 56 | Includes bibliographical references and index.
Identifiers: LCCN 2024059065 (print) | LCCN 2024059066 (ebook) | ISBN 9789004683280 (hardback) | ISBN 9789004726314 (ebook)
Subjects: LCSH: Islamic law—Saudi Arabia. | Wahhābīyah—Saudi Arabia. | Ijtihād (Islamic law)
Classification: LCC KBP285 .K74 2025 (print) | LCC KBP285 (ebook) | DDC 349.538—dc23/eng/20241212
LC record available at https://lccn.loc.gov/2024059065
LC ebook record available at https://lccn.loc.gov/2024059066

Typeface for the Latin, Greek, and Cyrillic scripts: "Brill". See and download: brill.com/brill-typeface.

ISSN 1384-1130
ISBN 978-90-04-68328-0 (hardback)
ISBN 978-90-04-72631-4 (e-book)
DOI 10.1163/9789004726314

This book is printed on acid-free paper and produced in a sustainable manner.

Contents

Acknowledgements

This book would not have been possible without the support of so many great people over the course of the last years, too many to name all. First and foremost, I want to thank Nadjma Yassari, who encouraged, supported, and inspired me in both good and bad times. I am very grateful to the Max Planck Institute for Comparative and International Private Law in Hamburg, its always helpful staff, and the rest of the *Hamburger Schule* for their support, valuable feedback, and endless conversations on Islamic law and jurisprudence: Lena-Maria Möller, Tess Chemnitzer, Dörthe Engelcke, Shéhérazade Elyazidi, Sina Torshizi, Khashayar Biria, and Hendrik Brecht. Lauan al-Khazail proved to be an excellent partner for discussing the ideas of Ibn Taymiyya and Ibn al-Qayyim, while my debates on Arabic legal terms with Mustafa Mohammad were of great help for my translations.

I want to thank all of my interview partners, who took their valuable time to explain their ideas, understandings, and practices of Islamic law to an outsider. I was always, with no exception, received with great hospitality, respect, and patience. My thanks also go to the King Faisal Center for Research and Islamic Studies (KFCRIS) and its staff in Riyadh, who kindly offered me a place to work and opened many doors for me in Saudi Arabia. I want to especially thank Majed bin Khunein, who tirelessly used all possible ways to put me in contact with Saudi jurists. I also want to express my gratitude to Sarah al-Dajani, who over the years shared her insights into the Saudi legal system with me and guided me through its complex structure. I am deeply indebted to Jan Krauser, without whom my fieldwork would not have been possible, who spontaneously offered me a place to stay in Riyadh, and with whom I shared many wonderful experiences.

Furthermore, I was lucky to receive great feedback from the academic community at conferences and in private conversations. I want to especially thank Rob Gleave for his support. I am deeply indebted to Frank Vogel. His groundbreaking work has paved the way for all further research on law in Saudi Arabia.

Last but not least, I want to thank Nina and my parents for their love and support.

Map

Saudi Arabia

On the Translations, the Transliteration, and the Calendar

1 A Note on the Translations

All translations, except if stated otherwise, are my own. Hence, all mistakes are also entirely mine. The translation of legal Arabic into English necessarily means a loss of accuracy since many terms or references do not have a direct English equivalent. To compensate for the loss of accuracy, I have added Arabic transliterations for many important technical legal terms and have used footnotes to explain any references an author makes to the Quran, the Sunna, or other *fiqh* books. For better readability, I have excluded eulogies, like *ṣalla Allāhu ʿalayhi wa-sallam* for the Prophet or *ʿazza wa-jall* for God, from the translations.

2 The Transliteration of Arabic Names

Arabic transliteration follows the standard established by the *International Journal of Middle Eastern Studies* (IJMES). Arabic words frequently used in English, like Quran, caliph, or sultan, are not transliterated. Likewise, the names of commonly known cities, such as Riyadh, Mecca, Medina, Dammam, or Jeddah, are not given in transliteration.

When referring to contemporary Saudi authors, I use the common naming system in Saudi Arabia, which includes the first name, the father's first name, and the family name (first name – father's name – last name). Saudi jurists are often members of large scholarly families. To know the father's name makes it easier to identify the author properly. When I cite non-Saudi writings, I only state the author's first and family name since legal publications outside of Saudi Arabia usually do not include the name of the author's father.

When it comes to premodern scholars, I refer to the name under which they are commonly known in contemporary Islamic jurisprudence, even if that name differs from their given name. For instance, I refer to Ibn al-Qayyim ("the son of the principal"[1]) instead of giving his full name, Shams al-Dīn Abī

1 His contemporaries, however, called him Ibn Qayyim al-Jawziyya in order to indicate that his father was the principal of the Ḥanbalī college al-Jawziyya in Damascus. See Catharina Bori and Livnat Holtzman, "A Scholar in the Shadow," Oriente Moderno 90 (1): 13, n. 1. We will discuss Ibn al-Qayyim's life and work in more detail in the first chapter.

ʿAbd Allāh Muḥammad bin Abī Bakr al-Zurʿī al-Dimashqī. For contemporary Arab authors who write in English, I use the transliteration they have chosen for their names.

3 The Two Calendars

For reasons of readability, I have deliberately refrained from using the Islamic Hijrī calendar throughout the text, even though it is the official calendar of the Saudi judiciary and Saudi legal writings generally only refer to Hijrī dates. Whenever an author provided a specific date in the Hijrī calendar, I converted it into the Gregorian calendar. However, whenever an author referred to a Hijrī year without specifying a day or a month, I estimated the Gregorian year based on the context. In the bibliography, I listed the year of publication in both calendars since this makes it easier to find and identify Arabic legal literature.

Introduction

Despite Muhammad bin Salman's reformist politics, Islamic jurists (*ʿulamāʾ*) continue to shape political and social life in Saudi Arabia. At the heart of this lies the legal system, which remains a stronghold of the religious establishment. While the vast majority of Muslim countries have adopted either a civil law or common law system, Saudi Arabia claims to maintain an Islamic legal system. This extends beyond simply applying Islamic law as a set of norms but encompasses a comprehensive Islamic understanding of the entire legal system.

Over the past two decades, the Saudi judiciary has experienced its most significant transformation in history: Islamic law has been partly codified, the court system has been expanded, and digital technology has been introduced to the courts. The aim of these reforms is to make the judiciary more efficient, professional, and transparent. While the recent reforms have increased the government's influence on Islamic law, the ʿulamāʾ continue to maintain their control of the legal system.

In this book, I provide an in-depth exploration of the workings of the Saudi legal system in order to offer a better understanding of these developments. I use the perspective of the judiciary's main protagonists, the ʿulamāʾ, to explore how Islamic law is understood and applied in Saudi Arabia today. I address two main questions: First, what is the jurists' understanding of an Islamic legal system? And second, how is this understanding reflected in the Saudi legal system, its laws, its institutions, and the courts' practice? The book focuses on family and criminal law, the most controversial areas of Islamic law in Saudi Arabia today, and covers the developments from the 1980s up to the codification of Islamic family law in 2022.

The jurists' discursive interaction with the Islamic legal tradition is a promising starting point for exploring the Saudi legal system because it is how the jurists understand the law themselves. From the perspective of Saudi ʿulamāʾ, there is no "Saudi law" (*qānūn Saʿūdī*), despite the recent codifications. Instead, the jurists see themselves as part of a global effort to understand the divine rulings, which are not restricted or connected to one nation-state. This is reflected in their writings: even though Saudi scholars and judges publish extensively today, only very few books explicitly mention Saudi Arabia in their titles. Whereas some scholars add a short chapter that discusses their topic in the context of the Saudi legal system, most books and articles only refer to supranational Islamic law.

DOI:10.1163/9789004726314_002

There is also another advantage of such an approach. By situating the Saudi legal discourse in the Islamic tradition, it is possible to overcome some of the binary oppositions that underlie many descriptions of the Saudi legal system: "modern" versus "archaic," "normal" versus "exceptional," "progressive" versus "traditional," and "liberal" versus "conservative."

1 Islamic Law as a Discursive Tradition

The understanding of Islamic law as a discursive tradition is informed by Talal Asad's work. Although Asad's approach has been fruitfully employed by anthropologists, sociologists, and historians of Islam, it has so far found little resonance among scholars of Islamic law. Asad argued that inquiries of Islam "should begin, as Muslims do, from the concept of a discursive tradition that includes and relates itself to the founding texts of the Quran and the Hadith."[1] By using the notion of a discursive tradition, Asad criticised scholarly understandings of Islam as a fixed set of rules and beliefs. Instead, Asad's approach puts the focus on the intellectual and applied practices of Islam.

His understanding of Islam was animated by a rethinking of the idea of tradition in the social sciences. From the 1980s onwards, Alasdair MacIntyre and others forwarded the idea that a tradition should not be seen as a set of timeless doctrinal or cultural givens, as it is commonly understood, but as a manifestation of the historicity of human practices and institutions.[2] Inspired by MacIntyre's approach, Asad defined a discursive tradition as follows:

> A tradition consists essentially of discourses that seek to instruct practitioners regarding the correct form and purpose of a given practice that, precisely because it is established, has a history. These discourses relate conceptually to a past (when the practice was instituted, and from which the knowledge of its point and proper performance has been transmitted) and a future (how the point of that practice can best be secured in the short or long term, or why it should be modified or abandoned), through a present (how it is linked to other practices, institutions, and social conditions). An Islamic discursive tradition is simply a tradition of Muslim discourse that addresses itself to conceptions of the Islamic past

1 Talal Asad, "The Idea of an Anthropology of Islam," *Qui Parle* 17, no. 2 (2009): 20.

2 See, for instance, Jerome Schneewind, "MacIntyre and the Indispensability of Tradition," *Philosophy and Phenomenological Research* 51, no. 1 (1991): 165–68.

> and future, with reference to a particular Islamic practice in the present. Clearly, not everything Muslims say and do belongs to an Islamic discursive tradition. Nor is an Islamic tradition in this sense necessarily imitative of what was done in the past.[3]

The notion of Islam as a discursive tradition comprises both doctrine and practice. Asad highlighted that both are interconnected since it is doctrine that authorises certain practices as Islamic. Doctrine, on the other hand, is not fixed but constantly negotiated. "The Islamic discursive tradition," Ovamir Anjum noted, "is characterised by its own rationality or styles of reasoning – couched in its texts, history, and institutions."[4] Hence, understanding Islamic law as a discursive tradition shifts the lens from a mere description of the Saudi jurists' doctrine to their use of Islamic jurisprudence, which forms the basis for their conceptions of the law.

Furthermore, the notion of Islam as a discursive tradition allows us to escape the dichotomy between "classical" and "modern" Islamic law that is still popular among scholars of Islam.[5] Asad reminds us that legal arguments, even if they are derived from a distant past, are always part of the tradition's present. The styles of reasoning, of course, differ over time.

Similarly, there cannot be a misinterpretation of the legal tradition from this perspective, nor can a tradition be inauthentic, since such an understanding would imply a fixed Islamic doctrine that is transmitted unchanged through time.[6] Like other traditions, Islam is continuously developing and always changing. Asad wrote:

> Talking of tradition ('Islamic tradition') as though it was the passing on of an unchanging substance in homogeneous time oversimplifies the problem of time's definition, experience, and event. Questions about the internal temporal structure of tradition are obscured if we represent it as the inheritance of an unchanging cultural substance from the past – as though 'past' and 'present' were places in a linear path down which that object was conveyed to the 'future'.[7]

---

3 Asad, "Idea of an Anthropology," 20.

4 Ovamir Anjum, "Islam as a Discursive Tradition: Talal Asad and His Interlocutors," *Comparative Studies of South Asia, Africa and the Middle East* 27, no. 3 (2007): 662.

5 See Asad, "Idea of an Anthropology," 21.

6 Anjum, "Islam as a Discursive Tradition," 671.

7 Talal Asad, *Formations of the Secular* (Stanford: Stanford University Press, 2003), 222.

To understand law, law-making, or legal interpretation as a tradition is not per se a new approach.[8] For instance, Niklas Luhmann noted that "law never has to 'begin'."[9] Every legal act, Luhmann claimed, could "join traditions as they are found."[10] In an influential article, Martin Krygier criticised that Western legal theorists would mostly understand law as a time-free instrument of regulation and would thereby ignore the role of references to the past made in judicial reasoning.[11] Instead, Krygier demanded, legal theorists should acknowledge law's traditionality and analyse the reasons why specific rules and practices have developed.[12] According to Krygier, the past plays a role in every legal argument, either explicitly or through the jurists' education, and hence, the tradition would always be inescapable. Every examination of the law, Krygier argued, should thus acknowledge law's traditionality.[13]

Understanding Islamic law as a *discursive* tradition does not mean simply adding the jurists' use of the past to the analysis but placing the jurists' connection of legal ideas through time in the center of the scholarly inquiry.[14] In the Saudi legal discourse, the way in which the jurists use the Sunni schools of Islamic jurisprudence (*madhāhib*, sing. *madhhab*) defines their legal reasoning. The madhāhib, most importantly the Ḥanbalī, the Mālikī, the Shāfiʿī, and the Ḥanafī schools, represent the established scholarship on Islamic law that forms the traditional understanding of fiqh.[15] Although the Quran and the Sunna constitute the starting point for every legal argument, legal reasoning in Saudi Arabia mainly consists of the evaluation of the schools' opinions on a specific issue. Most, but not all, legal reasoning takes place through the process of weighing (*tarjīḥ*) between already established opinions.

Samira Haj pointed out that Islamic jurists do not merely repeat the past but seek "rational coherence by making reference to a set of texts, procedures,

8 Nor is it a new approach to describe other human practices as traditions. Social theorists like Edward Shils have published extensively on the concept of tradition. See for an overview of Shils' ideas Struan Jacobs, "Edward Shils' Theory of Tradition," *Philosophy of the Social Sciences* 37, no. 2 (2007): 139–62.

9 Niklas Luhmann, *Law as a Social System* (Oxford: Oxford University Press, 2004), 153.

10 Ibid.

11 Martin Krygier, "Law as Tradition," *Law and Philosophy* 5, no. 2 (1986), 239.

12 Ibid., 243.

13 Ibid., 255.

14 As Krygier pointed out, legal theorists rarely make new discoveries about the law, but "focus attention on what was already familiar, frequently so familiar as to escape notice altogether." See Ibid., 238.

15 See for more information on the schools of Islamic jurisprudence Wael Hallaq, *An Introduction to Islamic Law* (Cambridge: Cambridge University Press, 2009) 31–37.

arguments and practices."[16] Like in any other tradition, the past in the Islamic legal tradition is not univocal. It consists of various voices that have been filtered through the transmission of knowledge or might even have been invented. Saudi jurists, as we will see throughout the book, accept pluralism as a natural element of Islamic law, through which they navigate. Pluralism enables them to adapt their doctrine to social, political, and technological developments.

At the heart of Asad's conception of Islam as a discursive tradition lies the idea of orthodoxy. For him, orthodoxy is not a particular set of beliefs, as it is commonly understood, but "the relationship between power and truth."[17] It is power, Asad argued, through which the "correct" Islamic understanding is established.[18] Hence, orthodoxy in the Saudi legal discourse is represented by those in power, namely leading scholars, influential judges, lawyers, and the Ministry of Justice as representatives of the Saudi king. However, political power alone is not sufficient in order to represent orthodoxy in the legal discourse. Every tradition provides its participants with a language through which they have to address the past. Only by using this language are participants admitted to the discourse. In the case of the Saudi legal discourse, this language consists most notably of the established methods of Islamic jurisprudence, the mastery of legal Arabic, and, more generally, the specific habitus of a trained Islamic jurist.

The focus of this book lies on Saudi orthodoxy, and thus on those in power – a distinct group of people, mostly influential scholars and judges – and explores their use of the legal discourse's language. This means that the book cannot represent the marginalized since those who either are not in power or cannot express their ideas through the discourse's complex language are not visible in the legal discourse. This includes Shia scholars, who are until now not represented in the legal system,[19] but also leads to an underrepresentation of female voices.

The Saudi legal discourse is still male-dominated. Although women are today admitted as lawyers, their opinions are still not considered authoritative. Of course, this does not mean that women do not utter legal opinions or demand legal reforms. Their struggle to be heard, however, is beyond the scope of this book.

---

16 Samira Haj, "Reordering Islamic Orthodoxy: Muḥammad ibn ʿAbdul Wahhāb," *The Muslim World* 92, no. 3/4 (2002): 336.

17 Asad, "Idea of an Anthropology," 22.

18 See also Saba Mahmood, *Politics of Piety: The Islamic Revival and the Feminist Subject* (Princeton: Princeton University Press, 2005), 116.

19 Anjum, "Islam as a Discursive Tradition," 671.

2 The Legal Discourse's Main Actors

The Islamic jurists, the ʿulamāʾ, form the backbone of the Saudi legal system.[20] Although most ʿulamāʾ publicly wear the same outfit – unlike other Saudis, they usually do not wear the traditional *ʿaqāl* – they are a diverse group and only share one common feature: their education in Islamic jurisprudence. Saudi ʿulamāʾ today have different ethnic and social backgrounds, although most jurists come from Central Arabia, especially from the Najd region. Whereas some ʿulamāʾ additionally hold degrees from foreign universities, others are deeply rooted in the Saudi tradition of Islamic jurisprudence.

For Western scholars, it is easy to idealise and exoticise the ʿulamāʾ. Until today, they describe themselves as the heirs of the Prophet and the guardians of faith. The Prophet supposedly said that "the scholar is superior to the regular believer like the full moon is superior to the rest of the planets."[21] Yet, the role of many ʿulamāʾ in the Saudi legal system is not always that glamorous. Like jurists in other countries, they work to maintain a functioning legal system that answers the complex demands of modern life. The everyday routine at Saudi courts, the president of the General Court in Riyadh, Nāyif bin Aḥmad al-Ḥamd, complained, would often be disconnected from the leading scholars' idealist description. "We have come to a different place," new judges would say when they arrived at his court after their training at the Higher Judicial Institute (al-Maʿhad al-ʿĀlī li-l-Qaḍāʾ). At court, al-Ḥamd reminded other ʿulamāʾ at a conference, people would show their emotions, cry, shout, lie, and cheat, an aspect that would be absent from the elitist legal debates.[22]

Even though it has become more difficult for Islamic scholars to express their opinions due to the increasingly imposed restrictions on freedom of speech, there is still considerable divergence of opinions in the legal discourse. One could say that there is a general rule: If an opinion is accepted in the Islamic tradition, it is generally safe to discuss it. Roughly speaking, the Saudi legal discourse consists of four different ideal types (in the Weberian sense):

---

20 Whereas in the context of the Saudi judiciary, *ʿulamāʾ* refers to Islamic scholars, the term is used in other contexts to describe scholars more generally.

21 Abū Dāwūd, *Sunan Abī Dāwūd* (Damascus: Dār al-Risāla al-ʿĀlamiyya, 1430/2009), 5:485 (No. 3641).

22 Lecture by Nāyif bin Aḥmad al-Ḥamd at the conference "Intiqāl Ḥaqq al-Ḥaḍāna fī Ḍawʾ Mutaghayyirāt al-ʿAṣr" (Transferring the Right to Custody in the Light of the Changes of the Century) at the Imām Muḥammad bin Saʿūd Islamic University in Riyadh on the 23.10.1433/10.9.2012. A recording of the conference is available on YouTube, www.youtube.com/watch?v=K8HOgry1j–s, min 31 [last access: 30 June 2020].

independent scholars, judges, lawyers, and jurists associated with the Ministry of Justice.

An independent scholar is a jurist who does not practice the law and is, therefore, relatively independent from the constraints of daily life in the Saudi judiciary.[23] A good example of an independent scholar is ʿAbd Allāh bin Muḥammad Āl Khunayn, who is arguably the leading Saudi jurist specialized in the Islamic judiciary (*qaḍāʾ*) today. Nevertheless, not only scholars who specialize in the legal system influence the way the law is understood in the Saudi legal system. Saʿd bin Nāṣir al-Shithrī, for example, another eminent contemporary Saudi scholar, specializes in Islamic legal theory (*uṣūl al-fiqh*) but also writes about issues that directly concern the Saudi judiciary.

To some extent, the role of most independent scholars resembles that of law professors in Western legal systems. Ibn Khunayn, for example, trains judges at the Higher Judicial Institute, and al-Shithrī teaches Islamic jurisprudence at several Saudi universities. In addition to their teaching appointments, independent scholars usually lecture in mosques, appear in television programs, answer fatwa requests, and publish books. Typically, independent scholars are members of influential families from the central region of Saudi Arabia, the Najd. The Khunayn family, for example, originates from the small town of Dilam south of Riyadh. Saʿd al-Shithrī's family has its roots in the Aflāj region, also in the southern Najd, and belongs to the powerful al-Qaḥṭānī tribe.[24] Other respected scholarly families come from the Qaṣīm area in the northern Najd.

Typically, the fathers and grandfathers of influential contemporary scholars have already been part of the scholarly establishment. Saʿd al-Shithrī's father, for example, Nāṣir bin ʿAbd al-ʿAzīz, was a trained Islamic jurist and powerful adviser to Saudi kings, most notably to King Khālid.[25] ʿAbd Allāh bin Muḥammad bin Khunayn is related to Rashīd bin Ṣāliḥ bin Khunayn, a famous scholar as well an adviser at the king's court. It is important to note that scholarly families should not be reduced to their religious representatives. Today, members of these families work in various sectors not at all related to Islam. Turkī Āl al-Shaykh, for example, a member of the most influential scholarly family, the al-Shaykhs, is a renowned sponsor of Saudi football, who

23 The ideal type of a Saudi independent scholar today to some degree resembles Wael Hallaq's concept of the author-jurist in premodern Islamic law. Hallaq distinguished between author-jurists, who compiled law manuals and theoretical treatises, and judges and muftis, who applied the law based on the author-jurists' writings. See Hallaq, "Introduction to Islamic Law," 11.

24 Muḥammad bin Nāṣir Al-Shithrī, *Āl al-Shithrī: ʿUlamāʾuhum wa-tārīkhuhum* (Riyadh: Dār al-Ḥabīb, 1430/2009), 63.

25 Ibid., 10.

was in 2016 appointed as the head of the controversial General Authority for Entertainment (al-Hayʾa al-ʿĀmma li-l-Tarfīh).[26]

Many independent scholars had worked in the judiciary before they focused on writing and teaching. For example, the former Grand Mufti Ibn Bāz served for twelve years as a judge in al-Kharj, a smaller city south of Riyadh.[27] Likewise, Ibn Khunayn had a long career in the judiciary. Before dedicating himself purely to writing and teaching, he served as a judge at the Riyadh Court of Appeal.[28]

Like other famous independent scholars, Ibn Khunayn and Saʿd al-Shithrī are members of the Council of Senior Scholars (Hayʾat Kibār al-ʿUlamāʾ), which is beside the Grand Mufti (Muftī al-ʿAmm), the kingdom's highest religious authority. The Council consists of a varying number of famous scholars, whom the king appoints, and is headed by the Grand Mufti.[29] Although the Council is funded by the Saudi king, it has in the past regularly disagreed with the king's plans and policies. In the context of the Saudi judiciary, one of the major issues in which the Council refused the king's policy was the question of codification.[30]

Like the Council, the Grand Mufti is a powerful institution. In practice, his authority largely depends on his charisma. Whereas the first two Grand Muftis, Muḥammad bin Ibrāhīm Āl al-Shaykh (d. 1969) and ʿAbd al-ʿAzīz bin ʿAbd Allāh bin Bāz (d. 1999), both were charismatic figures who are still regularly cited in Saudi legal writings, the current Grand Mufti, ʿAbd al-ʿAzīz bin ʿAbd Allāh Āl al-Shaykh, is less visible.[31] Besides the Grand Mufti and the Council of Senior Scholars, the Permanent Committee for Scholarly Research and Counselling (al-Lajna al-Dāʾima li-l-Buḥūth al-ʿIlmiyya wa-l-Iftāʾ) is the third main religious body in the kingdom. It consists of a small number of the Council's most

26 See www.english.alarabiya.net/en/life-style/entertainment/2018/12/27/Turki-al-Sheikh-new-Chairman-of-the-General-Authority-for-Entertainment [last access: 30 June 2022].

27 ʿAbd al-ʿAzīz bin ʿAbd Allāh Ibn Bāz, *Majmūʿ fatāwā wa-maqālāt mutanawwiʿa* (Riyadh: Dār al-Qāsim, 1420/1999), 1:10.

28 Ibn Khunayn spoke about his experiences in the judiciary in a lecture at the Saudi Association of the Judiciary (al-Jamaʿiyya al-ʿIlmiyya al-Qaḍāʾiyya). The recorded lecture can be found on YouTube, www.youtube.com/watch?v=Wa1PTeitSrQ [last access: 26 May 2022].

29 See Muhammad Al-Atawneh, *Wahhabi Islam Facing the Challenges of Modernity: Dār al-Iftā in the Modern Saudi State* (Leiden: Brill, 2010), 18.

30 In chapter 4, we will discuss the Council's decision and its main arguments in detail.

31 I have never seen ʿAbd al-ʿAzīz bin ʿAbd Allāh Āl al-Shaykh cited in any court judgements or legal writings. Frank Vogel shares this observation. See Frank Vogel, *Saudi Business Law in Practice: Laws and Regulations as Applied in the Courts and Judicial Committees of Saudi Arabia* (Oxford: Hart, 2019), 94.

respected scholars – for example, Ibn Khunayn is a former member – who prepare research papers for the Council's discussions and issue fatwas. Like the Council, the Permanent Committee is headed by the Grand Mufti and currently consists of only six members.

The second group of main actors in the legal discourse are the judges. Like most independent scholars, the ideal-typical Saudi judge comes from a respectable family, ideally from the Najd. He – women are still not admitted to judgeship – will have successfully studied Islamic jurisprudence and then transferred to the Higher Judicial Institute at Riyadh's Imām University. The judges typically earn a master's degree in Islamic jurisprudence, and some judges then join the Institute's PhD program. Non-Saudis are not admitted as judges, but foreign degrees in Islamic jurisprudence are recognized. Due to an extension of the court system in recent years, the Saudi government has appointed a large number of recent graduates as judges.

Generally, judges show their adherence to the group of the ʿulamāʾ by not wearing the traditional ʿaqāl. Even though they share a similar education, the judges, as we will see in the coming chapters, differ in their views considerably. Some Saudi judges additionally follow a career as preachers. For example, one judge from Dammam publishes on questions of family law and the Islamic judiciary and also holds public lectures in mosques, where he talks about questions of daily life and explains the Quran. The strong connection between ʿulamāʾ in different fields of religious life is very present, and some ʿulamāʾ even move between judicial and religious positions. For instance, Ṣāliḥ bin ʿAbd Allāh bin Ḥumayd served as head of the Higher Judicial Council (al-Majlis al-Aʿlā li-l-Qaḍāʾ) before he became imām at the Great Mosque in Mecca (al-Masjid al-Ḥarām).[32]

Thirdly, lawyers play an increasingly important role in the Saudi legal discourse. They are a relatively new phenomenon in Saudi Arabia. Although premodern scholars already allowed that parties are represented in court, Saudi Arabia did not have a formal framework that regulates the work of professional lawyers until 2002.[33] Today, lawyers form a heterogeneous group, including former judges, trained Islamic scholars, and jurists without any background in Islamic jurisprudence, although a formal degree in law is required.[34] Some identify as ʿulamāʾ by not wearing the traditional ʿaqāl, whereas others choose traditional Saudi dress or even wear Western-style clothes. Saudi universities

---

32 See Ibn Ḥumayd's website, www.ibnhomaid.af.org.sa [last access: 21 March 2023].

33 These were introduced by the 1422/2002 Code of Lawyering (Niẓām al-Muḥāmā).

34 Lawyers are required to register with the government and must hold a degree either in Islamic law or in the king's laws. See Article 3 of the Code of Lawyering.

have in the last decades started to offer degree programs in law, which focus on the codes issued by the king. The students take courses in civil and common law methodology, arbitration, international private law, and similar topics.[35]

In recent years, the number of female lawyers has been rising. Today, they are a natural part of the Saudi legal system and are increasingly respected by the judges. Since women are not admitted to the Higher Judicial Institute, many are educated in the king's codes and only took one or two classes in Islamic jurisprudence. Even though lawyers publish less than judges or independent scholars, they are very present in the legal discourse on the internet, where they comment on recent developments and share documents and legal literature. Some lawyers have become well known on social media and have thousands of followers.

Likewise, the Ministry of Justice, the fourth key actor in the Saudi legal discourse, is very active on the internet. Jurists with strong ties to the Ministry tend to be more reform-oriented than other actors in the legal discourse. Even though all Ministers of Justice until now were trained Islamic jurists, employees seem to have different backgrounds, depending on their work.

Beginning in the mid-2000s, the Ministry of Justice aimed to increase the transparency of the Saudi judiciary. One of the Ministry's primary goals is to establish a "culture of justice" (*thaqāfa ʿadliyya*). Manṣūr al-Ḥaydarī, an associate of the Ministry and former head of the Ministry's "Research Center" (Markaz al-Buḥūth), wrote that a culture of justice in Saudi Arabia would mean that every person knows about his or her rights and how to claim them in court.[36]

One result of the program to increase transparency is the publication of court judgements and other literature. As part of the establishment of a "culture of justice," the Ministry also aims to educate the judges on the "misinterpretations" (*tafsīr bi-shakl khāṭiʾ*) of the king's codes (*anẓima*).[37] De facto, this means a higher control of judges and other legal actors by the Ministry. Additionally, the Ministry promotes alternatives to adjudication before the sharīʿa courts, most importantly, arbitration (*taḥkīm*) and mediation (*waṣāṭa*).

35 I was able to get an impression of the courses through many conversations with lawyers and a talk I gave at the law faculty of the Prince Sultan University in Riyadh in October 2019.

36 Manṣūr bin ʿAbd al-Raḥmān Al-Ḥaydarī, "Al-taṭwīr fī al-jānib al-ijrāʾī," in *Al-niẓām al-ʿadl fī al-Saʿūdiyya*, ed. Markaz al-Fikr al-ʿĀlamī ʿan al-Saʿūdiyya (Riyadh: Markaz al-Fikr al-ʿĀlamī ʿan al-Saʿūdiyya, 1436/2015), 222.

37 Ibid., 223.

3 Sources and Methodology

Brinkley Messick recently pointed out that to approach Islamic law as a discursive tradition, and thereby to focus on the discursive interaction with legal texts, gives an "explicit mandate for textual inquiries."[38] This is especially true for Saudi jurists, who most importantly express their ideas through writing. The ʿulamāʾ traditionally preferred to transmit knowledge through personal interaction. Accordingly, Saudi scholars long refrained from publishing extensively. As a result, even thirty years ago, only a few books by Saudi scholars were available.[39]

This has changed fundamentally: like their European counterparts, Saudi jurists today communicate their ideas through writing articles and books. Several journals publish articles on Islamic law, PhD graduates upload their theses on the internet, students collect the fatwas of their older teachers, and the number of books written by Saudi jurists and scholars increases every year.

In the mid-2010s, court judgements became for the first time in Saudi history available in huge dimensions, which allowed for a detailed analysis of Saudi court practice. As part of their plan to establish a "culture of justice," the Ministry in 2007 published the first of three compilations (*mudawwanāt*) of cases from different fields, in particular criminal and private law. This step was remarkable since Saudi judges had long been very critical of releasing any information on their decision-making. Frank Vogel reported from his fieldwork in Saudi Arabia in the 1980s that he faced considerable resistance when trying to obtain case law. Vogel wrote that the large majority of his visits to the Supreme Judicial Council, the predecessor of the Higher Judicial Council, "produced only glasses of tea with court staff; a prized few of them led to quarter-hour oral or written exchanges of questions and answers."[40] Whereas the first three compilations merely allowed for a glimpse into the workings of the legal system, the Research Center at the Ministry of Justice in 2015 released the first substantial collection of court decisions (*Majmūʿat al-aḥkām al-qaḍāʾiyya*), in thirty volumes.[41] The collection includes selected decisions from the year

38 Brinkley Messick, *Sharīʿa Scripts: A Historical Anthropology* (New York: Columbia University Press, 2018), 35.

39 For example, during Frank Vogel's fieldwork in the 1980s, only a few books by Saudi scholars existed, and Saudi scholars were reserved towards foreign researchers. Personal conversation with Frank Vogel at a conference in Tampere, Finland, June 7, 2018.

40 Frank Vogel, *Islamic Law and Legal System: Studies of Saudi Arabia* (Leiden: Brill, 2000), 98.

41 Markaz al-Buḥūth, *Majmūʿat al-aḥkām al-qaḍāʾiyya li-ʿām 1434* (Riyadh: Markaz al-Buḥūth, 1436/2015).

1434/2012–13 of courts from all over the kingdom. Subsequently, in 2017, the Research Center published another massive collection of 1,154 court decisions from the year 1435/2013–14.[42] It is expected that more decisions will be released in the coming years. In total, several thousand decisions have been published so far.

Another important source is premodern legal writings: since Saudi ʿulamāʾ frequently refer to premodern authors, many quotes and translations of premodern legal writings can be found throughout this book. All translations are based on popular editions of the manuscripts. The question of the historical authenticity of premodern writings is beyond the scope of this book. I trusted the editors to use a plausible version of the manuscript and edit it correctly. To supplement my reading of legal literature, I conducted personal interviews with many leading Saudi scholars, judges, lawyers, and government officials in the course of three visits to the kingdom in 2018 and 2019. Additionally, I visited several Saudi courts in Riyadh.

I got to know most of my informants through my reading of Saudi legal literature. Once in Saudi Arabia, I either contacted potential interview partners directly by e-mail or managed to get in touch through friends, other jurists, or the always supportive King Faisal Center for Research and Islamic Studies. Whereas some interviews took place in a very formal context, others were more casual. It proved to be a good strategy to ask questions based on books that I had read. Due to the very detailed questions that were tailored to the individual interview partner, I decided not to structure the interviews.

Throughout the text, I refer to only some of the interviews that I conducted in the course of the research. This has two reasons: Firstly, many interviews or meetings informed my general understanding of the legal discourse and assured me that a particular idea is prevailing among most jurists but did not bring up new information. Secondly, many interviews addressed very detailed and technical questions that are not relevant to the topics addressed in this book but helped me understand the way the system works more generally. Occasionally, I only refer to the interview partner's position in the judiciary to keep them anonymous. I was able to visit the appeal court, the family court, and the general court in Riyadh several times. The visits gave me a better understanding of the procedural and structural reforms in the Saudi judiciary during the last decades. The courts' employees and judges explained the courts' procedures to me, and I was able to attend court sessions. However, these insights were only supplementary to my reading of Saudi legal literature and the interviews, and I will only sporadically refer to them.

42 Markaz al-Buḥūth, *Majmūʿat al-aḥkām al-qaḍāʾiyya li-ʿām 1435* (Riyadh: Markaz al-Buḥūth, 1438/2017).

The third main source for the book is videos and audio recordings. Over the course of more than five years, I watched hundreds of hours of recorded lectures, conferences, fatwa sessions, and TV interviews. These insights into the Saudi legal discourse proved to be especially helpful. Whereas an interview is limited to information that the interviewee wants to share with an outsider and the impression that he wants to give about the legal discourse, the massive amount of recorded material available allowed me to observe the communication between the legal discourse's participants without interfering. Moreover, the recordings helped me to understand the jurists' writings better. Saudi 'ulamā' often publish recordings of their lectures, in which they explain their writings in more detail. Whereas the scholars use the highly technical language of Islamic jurisprudence in their books, they often explain how their writings should be understood in their lectures and give examples for difficult concepts in order to make them more approachable. Furthermore, many lawyers upload videos on YouTube, in which they explain Saudi procedural law to students and the general public.

On Twitter and other social media, Saudi lawyers and judges discuss current topics and share literature and photos of court documents and judgements. For years, I followed many of the debates to identify the key developments and debates in the Saudi judiciary.

4 Outline of Chapters

The book starts by discussing the legal system's theoretical foundations and subsequently analyzes how they are reflected in the Saudi judicial institutions and the application of Islamic law in court.

Chapter 1 locates the Saudi judiciary in the overall structure of the Saudi state. It demonstrates how *siyāsa sharʿiyya*, a state doctrine that links the ruler's legitimacy to his commitment to apply and enforce Islamic law, obliges him to uphold an Islamic judiciary. The right to interpret Islamic law, on the other hand, remains in the hand of the Islamic jurists and thereby allows them to control the legal system.

Chapter 2 explores the roots of the Saudi jurists' understanding of Islamic law. It shows that contemporary Saudi Islamic jurists, contrary to what is commonly assumed, do not feel bound to a single school of Islamic jurisprudence. The Saudi jurists' critique of the established schools of law, the chapter demonstrates, can be traced back to the reformist agenda of Ibn ʿAbd al-Wahhāb (d. 1792) and to nineteenth-century modernist scholars from Egypt.

Chapter 3 investigates the jurists' resistance to the codification of Islamic law. Whereas many observers see the debate on codification mostly as a power struggle between the Islamic jurists and the king, the chapter takes the jurists' perspective and explores the reasons for their longstanding refusal of codified Islamic law. It shows that the main reason for the jurists' refusal is not the transformation of Islamic law into state law but their fear that a binding codification would deprive Islamic law of its flexibility and normative plurality, which would lead to unjust court decisions.

Chapter 4 analyzes how Saudi jurists have extended the scope of the premodern idea of the prevailing practice (*mā jarā ʿalayhi al-ʿamal*) of the courts into a de facto system of judicial precedent and, contrary to the prevalent opinion in classical doctrine, have allowed for the introduction of a hierarchical court system. The chapter argues that the prevailing practice, which is enforced by the appellate courts, constituted a form of proto-codification that stabilized the legal system and acted as a counterweight for the judges' emphasis on *ijtihād*.

Chapter 5 shows how the jurists' understanding of Islamic law was reflected in Saudi court practice prior to codification. By using the example of child custody, the chapter demonstrates how Saudi judges related to the tradition of Islamic jurisprudence in their judgements, how they moved away from dominant doctrines in Islamic jurisprudence and thereby adapted custody law to the changing social and technological circumstances in twenty-first-century Saudi Arabia.

Chapter 6 uses two case studies to explore how Saudi Islamic jurists initiated legal reforms in the middle of the twentieth century and how they unfold today. The first case study analyses the ways through which leading Saudi Islamic jurists have expanded the scope of the severe Quranic punishment of *ḥirāba*, usually understood as highway robbery, to also include drug trafficking. This eventually led to the introduction of harsh penalties for drug trafficking in the Code against Drugs and Mind-affecting Substances (Niẓām Mukāfaḥat al-Mukhadirāt wa-l-Muʾathirāt al-ʿAqliyya). The second case study traces the jurists' reinterpretation of women's unilateral *khulʿ* divorce from the primary sources of Islamic law to contemporary court practice. By gradually allowing women to divorce against the will of their husbands, Saudi Islamic jurists have diverged from the consensus of the four major schools of jurisprudence.

Chapter 7 analyzes the codification of Islamic family and inheritance law in 2022. It shows that the law of personal status (Niẓām al-Aḥwāl al-Shakhṣiyya) deviates in several key aspects from Ḥanbalī teachings. These deviations, as the chapter demonstrates, are not the result of state reform but the codification of the prevailing practice of the courts. By pointing to the continuities between the codification and the Islamic jurists' writings, the chapter challenges common understandings among scholars of Islam, who describe the codification of Islamic law as a turning point in Islamic history.

CHAPTER 1

The Foundations of the Saudi Legal System

1 Introduction

From the perspective of premodern ʿulamāʾ, there was one ideal form of Islamic governance: the caliphate (*khilāfa*).[1] Although many different conceptions of the caliphate exist, all agree that it should unite all Muslims under one rule. As successor of the Prophet, the caliph should lead the Islamic community. While some caliphs became renowned for their charisma and just rule, the institution's symbolic power always transcended the individual caliph's personality. There is even a debate among the ʿulamāʾ whether an unjust ruler could be considered a legitimate caliph.

When the last caliphate ended, with the fall of the Ottoman empire in 1924, some Muslim scholars and activists, like Rashīd Riḍā, hoped that the Saudi king ʿAbd al-ʿAzīz, who later that year conquered the holy cities of Mecca and Medina, would fill that void and declare himself the leader of the Muslim community.[2] However, King ʿAbd al-ʿAzīz did not try to establish himself as a caliph, nor did he claim religious leadership.[3] Whereas other Arab rulers, like the Jordanian and the Moroccan kings, trace their genealogy back to the Prophet Muḥammad, the Saudi kings never tried to legitimize their rule genealogically by linking themselves to great Islamic leaders. Although the Saudi king claims the title of the custodian of the two holiest places in Islam (*khādim al-ḥaramayn al-sharīfayn*), the simple act of governing Mecca and Medina alone provides him with little religious authority.

The Saudi kings legitimize their rule in a different way: since the foundation of the first Saudi emirate on the Arabian Peninsula, in 1744, the Saudi rulers have derived their legitimacy from siyāsa sharʿiyya, a state doctrine that was

1 Baber Johanson, "A Perfect Law in an Imperfect Society: Ibn Taymiyya's Concept of 'Governance in the Name of the Sacred Law,'" in *The Law Applied: Contextualizing the Islamic Shariʿa*, ed. Peri Bearman, Wolfhart Heinrichs, and Bernard Weiss (London: I.B. Tauris, 2008), 276.

2 See Henri Lauzière, *The Making of Salafism: Islamic Reform in the Twentieth Century* (New York: Columbia University Press, 2015), 65.

3 There are different ways through which a political leader can show his aspiration to the role of a religious leader without claiming the title of caliph. For instance, rulers have adopted the honorary title "commander of the faithful" (*amīr al-muʾminīn*). Today, for instance, the Moroccan king serves, at least according to the country's constitution, as amīr al-muʾminīn.

© DOMINIK KRELL, 2025 | DOI:10.1163/9789004726314_003

mainly developed by the controversial medieval Ḥanbalī scholar Ibn Taymiyya (d. 1328).[4] The doctrine puts the focus on Islamic law. A ruler can gain religious legitimacy if he ensures that all of his policies follow Islamic law.

This chapter explores how leading Saudi Islamic scholars understand siyāsa sharʿiyya. While the doctrine is essential for the constitution of the Saudi state as such, we will pay special attention to how the ʿulamāʾ's understandings of siyāsa sharʿiyya are reflected in the conceptualization and structure of the judiciary.

2 The Doctrine of Siyāsa Sharʿiyya

2.1 *The Development of the Doctrine by Ibn Taymiyya*

Ibn Taymiyya was born in 1263 into a family of jurists in Ḥarrān in present-day Turkey, where both his uncle and grandfather were famous Ḥanbalī scholars. As a six-year-old, he fled from the Mongol invasion to Damascus with his father, where he later became one of the leading Ḥanbalī scholars.[5] Ibn Taymiyya was not only a prolific scholar who authored several books on Islamic law and creed, he was also a political activist in turbulent times. When the Mongols conquered Damascus in 1300, Ibn Taymiyya remained in the city, whereas the ruling Mamlūk prefects and most notables fled. Despite not holding a public office, he played a crucial role in the subsequent negotiations with the Mongols.[6]

His relationship with the Mamlūk rulers was troubled. On the one hand, he acted as advisor to Sultan Qalāwūn (d. 1290) and was in close contact with several Mamlūk governors. On the other hand, he clashed with the political elite of his times on various occasions, mostly because he insisted on his unconventional theological and legal positions.[7] As a result, Ibn Taymiyya was

4 It is important to note that the political realities differ from the concepts and ideas prevailing in the legal discourse. In practice, the Saudi kings also build their rule on tribal structures and alliances. See Muhammad Al-Atawneh, "Is Saudi Arabia a Theocracy? Religion and Governance in Contemporary Saudi Arabia," *Middle Eastern Studies* 45, no. 5 (2009): 726.

5 Ann Lambton, *State and Government in Medieval Islam* (London: Routledge, 1981), 143.

6 Reuven Amitai, "The Mongol Occupation of Damascus in 1300: A Study of Mamluk Loyalties," in *The Mamluks in Egyptian and Syrian Politics and Society*, ed. Michael Winter and Amalia Levanoni (Leiden: Brill, 2004), 26–34.

7 Ibn Taymiyya was not only controversial because of his legal reasoning but also because of his personality. Contemporaries, like the famous traveler Ibn Baṭṭūṭa, described him as erratic and extravagant. See Donald Little, "Did Ibn Taymiyya Have a Screw Loose?" *Studia Islamica* 41 (1975): 93–111.

imprisoned several times by Mamlūk rulers in Cairo and Damascus and eventually died in the citadel of Damascus in 1328.

The Mongol conquests, the destruction of Baghdad, and the end of the Abbasid Caliphate, which had occurred five years after Ibn Taymiyya's birth, had led to a feeling of crisis in the Muslim world. Ibn Taymiyya saw corruption spreading and feared that, like the institution of the caliphate, the authority of Islamic law as a whole was in decline. As a pragmatic thinker, he developed a new approach to Islamic governance. By the early thirteenth century, the jurists' debate on the caliphate had become detached from everyday politics and power structures in the Mamlūk Sultanate. Although Ibn Taymiyya recognised the jurists' agreement on the necessity of the caliphate, he saw the need to address the political realities, which had been ignored by the scholars of his time.[8] His idea was to shift the focus away from the ruler to the sovereignty of Islamic law. It would be the just application of Islamic law, he argued, that would legitimize the ruler. Thereby, he developed what has been called an "Islamic rule of law."[9]

The Mamlūks had trouble legitimizing their rule. They were military slaves who were mostly captured as boys in the Caucasus, Turkey, or among the Turkic people of Eastern Europe and then brought to Egypt, where they were trained as soldiers. In the middle of the thirteenth century, the Mamlūks, who had already been an important political actor in the Abbasid Caliphate, rose to power in Egypt. As outsiders to the political and religious establishment, they could not base their sultanate on a religious genealogy, as the Fatimids or the Abbasids had done. Instead, their authority depended on their military, political, and economic success and their support for Sunni Islam. Mamlūk sultans fostered Islamic scholars from all Sunni schools in search of religious legitimacy, and in turn, different groups of ʿulamāʾ sought the sultan's support for their doctrines.[10]

Ibn Taymiyya was one of them. Around 1309–12, he was asked by a Mamlūk ruler, most likely the Damascene Jamāl al-Dīn Āqqush al-Manṣūrī (d. 1320),

8 Ovamir Anjum, *Politics, Law and Community in Islamic Thought: The Taymiyyan Moment* (Cambridge: Cambridge University Press, 2012), 257.

9 Clark Lombardi, *State Law as Islamic Law in Modern Egypt: The Incorporation of the Sharīʿa into Egyptian Constitutional Law* (Leiden: Brill, 2006), 54.

10 Johanson, "Perfect Law," 260. The Abbasids had already followed a similar strategy to influence the legal discourse, see Norbert Oberauer, *Religiöse Verpflichtung im Islam: Ein ethischer Grundbegriff und seine theologische, rechtliche und sozialgeschichtliche Dimension* (Würzburg: Ergon, 2004), 97–106.

to give him advice (*naṣīḥa*) on his role in the state.[11] Ibn Taymiyya's main ideas on governance can be found in the treatise, which he wrote as a response to the Mamlūk ruler's request. He called the treatise *Al-Siyāsa al-sharʿiyya fī iṣlāḥ al-rāʿī wa-l-raʿiyya* (Governance in Accordance with Islamic Law for the Righteousness of the Shephard and the Flock). Siyāsa sharʿiyya, the term Ibn Taymiyya used to describe his approach to Islamic governance, has been translated as "governance in accordance with the sharīʿa,"[12] "governance in the name of the sacred law,"[13] "Islamic public policy,"[14] or "sharīʿa compliant policy".[15]

Earlier Islamic jurists had already used the expression siyāsa sharʿiyya, however in a much broader way. They understood siyāsa sharʿiyya as the management of the Islamic community as a whole. For them, the term referred more generally to all rulings that guide the Islamic community (*umma*), not only to governance.[16] It was, as Bernard Lewis put it, "a skill or a craft rather than a doctrine or a philosophy."[17]

Ibn Taymiyya developed siyāsa sharʿiyya from a set of general ideas on statecraft into a theory of Islamic governance. However, as Ovamir Anjum pointed out, Ibn Taymiyya's contribution to Islamic jurisprudence did not lie "in elaborating robust political institutions," but in making "such thinking possible by deconstructing the doctrines and developments that had foreclosed the very possibility of political thinking."[18]

2.2 *The Obligation to Command Good and Forbid Wrong*

Ibn Taymiyya never explicitly defined siyāsa sharʿiyya.[19] At the heart of his conception of the doctrine lies the Quranic obligation to command good and

11 Henri Laoust, *Le Traité de droit public d'Ibn Taymiyya* (Beirut: Institut Français de Damas, 1948), xii. See also Ibn Taymiyya, Al-Siyāsa al-sharʿiyya fī iṣlāḥ al-rāʿī wa-l-raʿiyya (Riyadh: Wizārat al-Shuʾūn al-Islāmiyya, 1419/1998), 5.

12 Benjamin Jokisch, *Islamic Imperial Law: Harun Al-Rashid's Codification Project* (Berlin: Walter de Gruyter, 2007), 396, similarly: Lombardi, *State Law*, 49.

13 Johanson, "Perfect Law," 259.

14 Abdessamad Belhaj, "Law and Order According to Ibn Taymiyya and Ibn Qayyim al-Jawziyya: A Re-Examination of Siyāsa Sharʿiyya," in *Islamic Theology, Philosophy and Law: Debating Ibn Taymiyya and Ibn Qayyim al-Jawziyya*, ed. Birgit Krawietz and Georges Tamer (Berlin: De Gruyter, 2012), 400.

15 Article "Siyāsa" in the *Encyclopedia of Islam, Second Edition*. Available online: dx.doi.org/10.1163/1573-3912_islam_COM_1096 [last access: 24 June 2022].

16 ʿAbd al-ʿĀl bin Aḥmad ʿAṭwa, *Al-Mudkhal ilā al-siyāsa al-sharʿiyya* (Riyadh: Jāmiʿat al-Imām Muḥammad bin Saʿūd al-Islāmiyya, 1414/1993), 22.

17 Bernard Lewis, *Political Words and Ideas in Islam* (Princeton: Markus Wiener, 2008), 32.

18 Anjum, *Politics, Law and Community*, 273.

19 See ʿAṭwa, *Al-Mudkhal ilā al-siyāsa al-sharʿiyya*, 23.

to forbid wrong (*al-amr bi-l-maʿrūf wa-l-nāhī ʿan al-munkar*).[20] According to the concept of al-amr bi-l-maʿrūf, every Muslim is obliged to rebuke behaviour that is considered a violation of Islamic teachings.[21] In Ibn Taymiyya's understanding, the fulfilment of the obligation forms the basis for the joint leadership of the ruler (*amīr*) and the scholars (*ʿulamāʾ*), it is the state's raison d'être.[22] The doctrine demands that every person in a public office commands good and forbids wrong, irrespective of the function of his office. All public offices are thereby assigned a religious dimension.[23] Siyāsa sharʿiyya is, as Johansen highlighted, not "a system of rules and norms but the religious purpose underlying these norms in its practical political form."[24]

According to Ibn Taymiyya's conception of siyāsa sharʿiyya, the ruler's obligations do not differ from those of the common believer. Both are united in their striving for a more just world. The ruler does not have to declare a caliphate or claim a religiously significant genealogy. It is the simple enforcement of Islamic law's commands that grants him legitimacy. Ibn Taymiyya saw the ruler's main task in the execution of the penalties (*ʿuqūbāt*) prescribed by Islamic jurisprudence, and the administration of the community's wealth.[25] Many later jurists also associated siyāsa sharʿiyya with punishments. It is through controlled violence, the jurists argued, that the ruler would defend the community and thereby fulfil his prime task.[26] Those jurists, however, did not understand punishment in the modern sense, as retribution for wrongdoing, but more broadly, as every form of violent action a ruler takes for the benefit of the Muslim community.[27] Other later jurists not only focused on repression but also on the well-being of the Muslim community. The influential Ḥanafī

20 Most importantly, the command is mentioned in Q 3:104, Q 3:110 and Q 9:71. See Michael Cook, *Forbidding Wrong in Islam: An Introduction* (Cambridge: Cambridge University Press, 2003), 3.

21 The concept of al-amr bi-l-maʿrūf is widely acknowledged. However, the jurists debated extensively about what would constitute wrong behavior. Most importantly, they disagreed on three points: Can the following of one's school constitute a wrong? Can disapproved behaviour also be forbidden? And at what point can immanent wrongdoing be stopped? See Cook, *Forbidding Wrong*, 22–25.

22 Anjum, *Politics, Law and Community*, 268–69.

23 Baber Johansen, "Signs as Evidence: The Doctrine of Ibn Taymiyya (1263–1328) and Ibn Qayyim al-Jawziyya (d. 1351) on Proof," *Islamic Law and Society* 9, no. 2 (2002): 181.

24 Ibid.

25 Ibn Taymiyya, *Al-Siyāsa al-sharʿiyya*, 21.

26 Ḥamūd bin Muḥammad Al-Ghashīmī, "Mabādiʾ al-siyāsa al-sharʿiyya wa-athāruhā fī al-niẓām al-asāsī li-l-ḥukm fī al-Mamlaka al-ʿArabiyya al-Saʿūdiyya," *Majallat al-Jāmiʿa al-Islāmiyya li-l-ʿUlūm al-Sharʿiyya* 185, no. 1 (1439/2017): 334.

27 Fuʾād bin ʿAbd al-Munʿim Aḥmad, *Shaykh al-Islām Ibn Taymiyya wa-l-wilāya al-siyāsiyya al-kubrā fī al-Islām* (Riyadh: Dār al-Waṭan, 1417/1996), 72.

Ibn Nujaym (d. 1563), for instance, defined siyāsa sharʿiyya very broadly as all actions that a ruler takes for the benefit (*maṣlaḥa*) of the Muslim community.[28]

2.3 *Ibn al-Qayyim's Understanding of Siyāsa Sharʿiyya*

One of the important jurists to further develop the doctrine was Ibn Taymiyya's most prominent student, Ibn al-Qayyim (d. 1351). Until today, Ibn al-Qayyim stands in his teacher's shadow, despite being an innovative and independent thinker himself. Like his father, a renowned Damascene Ḥanbalī scholar, he was trained in Ḥanbalī jurisprudence, before Ibn Taymiyya introduced him to comprehensive jurisprudential books that included views from all schools of Islamic law.[29] Although not as controversial as his teacher, Ibn al-Qayyim also developed unconventional views on various key questions in Islamic jurisprudence.

His ideas on siyāsa sharʿiyya can be found in his writings on judicial procedure, which he considered one of the core elements of the doctrine. His main work, the book *Al-Ṭuruq al-ḥukmiyya fī al-siyāsa al-sharʿiyya* (*The Judicial Process in Governance in Accordance with Islamic Law*), influences court practice in Saudi Arabia until today.[30]

Ibn al-Qayyim shared his teacher's belief that Islamic law's role in the state was highly political. He, too, criticized the judicial establishment of his time for their formalism. Ibn al-Qayyim felt that the schools' formalism had led the Mamlūk authorities to believe that Islamic law could not guarantee law and order. This, he argued, was especially true for procedural law. In his writings, he advocated for a fundamental rethinking of Islamic procedural law, which he considered impractical. By reforming procedural law, Ibn al-Qayyim hoped that the Mamlūk authorities could be convinced of the practicability of Islamic law.[31]

The starting point of his book *Al-Ṭuruq al-ḥukmiyya* is the question of whether a judge could base his judgement on circumstantial evidence (*qarāʾin*) and physiognomy (*firāsa*), a question of high practical importance.[32]

---

28 Ibn Nujaym, *Al-Baḥr al-rāʾiq sharḥ kanz al-daqāʾiq* (Beirut: Dār al-Kutub al-ʿIlmiyya, 1434/2013), 5:118.

29 Bori and Holtzman, "Scholar in the Shadow," 18.

30 See, for example, the interview with the president of the General Court in Riyadh, Nāyif bin Aḥmad Al-Ḥamd, in an episode of the TV program "Riḥlat Kitāb" on Ibn al-Qayyim's *Al-Ṭuruq al-ḥukmiyya*, available on YouTube: www.youtube.com/watch?v=AsxwR86Anis, min 7–8 [last access: 10 July 2020].

31 Johansen, "Signs as Evidence," 186.

32 Ibn al-Qayyim, *Al-Ṭuruq al-ḥukmiyya fī al-siyāsa al-sharʿiyya* (Beirut: Dār al-Kutub al-ʿIlmiyya, 1415/1995), 3.

At the time, most jurists held that proof (*bayyina*) could only consist of two witnesses, whereas other forms of evidence could not be admitted.[33] This meant that, for instance, a person who is apprehended near a corpse with a bloody knife could only be convicted of manslaughter if there are witnesses to the act of killing itself. In the course of *Al-Ṭuruq al-ḥukmiyya*, Ibn al-Qayyim argued that such a formalistic understanding of evidence would contradict the sources of Islamic law and laid down a more pragmatic understanding of the Islamic law of evidence.

3 Siyāsa Sharʿiyya in the Saudi Legal Discourse

3.1 *Ibn Taymiyya's Legacy in Saudi Arabia*

Ibn Taymiyya's and Ibn al-Qayyim's pragmatic legal reasoning has deeply affected the Saudi legal discourse, as we will see in more detail in the next chapters. The jurists of his time only slowly accepted Ibn Taymiyya's ideas. Scholarship on Ibn Taymiyya differs in the impact that he had on premodern Islamic jurisprudence. El-Rouayheb claimed that for five centuries after his death, Ibn Taymiyya had little influence on mainstream Sunni law.[34] Other scholarship indicates that his writings already played an influential role in the decades and centuries after his death, especially in the intellectual life of Damascus.[35]

Undeniably, Ibn Taymiyya's ideas rose to prominence with the Wahhābī movement and the political success of the Saudi kings, especially in the twentieth century. The movement's founder, Ibn ʿAbd al-Wahhāb (d. 1792), an eighteenth-century preacher from the Najd region, whose ideas we will discuss in more detail in the next chapter, admired Ibn Taymiyya. Both Ibn ʿAbd al-Wahhāb's political agenda and his views on governance were strongly influenced by Ibn Taymiyya's concept of siyāsa sharʿiyya.[36]

---

33 Johansen, "Signs as Evidence," 187.

34 Khaled El-Rouayheb, "From Ibn Hajar al-Haytami (d. 1566) to Khayr al-Din al-Alusi (d. 1899): Changing Views of Ibn Taymiyya amongst Sunni Islamic Scholars," in *Ibn Taymiyya & His Times*, ed. Shahab Ahmed and Yossef Rapoport (Karachi: Oxford University Press, 2010), 269–318.

35 Caterina Bori, "Ibn Taymiyya (14th to 17th Century): Transregional Spaces of Reading and Reception," *The Muslim World* 108, no. 1 (2018), 122.

36 Nabil Mouline, *The Clerics of Islam: Religious Authority and Political Power in Saudi Arabia* (Yale: Yale University Press, 2014), 66.

3.2 *The Troubles of Defining Siyāsa Sharʿiyya*

Saudi ʿulamāʾ share with Ibn Taymiyya the feeling that Islamic law is in decline. Siyāsa sharʿiyya offers them a way to ensure the application of Islamic law without waiting for the establishment of the caliphate.[37] Over the last decades, the jurists have adjusted the doctrine in order to make it compatible with the political realities in a twenty-first-century nation-state.

Like Ibn Taymiyya, Saudi scholars have trouble defining siyāsa sharʿiyya. Saʿd al-ʿUtaybī, a teacher at the Higher Judicial Institute in Riyadh and a prominent specialist on the doctrine, argued that the reason for this would be the doctrine's fluidity. Similar to other scholarly fields, siyāsa sharʿiyya would be hard to define in absolute terms because the doctrine addresses new facts and needs continuously.[38] Likewise, the high-ranking government official and author of a book on siyāsa sharʿiyya ʿĀlī bin Sulaymān al-ʿAṭṭiya held that the doctrine could not be seen as a fixed set of rulings, but its understanding would differ with the changing needs and customs of the Islamic community.[39] For al-ʿAṭṭiya, it is the changing nature of siyāsa sharʿiyya that defines it. The doctrine, he argued, would primarily consist of the process through which the scholars and the rulers adjust considerations of benefits. It would be the ruler's obligation to interfere and find new solutions if circumstances change that legitimized a specific practice.[40] Al-ʿAṭṭiya illustrated this with an example: the state would face higher expenses today than in earlier centuries since it has to build bridges or maintain universities. Following siyāsa sharʿiyya, the state should thus be entitled to collect higher taxes.[41]

Despite the doctrine's fluidity, Saudi jurists agree on a very general description of siyāsa sharʿiyya. They understand it as all actions that are taken for the benefit (*maṣlaḥa*) of the Muslim community whenever there is no specific textual evidence (*dalīl*) in the revelation that addresses the issue.[42] Some jurists limit siyāsa sharʿiyya only to actions that are taken by the ruler,[43] whereas others

---

37 See for example Muḥammad bin Ṣāliḥ Ibn ʿUthaymīn, *Sharḥ kitāb al-siyāsa al-sharʿiyya li-Shaykh al-Islām Ibn Taymiyya* (Beirut: Dār Ibn Ḥazm, 1425/2004), 5.

38 Saʿd bin Maṭar Al-ʿUtaybī, *Aḍwāʾ ʿalā al-siyāsa al-sharʿiyya* (Riyadh: Dār al-Alūka, 1434/2013), 17.

39 ʿĀlī bin Sulaymān Al-ʿAṭṭiya, *Al-Siyāsa al-sharʿiyya fī al-niẓām al-asāsī li-l-ḥukm* (Riyadh, 1432/2011), 43.

40 Ibid., 44–45.

41 Ibid., 47–48.

42 The Saudi jurists' formulation of the definition resembles that of the Ḥanbalī scholar Ibn ʿAqīl (d. 1119), which Ibn al-Qayyim referred to in his *Al-Ṭuruq al-ḥukmiyya*. See Ibn al-Qayyim, *Al-Ṭuruq al-ḥukmiyya*, 11.

43 See al-ʿAṭṭiya, *Al-Siyāsa al-sharʿiyya*, 54.

include the rulings and actions of both scholars and the ruler.[44] According to those jurists, a scholar who issues a fatwa is, in some instances, also practising siyāsa sharʿiyya.[45]

3.3 *Siyāsa Sharʿiyya in the Writings of Saudi Scholars*

In contemporary Saudi Arabia, siyāsa sharʿiyya is considered one of the main areas of Islamic jurisprudence, like the law of sales or marriage.[46] Some Saudi universities even offer degree programs in siyāsa sharʿiyya. However, the doctrine is considered a rather abstract and theoretical subject and is therefore seen as closer to legal theory (*uṣūl al-fiqh*) than other fields of Islamic jurisprudence.[47]

The conceptual fluidity of siyāsa sharʿiyya is also reflected in the way in which Saudi scholars discuss the doctrine in their works. Although the doctrine is recognised as a distinct field of Islamic jurisprudence, some Saudi jurists refrain from treating matters of siyāsa sharʿiyya as a separate category. For instance, ʿAbd al-Raḥmān bin Nāṣir al-Saʿdī (d. 1957), one of the leading Najdī scholars in the first half of the twentieth century, wrote extensively on key questions of siyāsa sharʿiyya; however, his thoughts are scattered all over his Quran commentaries and fatwas.[48] Moreover, following the example of Ibn al-Qayyim and other Ḥanbalī scholars, some Saudi ʿulamāʾ still associate siyāsa sharʿiyya with judicial proceedings.[49]

3.4 *The Main Areas of Siyāsa Sharʿiyya*

According to al-ʿUtaybī, siyāsa sharʿiyya today constitutes the basis for six main areas of governance: the state's overall organization, its financial administration, trade regulations, the organization of the judicial system, the penal

44 See al-ʿUtaybī's introduction to Muḥammad bin Ṣāliḥ Ibn ʿUthaymīn, *Al-Taʿlīq ʿalā al-siyāsa al-sharʿiyya fī iṣlāḥ al-rāʿī wa-l-raʿiyya* (ʿUnayza: Madār al-Waṭan, 1427/2006), 8. For al-ʿUtaybī, the Quranic term *ulū al-amr* includes not only the ruler (*walī al-amr*) but also the ʿulamāʾ.

45 Al-ʿUtaybī, *Aḍwāʾ ʿalā al-siyāsa al-sharʿiyya*. 21.

46 Id., *Maqālāt fī al-siyāsa al-sharʿiyya* (Riyadh: Al-Bayān, 1434/2012), 50.

47 See, for example, a lecture by Saʿd bin Maṭar al-ʿUtaybī in the Saʿīd bin Zayd mosque in Riyadh on the 15.2.1437/28.11.2015. The lecture is available on YouTube, www.youtube.com/watch?v=gerVUJx7bNk&t=5365s, min. 66 und 70. [last access: 30 June 2020].

48 Ṣaghīr bin Muḥammad Al-Ṣaghīr, *Maʿālim min al-siyāsa al-sharʿiyya ʿand al-ʿalāma Ibn Saʿdī*, in *Al-Sijll al-ʿilmī li-muʾtamar al-shaykh al-ʿalāma ʿAbd al-Raḥmān bin Nāṣir al-Saʿdī*, ed. Jāmiʿat al-Qaṣīm (ʿUnayza: Jāmiʿat al-Qaṣīm, 1441/2019), 1945.

49 See, for instance, Yāsir bin Ḥamd al-Ḥaqīl, "Al-Siyāsa al-sharʿiyya fī mukāfaḥat al-fasād wa-l-wiqāya minhu," *Majallat al-Qaḍāʾiyya* 3 (1433/2011): 138.

system, and international relations.[50] Other areas of life could become relevant for siyāsa sharʿiyya if they relate, at least partly, to these main subjects. All jurists, however, agree that the ruler can under no circumstances decide on matters of worship.

In al-ʿAṭṭiya's understanding, siyāsa sharʿiyya applies to Saudi society as a whole. The doctrine, al-ʿAṭṭiya argued, not only regulates state policies but sets Islam as the foundation for life in Saudi Arabia, preserves the kingdom's Arab identity, facilitates patriotism, and strengthens family structures.[51] Siyāsa sharʿiyya, al-ʿAṭṭiya continued, would oblige Saudi citizens to obey the king. In return, the king would protect their health, their environment, their safety, and their individual rights.[52] For al-ʿAṭṭiya, all of this is related to the king's obligation to command right and to forbid wrong.

The main objective of both the ruler and the scholars should be, the doctrine demands, to bring the Islamic community as close to rectitude (*ṣalāḥ*) and as far from corruption (*fasād*) as possible. The legitimacy of any act by the ruler is evaluated according to the established sources of Islamic law, most importantly the Quran, the Sunna, the jurists' consensus (*ijmāʿ*), and legal analogy (*qiyās*). Saʿd al-ʿUtaybī stated that one example of an established consensus in siyāsa sharʿiyya today would be the permissibility of female state schoolteachers in female-only schools.[53] Another example would be the permissibility of (local) elections in Saudi Arabia. For al-ʿUtaybī, this is, among other things, the result of an analogy with the election of twelve representatives during the second pledge of ʿAqaba.[54] At ʿAqaba, a town near Mecca, a group of seventy-five citizens of Medina met the Prophet and pledged alliance to him. The Prophet then commanded them to elect representatives who should lead their group and spread Islam in Medina.[55]

3.5 *The Relationship between the Scholars and the Ruler*

In Ibn Taymiyya's ideal conception of a state governed by siyāsa sharʿiyya, the ʿulamāʾ and the ruler lead the Islamic community together by forming a symbiotic relationship. The scholars advise the ruler based on their understanding of Islamic law, and the ruler is then expected to follow their advice.[56]

---

50 Al-ʿUtaybī, *Aḍwāʾ ʿalā al-siyāsa al-sharʿiyya*, 121–24.

51 Al-ʿAṭṭiya, *Al-Siyāsa al-sharʿiyya*, 591–655.

52 Ibid., 659–99.

53 Al-ʿUtaybī, *Aḍwāʾ ʿalā al-siyāsa al-sharʿiyya*, 41.

54 Ibid., 45.

55 Yaser Ellethy, *Islam, Context, Pluralism and Democracy: Classical and Modern Interpretations* (London: Routledge, 2015), 247.

56 Johansen, "Signs as Evidence," 181.

In practice, Frank Vogel argued, the scholars and the ruler would be in competition. Siyāsa sharʿiyya, he maintained, would be a way to organize the relationship between the scholars and the ruler, since the doctrine offers "a constitutional theory by which the excesses of rulers may be curtailed and sharīʿa legitimacy extended to actual states."[57] Similarly, Benjamin Jokisch emphasized the conflict between the jurists and the ruler. Since the doctrine of siyāsa sharʿiyya does not assign the ruler the power to legislate, the ʿulamāʾ could limit the ruler's power through their interpretation of Islamic law. Jokisch claimed that this power struggle was the reason for several conflicts in Islamic history after Ibn Taymiyya.[58]

Like Ibn Taymiyya, Saudi scholars generally maintain that the ʿulamāʾ and the ruler jointly lead the Islamic community by following what God has instructed. For the Saudi jurists, both are, in the Quranic sense (Q 4:59), the commanders (*ulū al-amr*) of the community. However, the ʿulamāʾ differ in their relationship with the ruler. For instance, Ibn ʿUthaymīn (d. 2001), another eminent twentieth-century Saudi scholar, argued that the jurists would be the community's true leaders, whereas the ruler would merely enforce their decision. In his ḥadīth commentary, he writes:

> The leaders [*aʾimma*] of the Muslims are two groups of people:
>
> First, the scholars, by that it is meant religious scholars [*ʿulamāʾ rabāniyūn*], who inherited the Prophet in his knowledge, worship, morals [*akhlāq*] and his mission [*daʿwa*]. Those are the true leaders [*hum ulū al-amr ḥaqīqatan*] because they address the public [*al-ʿāmma*], and the rulers [*umarāʾ*], and they define [*yubayyinūn*] the religion and call to [follow] it.
>
> The second group of the leaders of the Muslims are the enforcing rulers [*umarāʾ munaffidhūn*] of the sharīʿa. Because of that, we say the ʿulamāʾ define, and the rulers enforce, they have to enforce God's law in their rule and their worship to God.[59]

Ibn al-Qayyim had already distinguished between the ʿulamāʾ as messengers (*muballighūn*) of the Prophet's command and the purely executing rulers

57 Article "Siyāsa" in the *Encyclopedia of Islam, Second Edition*. Available online: dx.doi.org/10.1163/1573-3912_islam_COM_1096 [last access: 24 June 2022].

58 Benjamin Jokisch, *Islamic Imperial Law: Harun Al-Rashid's Codification Project* (Berlin: Walter de Gruyter, 2007), 396.

59 Muḥammad bin Ṣāliḥ Ibn ʿUthaymīn, *Sharḥ al-arbaʿīn al-nabawiyya* (Dār al-Thurayyā, 1425/2004), 138.

(*munaffidhūn*).[60] Unlike Ibn ʿUthaymīn, who saw the ʿulamāʾ as the "true leaders," Ibn al-Qayyim did not rank the ʿulamāʾ above the rulers. Nevertheless, in the contemporary Saudi legal discourse, the notion of cooperation between the scholars and the ruler is prevailing in the jurists' writings, speeches, and lessons. To some extent, this may be due to the increasingly authoritative climate in Saudi Arabia. In recent years, famous ʿulamāʾ have been imprisoned; however, until now, none of these scholars was part of the core Saudi scholarly establishment.

The jurists' reluctance to explicitly elevate themselves over the king is also grounded in their belief that every Muslim and, therefore, also the ʿulamāʾ, must obey the ruler. Although a sense of superiority towards the king can be felt among some of the ʿulamāʾ, most of them acknowledge (at least publicly) that they are not more than consultants, first to the king and second to society at large. Ṣāliḥ bin Fawzān al-Fawzān, one of the most influential members of the Council of Senior Scholars, maintained that the ʿulamāʾ would occupy a unique position in the society due to their role as inheritors of the prophets (*anbiyāʾ*). However, in contrast to the ruler, the scholars would not express their own opinions but only report what was transmitted to them from the Prophet. Their role, al-Fawzān stated, would be limited to informing the community and the ruler on what has been passed down to them.[61]

In practice, the power relationship between the ruler and the ʿulamāʾ is far more complex. Often, the ʿulamāʾ and the king share an agenda, especially when it comes to the kingdom's religious legitimation. We have already seen that the ʿulamāʾ are a very diverse group. Whenever a conflict arises, parts of the ʿulamāʾ tend to join the king's agenda for ideological or pragmatic purposes, whereas others insist on their positions. The debate on codification, which we will discuss in detail in Chapter 4, is a good example of the multilayered interactions between the ʿulamāʾ and the king.

4 The Expression of the Doctrine in the Saudi Legal System

4.1 *The 1992 Basic Law of Governance*

Technically, Saudi Arabia still does not have a written constitution. Although King ʿAbd al-ʿAzīz announced a Saudi constitution in 1932, despite many

---

60 Ibn al-Qayyim, *Iʿlām al-muwaqqiʿīn ʿan Rabb al-ʿĀlamīn* (Beirut: Dār al-Kutub al-ʿIlmiyya, 1425/2004), 376.

61 Al-Fawzān's fatwa on the issue can be found on his official homepage, www.alfawzan.af.org.sa/en/node/2018 [last access: 7 June 2022].

promises no such text was produced for the following sixty years. The First Gulf War, which started in 1990, put Saudi Arabia in the spotlight of international media, Western governments, and human rights groups. King Fahd reacted to increasing demands for reform and on March 1, 1992 eventually issued the Basic Law of Governance (al-Niẓām al-Asāsī li-l-Ḥukm).[62]

However, in Article 1, the Basic Law states that it is not intended to serve as a constitution. The only constitution (*dustūr*) of the kingdom would be the Quran and the Sunna of the Prophet Muḥammad. Nevertheless, the Basic Law's eighty-three articles address many issues that can usually be found in modern constitutions. A Saudi lawyer jokingly remarked that the Basic Law of Governance is a constitution which states in its first article that it is not one.[63]

There are considerable differences between the Basic Law of Governance and modern constitutions. Whereas most constitutions in the Arab world promise rights to the country's citizens that are in practice rarely guaranteed, the Basic Law of Governance is, as Abdulaziz Al-Fahad put it, "unabashedly honest, promulgating no rights that will not be protected, promising no elections, and not conceding the principle of accountable governance in any direct way."[64]

The Basic Law is not meant to grant constitutional rights to Saudi citizens, at least not directly. Instead, it is an expression of the Saudi king's commitment to siyāsa sharʿiyya. In several of its articles, the Basic Law lays down the king's obligation to implement and follow Islamic law.[65] For instance, in Article 55, the Basic Law specifies:

> The king manages the affairs of the community [*umma*] according to siyāsa sharʿiyya by applying the rulings of Islam. He oversees the application of the Islamic sharīʿa, the state laws [*anẓima*], the general state policies, and the country's protection and defence.

The former head of the Higher Judicial Institute, Zayd al-Zayd, argued that it was not so much its content but its legal nature that distinguished the Basic Law from a modern constitution. In contrast to modern constitutions, al-Zayd

62 Abdulaziz Al-Fahad, "Ornamental Constitutionalism: The Saudi Basic Law of Governance," *Yale Journal of International Law* 39, no. 2 (2005), 377.

63 However, the kingdom is not the only country that refrains from using the term constitution. For instance, after the Second World War, West Germany's constitution was called Basic Law in order to emphasize its provisional character until a true German constitution was issued after Germany's reunification.

64 Al-Fahad, "Ornamental Constitutionalism," 376.

65 See also Vogel, *Saudi Business Law*, 28.

wrote, the Basic Law was not the highest-ranking law, since it is surpassed by Islamic law.[66]

The Basic Law specifies that it is only the implementation of Islamic law, not the will of the people, that binds the Saudi government. In Article 7, the Basic Law stipulates:

> The government of the Saudi kingdom derives its authority from the Quran and the Sunna of the Prophet. They are the sovereign of this law and all other state laws.

Yet, the Basic Law assigns both the ruler (*ḥākim*) and the ruled (*maḥkūm*) rights and duties which are very different to those usually laid down in modern constitutions. Whereas the ruler can demand obedience, the ruled can insist that the ruler follows his obligation to command right and forbid wrong in order to establish justice. The law expresses this principle in Article 23:

> The state protects the Islamic creed and the sharīʿa, and it commands good and forbids wrong, and carries out the duty of propagating Islam [*daʿwa ilā Allāh*].

The doctrine of siyāsa sharʿiyya is thus not only a theory of the ʿulamāʾ but is incorporated into Saudi state legislation. Therefore, Article 1 of the Basic Law is not only symbolic. It articulates that the Basic Law is nothing more than the king's public declaration to follow the teachings of Islamic law. Laws and the legal system, as the Basic Law emphasizes several times, play a primary role in the king's commitment to siyāsa sharʿiyya. Article 48 of the Basic Law lays down:

> The courts apply the rulings of the Islamic sharīʿa in cases that are brought before them in accordance with what the Quran and the Sunna prescribe and in accordance with the codes issued by the ruler [provided that they] do not contradict the Quran and the Sunna.

This means that every legal act in the kingdom, whether by a judge or the king, has to be legitimated from the perspective of the Islamic legal tradition.

---

66 Zayd bin ʿAbd al-Karīm al-Zayd, "Maṣādir istimdād al-anẓima al-ʿadliyya," in *Al-Niẓām al-ʿadl fī al-Saʿūdiyya*, ed. Muḥammad bin Saʿūd al-Bashr and Manṣūr bin ʿAbd al-Raḥmān al-Ḥaydarī (Riyadh: Markaz al-Fikr al-ʿĀlamī, 1436/2010), 19.

4.2 *The Relationship between the King and the Judge*

According to siyāsa sharʿiyya, all public offices are similarly obliged to implement Islamic law, the rulers, the governors, and the judges alike.[67] Since all share the same responsibility, the tasks of the administration and the judiciary blur. For Ibn Taymiyya, judgeship is not merely an office at court, but every decision-maker can act as a judge. He wrote that the term *qāḍī*

> applies to each and every one who issues a decision in a conflict between two parties or who arbitrates between them, no matter whether he is a caliph, a sultan, a deputy or a governor, whether he was appointed in order to judge according to the sacred law; or as the deputy of such a judge deciding in a conflict between parties, even if he judges nothing more than the quality of the handwriting among children who turned to him for his purpose.[68]

The judiciary is not conceptualized as the ruler's antagonist. Instead, the ruler and the judges are supposed to work hand in hand in the judiciary towards the full implementation of Islamic law. From the perspective of classical European constitutional theory, we could say that the executive and the judicial branch of the state fall together. Jurists, therefore, do not consider the Saudi judiciary to be independent from the ruler. However, both the ruler and the judiciary are controlled by the strong authority of the ʿulamāʾ's interpretation of Islamic law.

Leading ʿulamāʾ encourage their peers to join the judiciary. It is the individual duty (*farḍ ʿayn*) of every capable Muslim, the jurists argue, to work as a judge when needed.[69] Judges are obliged to follow the judicial procedures and respect the court system that the ruler has established. According to siyāsa sharʿiyya, the rulers' task is to address general questions of the community, whereas the judge only decides cases that are brought before him. Thus, from the perspective of the doctrine, a judge in court is not more than a delegate (*nāʾib*) of the ruler.

The ruler, on the other hand, is the guarantor of the legal system. As such, the king issues laws and regulations that the judges are obliged to follow.

---

67 Johansen, "Signs as Evidence," 185.

68 Cited after Johanson, "Perfect Law," 268. For the original text in Arabic, see Ibn Taymiyya, *Al-Siyāsa al-sharʿiyya*, 12–13.

69 See, for example, Ibn Qudāma, *Al-Mughnī* (Beirut: Dār ʿĀlam al-Kutub, 1417/1997), 14:5. However, judgeship is, as we will see in more detail in Chapter 4, considered a dangerous endeavor, and Islamic history is full of examples of scholars who tried to escape it.

Saudi jurists today acknowledge that there is a Saudi legislative power (*sulṭa tanẓīmiyya*). This is also expressed in Article 44 of the Basic Law of Governance:

> The powers (*sulṭāt*) of the state consist of:
> – The judicial power
> – The executive power
> – The legislative power
> These powers work together in fulfilling their tasks according to this and other laws. The king is the source (*marjiʿ*) of these powers.

Since it ultimately grants all power to the king, the Basic Law of Governance explicitly refrains from establishing a checks and balances system similar to European constitutions. Maḥmūd bin ʿAlī Wāfī, a lecturer at Qaṣīm University, therefore argued that the king cannot be considered to hold only the state's executive power, but, since the judges are the king's delegates, he also represents the judicial system.[70] The king's powers are, of course, limited by his obligation to implement Islamic law as interpreted by the jurists.

The ruled can demand that the ruler oversees the courts and ensures that they apply Islamic law. Despite Article 44 of the Basic Law, Saudi jurists regularly emphasize that the Saudi judiciary is independent.[71] Likewise, Article 46 of the Basic Law stipulates:

> The judiciary is an independent power. There is no authority over the judges in their adjudication other than the Islamic sharīʿa.

However, judicial independence is understood very differently: in the writings of Saudi jurists, it means that the government is not allowed to intervene in the adjudication of an individual case,[72] not that the judiciary itself is a separate and independent entity.

4.3 *The King's Power to Legislate*

Notwithstanding its central role in the formation of the Saudi state, Islamic law is not the only type of law applied in the Saudi legal system today. As we

70 Maḥmūd bin ʿAlī Wāfī, *Al-Qaḍāʾ al-ʿāmm fī al-Mamlaka al-ʿArabiyya al-Saʿūdiyya* (Riyadh: Maktabat al-Rushd, 1436/2015), 260–61.

71 See, for example, Nāṣir bin Muḥammad Jawfān, "Istiqlāl al-qaḍāʾ fī al-Mamlaka al-ʿArabiyya al-Saʿūdiyya," *Majallat al-ʿAdl* 1 (1420/1999): 143–65.

72 At least in theory, ministers face a prison sentence of a minimum of five years when they use their power to interfere with the judiciary for personal reasons. See Article 5 w) of the Code of the Prosecution of Ministers (Niẓām Muḥākamat al-Wuzarāʾ).

have seen, the doctrine of siyāsa sharʿiyya only grants the ruler the right to uphold and enforce Islamic law, not to create or interpret it.[73] However, legislation that supplements Islamic law has been known since early Islam. As part of his role as the community's leader, the ruler may issue laws as long as they do not conflict with the prevailing interpretation of Islamic law. While the first caliphs had already issued tax laws based on their authority as successors of the Prophet, it was the Ottoman rulers who, beginning in the late fifteenth century, systematically used their power to issue laws.[74] In the nineteenth century, the Ottoman sultans made extensive use of codes, on the one hand, to modernize their legal system and, on the other hand, to react to new legal phenomena that arose with modern life, especially with modern capitalism.

The Ottoman codes were applied in the Ḥijāz before the Saudi conquest. In the Najd, however, only a few regulations issued by the king were in force at that time. After King ʿAbd al-ʿAzīz had conquered the Ḥijāz in 1926, he had to decide on the future of Ottoman laws in the newly founded third Saudi kingdom. On 11 February 1927, leading Saudi ʿulamāʾ released a fatwa according to which the courts in the Ḥijāz should immediately stop the application of positive laws and return to what they understood as the "pure" sharīʿa.[75] However, the ʿulamāʾ could not provide solutions for the numerous issues addressed in the Ottoman codes. Moreover, they were not used to quickly developing answers to new legal problems. As a result, the king did not consider their call to return to the "pure" sharīʿa a realistic option. A few months after the issuing of the fatwa, on 28 June 1927, King ʿAbd al-ʿAzīz announced that the Ottoman laws would continue to be applied until they were replaced with new regulations.[76]

In the following years and decades, the Saudi kings not only replaced the Ottoman laws but issued a large number of different codes themselves, which now regulate many areas of the law comprehensively. For Saudi jurists, this is a necessary and desired facet of the king's role as leader of the state. Ibn Khunayn, for instance, wrote in his commentary on the sharīʿa procedural code (Niẓām al-Murāfaʿāt al-Sharʿiyya):

---

73 Bernard Weiss, "Interpretation in Islamic Law: The Theory of Ijtihad," *American Journal of Comparative Law* 26, no. 2 (1978): 201.

74 See for an overview of the development of codes in early Islam the Article "Kānūn" in the *Encyclopedia of Islam, Second Edition*. Available online: dx.doi.org/10.1163/1573-3912_islam_COM_0439 [last access: 4 June 2022].

75 Muḥammad bin Barrāk al-Fawzān, *Al-Tanẓīm al-qaḍāʾī al-jadīd fī al-Mamlaka al-ʿArabiyya al-Saʿūdiyya* (Riyadh: Maktabat al-Qānūn al-Iqtiṣād, 1431/2010), 57–58.

76 Ibid., 58.

> The codes are issued by the ruler or his deputies, depending on [their] competence, in order to guarantee the protection of the five necessities[77] [*al-ḍarūriyāt al-khams*], and they are consistent with the objectives [*maqāṣid*] of the sharīʿa and its general principles [*qawāʿid*]. They do not deviate from the [respective] texts in the Quran and the Sunna. Such deviation makes the code invalid. The Prophet says what ʿAlī bin Abī Ṭālib narrated: "No obedience in the wrong, but obedience in the commanded." Ibn Taymiyya (d. 728 [*hijrī*]) says: No one has the right to deviate from the Quran and the Sunna of the Prophet, neither the shaykhs [*mashāʾikh*] and the poor, nor the kings and the rulers [*umarāʾ*], nor the scholars [*ʿulamāʾ*] and the judges and others, rather all mankind has to obey God and his Prophet.[78,79]

The kings carefully avoid giving the impression that they would replace Islamic law with positive law. On 2 March 1976, the Saudi Council of Ministers decided that the Arabic word *musharriʿ* (usually translated as "legislator") could not be applied to the Saudi kings.[80] Moreover, the kings explicitly refrain from using the common Arabic term for positive law (*qānūn*) but instead employ the less controversial word *niẓām* (pl. *anẓima*), which is often translated as "statute" or "code."

Until today, Saudi scholars discuss the differences between qānūn and niẓām. While a few jurists argue that the terms are synonyms and that Islamic scholars used the word qānūn in the past, the majority see a difference in meaning between the two terms. They argue that qānūn is generally used to distinguish positive law from revealed Islamic law. It is mostly the association with the idea of positive law that makes the term qānūn problematic. In contrast, the word niẓām refers to a subcategory of Islamic law and thus signifies that the written law is in line with Quran and Sunna. Hence, the use of the term ensures that everyone understands the superiority of Islamic law in the Saudi legal system.[81] Anẓima are seen as a part of the sharīʿa, which means

77 The five necessities are religion, life, intellect, progeny, and property. See Felicitas Opwis, *Maṣlaḥa and the Purpose of the Law: Islamic Discourse on Legal Change from the 4th/10th to 8th/14th Century* (Leiden: Brill, 2010), 4.

78 See Ibn Taymiyya, *Majmūʿat al-fatāwā* (Beirut: Dār Ibn Ḥazm, 1432/2011), 11:465.

79 ʿAbd Allāh bin Muḥammad Āl Khunayn, *Al-Kāshif fī sharḥ niẓām al-murāfaʿāt al-sharʿiyya al-Saʿūdī* (Riyadh: Dār Ibn al-Farḥūn, 1433/2012), 1:17.

80 Bakr bin ʿAbd Allāh Abū Zayd, *Muʿjam al-manāhī al-lafẓiyya* (Riyadh: Dār al-ʿĀṣima, 1417/1996), 509.

81 Al-ʿUtaybī, *Maqālāt fī al-siyāsa al-sharʿiyya*, 23.

that there is, at least in theory, no significant difference between the authority of a niẓām and that of fiqh treatises. For the jurists, both are equally valid as long as they do not contradict the revelation. Like jurisprudential writings, Zayd al-Zayd argued, a niẓām is a direct product of the sources of Islamic law.[82]

Today, the vast majority of anẓima can be found in the fields that al-ʿUtaybī described as the main areas of siyāsa sharʿiyya: the overall system of governance, the state's financial administration, trade, the organization of the judicial system, the penal system, and international relations.[83] In other areas, only a few legal issues, mostly related to judicial procedure, are addressed by anẓima. In areas that are traditionally not much discussed by Islamic jurists, the kings often turned to Egyptian, European, or North American law to develop anẓima, especially since the 1970s.[84] After the millennium, the number of statutes increased immensely, and in 2023, 447 anẓima were in force.[85] The oldest niẓām still in effect is the commercial code (*niẓām tijārī*), which was issued on 18 May 1931. Most anẓima can today be found in state and administrative law. For example, anẓima regulate the regional government, court administration, public services, and the military. Apart from that, statutes play an increasingly important role in criminal and commercial law. As we will see in Chapter 7, there is not yet a single criminal niẓām, but separate statutes regulate key areas of contemporary criminal law. Relevant criminal anẓima address, among other things, money laundering, counterfeiting, drug trafficking, and corruption. In commercial law, the most relevant anẓima regulate company and competition law.

While the term anẓima was long used only for laws that are not based on fiqh, this changed with the introduction of the first codifications of Islamic law in the 2020s. The new codifications are now also called anẓima, notwithstanding their origin in Islamic jurisprudence.

82 Zayd bin ʿAbd al-Karīm al-Zayd, "Maṣādir istimdād al-anẓima al-ʿadliyya," in *Al-Niẓām al-ʿadl fī al-Saʿūdiyya*, ed. Muḥammad bin Saʿūd al-Bashr and Manṣūr bin ʿAbd al-Raḥmān al-Ḥaydarī (Riyadh: Markaz al-Fikr al-ʿĀlamī, 1436/2010), 36.

83 Al-ʿUtaybī, *Aḍwāʾ ʿalā al-siyāsa al-sharʿiyya*, 121–24.

84 All anẓima can be accessed through the Bureau of Experts' (Hay'at al-Khubarāʾ) website: laws.boe.gov.sa/BoeLaws/Laws/Folders/1 [last access: 21 April 2023].

85 According to the website of the Bureau of Experts: laws.boe.gov.sa/BoeLaws/Laws/ [last access: 21 April 2023].

5 The Structure of the Saudi Court System

5.1 *Administrative Courts*

Generally speaking, the Saudi court system consists, on the one hand, of administrative courts, called the Board of Grievances (Dīwān al-Maẓālim) and, on the other hand, of the sharīʿa courts.[86] Additionally, specialized courts, like the counterterrorism courts, have been introduced, which only apply the controversial Counter-Terrorism Act (Niẓām Mukāfaḥat Jarāʾim al-Irhāb wa-Tamwilihi). Furthermore, more than one hundred semi-administrative tribunals can be found, which usually only adjudicate a narrow field of the law. They originate from subdivisions of ministries or other administrative bodies and have, over time, become individual institutions. Among them are disciplinary tribunals for the military and police, but also commercial tribunals, like the Banking Disputes Committee or the Committees for the Settlement of Finance Disputes.[87]

The idea and the name of the Board of Grievances have their roots in premodern Islamic jurisprudence. In medieval Islam, commoners were given the opportunity to report injustices (*maẓālim*) they had suffered by others to the ruler and ask him to interfere.[88] Following this idea, the Saudi Board of Grievances was established in 1955 as a way for Saudi citizens to complain about any injustices they experience, whether by government employees or others.[89] Initially, the board's office registered the complaints, proposed a solution, and brought the issue in front of the king. Over the next decades, the board became more powerful and independent. In 1982, the board was transformed into an independent administrative court that could decide on cases without direct interference from the king.[90] From 1987 until 2018, moreover, it had jurisdiction over all commercial disputes.[91] Today, the board is no

86 A detailed analysis of the court system is not our primary focus. For a more comprehensive, but still brief, overview of the Saudi court system, see Vogel, *Saudi Business Law*, 36–54.

87 See ibid., 46–52 for more information on these and other specialized tribunals.

88 Ibid., 39.

89 Fādī bin Muḥammad Shaʿīshaʿ, *Al-Tanẓīm al-qaḍāʾī al-jadīd fī al-Mamlaka al-ʿArabiyya al-Saʿūdiyya* (Riyadh: Maktabat al-Rushd, 1435/2014), 265.

90 Ibid., 267.

91 Commercial law always had a special place in the Saudi legal system. After the foundation of the third Saudi kingdom in 1926, commercial cases were adjudicated by a special commercial tribunal (Majlis al-Tujjār), which consisted not only of judges, but also of businessmen. In addition to Islamic law, the courts also referred to commercial customs. See ʿAlī bin Ramaḍān Barakāt, *Al-Wasīṭ fī sharḥ niẓām al-qaḍāʾ al-Saʿūdī al-jadīd* (Riyadh: Maktabat al-Qānūn wa-l-Iqtiṣād, 1433/2012), 248.

longer a single court but consists of several courts, which are divided into three instances.[92] The courts hear common issues of administrative law, like appeals of administrative decisions or public-private partnerships, and also adjudicate criminal offences committed by officials.[93]

5.2 *The Sharīʿa Courts*

Generally, civil and criminal cases are handled by the sharīʿa courts, our main area of interest. The trial courts are divided into four branches: the general courts (*maḥākim al-ʿāmma*), personal status courts (*maḥākim al-aḥwāl al-shakhṣiyya*), labor courts (*maḥākim ʿummāliyya*), and commercial courts (*maḥākim tijāriyya*).[94] The specialized courts were introduced with the 2007 Code of the Judiciary (Niẓām al-Qaḍāʾ). Before the 2007 reform, a judge at the first instance court could face such diverse topics as child custody, transfer of property, and manslaughter on a single day.[95] The sharīʿa courts' general jurisdiction stemmed from premodern Islamic jurisprudence, where an Islamic judge generally handled all cases that were brought in front of him, regardless of the subject.[96]

The introduction of specialized courts was considered by many a major step towards the professionalization of the judiciary. The judges now receive extra training in all legal areas that fall in the competence of their courts. The Ministry of Justice hopes that the specialization would ensure faster handling of complex cases. Manṣūr al-Ḥaydarī even called the 2007 reform the beginning of a "new age" (*ḥiqba jadīda*) for the Saudi judiciary.[97] However, the reform was slowly implemented, and only in 2018 were the first specialized courts opened. It is still to see to what extent the specialization of the courts changes the way the law is applied. The general courts' decisions can be appealed at the appeal courts (*maḥākim al-istiʾnāf*), which we will discuss in detail in Chapter 5.

---

92 Article 8 of the 1428/2007 Code of the Board of Grievances (Niẓām Dīwān al-Maẓālim).

93 Article 13 of the 1428/2007 Code of the Board of Grievances.

94 Article 9 of the 1428/2007 Code of the Judiciary.

95 Article 26 of the 1395/1975 Code of the Judiciary granted the courts jurisdiction in all disputes and crimes.

96 Muhammad Khalid Masud, Rudolph Peters, and David Powers, "Qāḍīs and Their Courts: An Historical Survey," in *Dispensing Justice in Islam: Qadis and their Judgments*, ed. Muhammad Khalid Masud, Rudolph Peters, and David Powers (Leiden: Brill, 2006), 21.

97 Manṣūr bin ʿAbd al-Raḥmān al-Ḥaydarī, "Muʾassasat al-qaḍāʾ al-ʿāmm," in Markaz al-Fikr al-ʿĀlamī ʿan al-Saʿūdiyya, *Al-Niẓām al-ʿadl fī al-Saʿūdiyya* (Riyadh: Markaz al-Fikr al-ʿĀlamī ʿan al-Saʿūdiyya, 1436/2015), 129.

5.3 *The Higher Judicial Council*

The Higher Judicial Council (al-Majlis al-Aʿlā li-l-Qaḍāʾ) plays a vital role in the Saudi legal system, especially regarding the sharīʿa courts. It consists of the minister of justice, the minister's deputy, the chief public prosecutor, the president of the High Court, four appeal court presidents, and three appeal court judges.[98]

The Council has broad administrative competences. For example, it chooses judges and court presidents and handles all their employment issues. However, the Council is also responsible for the "supervision" (*ishrāf*) of the courts and the judges.[99] It issues statements that are circulated among the judges, in many of which the judges are prompted to follow a particular legal opinion. The binding nature of the Council's decisions is disputed, as we will see in detail in Chapter 5, but Saudi judges nevertheless regularly refer to them in their verdicts.

The Council is funded independently from the Ministry of Justice, which gives the Council some discretionary power.[100] Some argue that the Council's existence proves that the Saudi judiciary is independent. For instance, one Saudi author claimed that the fact that the Council, not the king, chooses the judges would show that the king's power over the judiciary is limited.[101] However, since the minister of justice heads the Council, it is not independent from government policies in practice nor in theory.

5.4 *Saudi State Legislation on the Judiciary*

Until the 1970s, the Saudi kings only issued a few laws that addressed the judiciary. The first procedural code for the sharīʿa courts (Niẓām Sayr al-Muḥākamāt al-Sharʿiyya) was issued in 1927 and only consisted of thirty-six articles.[102] Whenever the code was silent, the judges continued to apply the procedural rules that they found in premodern fiqh manuals. A more extensive procedural code (Niẓām al-Murāfaʿāt al-Sharʿiyya) was introduced in 1936, which comprised of 142 articles.[103] The code remained in force until it was succeeded by the 2000 Code of Procedure. Its 266 Articles for the first time

98 Article 5 of the 1428/2007 Code of the Judiciary.

99 Article 6 of the 1428/2007 Code of the Judiciary.

100 Shaʿīshaʿ, *Al-Tanẓīm al-qaḍāʾī al-jadīd fī al-Mamlaka al-ʿArabiyya al-Saʿūdiyya*, 276.

101 Wāfī, *Al-Qaḍāʾ al-ʿāmm fī al-mamlaka al-ʿArabiyya al-Saʿūdiyya*, 260.

102 ʿAbd Allāh bin Muḥammad Āl Khunayn, *Al-Kāshif fī sharḥ niẓām al-murāfaʿāt al-sharʿiyya al-Saʿūdī* (Riyadh: Dār Ibn al-Farḥūn, 1433/2012), 1:5.

103 Ibid.

regulated the different stages of the judicial process in detail. In 2013, the Code of Procedure was further extended and refined.

In general, the Code of Procedure both applies to civil and criminal cases. However, in 2013, a special Code of Criminal Procedure (Niẓām al-Ijrā'āt al-Jazā'iyya) was issued, which addresses procedural questions that are unique to criminal law. If the Code of Criminal Procedure remains silent on an issue, the judge still has to refer to the more general Code of Procedure. Areas that were extensively discussed by the 'ulamā', most importantly, the rules of evidence, are not addressed by both codes. For instance, the Code of Procedure only regulates the formalities of a witness's testimony but remains silent on whether a person can be admitted as a witness. The judges have to resort to Islamic jurisprudence, which has developed detailed rules of evidence.[104]

Nevertheless, Islamic jurisprudence also plays an important role when judges apply a specific provision of the code since the judges use the methodology and terminology of Islamic law to interpret the code.[105] It would be a mistake, Sa'd al-'Utaybī argued, to understand the *anẓima* the same way as positive law. Instead, they have always to be seen in the light of the sources of Islamic law.[106]

5.5 *The Role of Digital Technology*

Over the last decade, digital technology has been introduced to an impressive extent. In 2017, the Ministry of Justice started a project to establish a "paperless court" (*maḥkama bi-lā waraq*). By 2018, some parts of the appeal courts were already working almost fully digitally, which significantly changed the proceedings in court. In case one of the parties appeals the first instance court's decision, the judge uploads his decision to the Ministry of Justice's computer system. The administrative staff at the appeal court then accesses the first instance judge's decision through the computer system and either print the files or forwards them directly to the appeal court judges' computers. Some older judges still prefer to work on paper. In this case, the court staff has to enter the appeal

104 The application of Islamic law in procedural questions can be seen in the published court judgements. Whereas in most issues, the judges refer to the Code of Procedure, there are some issues, especially when it comes to the admissibility of witnesses, in which they directly refer to fiqh books.

105 'Abd Allāh bin Muḥammad Āl Khunayn, *Al-Madkhal ilā fiqh al-murāfa'āt* (Riyadh: Dār Ibn al-Farḥūn, 1431/2010), 187–94.

106 Sa'd bin Maṭar al-'Utaybī, "Khaṣā'iṣ al-anẓima fī al-Mamlaka al-'Arabiyya al-Sa'ūdiyya," in *Al-Niẓām al-'adl fī al-Sa'ūdiyya*, ed. Markaz al-Fikr al-'Ālamī 'an al-Sa'ūdiyya (Riyadh: Markaz al-Fikr al-'Ālamī 'an al-Sa'ūdiyya, 1436/2015), 76.

court judge's written comments into the system. The court staff in Riyadh explained to me that before the introduction of the online system, files had to be transported between the different courts, a process that could take several days.[107]

Digital technology today also plays a crucial role at the first instance courts. Lawsuits, for example, can be filed through the Ministry of Justice's website. Once the lawsuit is filed, the online system enables the parties to access information on the trial. Moreover, judgments can be enforced through an online procedure, and, more recently, the Ministry even allowed that marriages can be registered online instead of at the court.[108]

Some judges also use digital technology in their everyday work in court. Until now, however, this seems to depend on the way the individual judge organizes his courtroom. In July 2018, I spent a day attending trials in the courtroom of a young judge at the General Court in Riyadh. The judge and both of his assistants divided their attention between the parties' statements and the big computer screen that was set up at the bench. At one point, all three were sitting around the screen and only every now and then turned to the parties and asked for details on the case. The courtroom staff saved all documents on USB sticks, which had replaced the paper court files.

The Ministry's goal is to speed up the trials and make them more transparent. However, the increasing digitalization also has downsides. Data security, for instance, seems to play only a minor role. Moreover, as we will discuss in more detail in Chapter 5, the digitalization of court infrastructure not only allows the Ministry of Justice to access the parties' data easily but also the judges' decisions. Thereby, digitalization helps the Saudi government to increasingly control the judiciary.

6 Conclusion

The doctrine of siyāsa sharʿiyya requires that all state actions have to be based on Islamic law. Only then can a ruler who otherwise lacks religious justification establish himself as the leader of the Islamic community, regardless of how he came to power. Today, siyāsa sharʿiyya still forms the legal basis for Saudi rule.

107 In the summer of 2018, I had the chance to visit several courts in Riyadh and both the court staff and the judges were happy to explain the procedure in detail.

108 All online services can be accessed through the Ministry of Justice's official website, see www.moj.gov.sa.

The doctrine allows the Saudi king to demand obedience from his subjects in return for the implementation of Islamic law.

Outside the legal sector, the doctrine's influence has diminished significantly over the last decades. Siyāsa sharʿiyya also demands that the king upholds Islamic morality in the public sphere. The emergence of public dance music festivals, among other things, illustrates how much public morality has diverged from the ʿulamāʾ's interpretation of Islamic law

When it comes to the legal system, however, the doctrine still limits the kings' powers and leaves the courts largely in the hands of the ʿulamāʾ. The king's only task is to ensure due process and organize the court administration. Every reform of the court system thus must, at least in theory, be consistent with the ʿulamāʾ's interpretation of Islamic law.

CHAPTER 2

Ibn ʿAbd al-Wahhāb, Salafī Islam, and the Saudi Judiciary

1 Introduction

The Saudi judiciary is commonly described as one of the strongholds of Wahhābī Islam – a reform movement that was started by the eighteenth-century Najdī preacher Muḥammad bin ʿAbd al-Wahhāb (d. 1792). Ibn ʿAbd al-Wahhāb called for the return to *tawḥīd*, the belief in the absolute singularity of God. He and his followers forbade the worshipping of Sufi graves and other practices that they considered forbidden innovations (*bidʿa*, sing. *bidaʿ*) in the Islamic creed. The strict focus on tawḥīd served as the blueprint for Ibn ʿAbd al-Wahhāb's idea of a perfect Islamic community. Around the year 1744, he famously made a deal with Muḥammad bin Saʿūd (d. 1765), the chieftain of the small town of Darʿiya in the center of the Najd, in order to establish a state that would bring the people of the Arabian Peninsula back to tawḥīd. This was the beginning of the institutionalization of what has since been known as "Wahhābism."

At the time of Ibn ʿAbd al-Wahhāb, the center of the Arabian Peninsula was forgotten by the big empires. Strategically of minor importance, it was left by the Ottomans to several local rulers who regularly engaged in feuds with each other.[1] With the support of Ibn ʿAbd al-Wahhāb's followers, Muḥammad bin Saʿūd's military and political influence rose. Eventually, his son ʿAbd al-ʿAzīz bin Muḥammad for the first time unified the Najd under one reign. The kingdom flourished until Muḥammad bin Saʿūd's grandson, Saʿūd bin ʿAbd al-ʿAzīz conquered the Ḥijāz. The Ottoman rulers realized the threat that the Saudi emirate and its Wahhābī allies presented to the Ottoman sultan's claim to protect the two holiest cities in Islam, Mecca and Medina. Ottoman troops attacked the Saudi emirate and eventually conquered the Najd. In 1818, the first Saudi state was defeated.[2]

What initially was a bond between a local ruler and an unconventional preacher had by that time already become a pact between two families that

---

1 For an overview of the situation in the Najd before Ibn ʿAbd al-Wahhāb, see David Commins, *The Wahhabi Mission and Saudi Arabia* (London: I.B. Tauris, 2006), 7–10.

2 Ibid., 37.

shapes Saudi Arabia until today. Although he had many disciples, Ibn ʿAbd al-Wahhāb preferred that his children and grandchildren carry on his legacy and gave them the best possible education.[3] Over the next decades and centuries, his descendants held key positions in the kingdom and functioned as advisers and judges. They adopted the patronym Āl al-Shaykh, the "house of the shaykh." When the second Saudi kingdom was founded, after the withdrawal of Ottoman troops from the Najd in 1824, it was the scholars from the house of the shaykh who legitimized the rule of King Turkī bin ʿAbd Allāh. When King ʿAbd al-ʿAzīz finally unified the Arabian Peninsula again in 1932 and declared the third Saudi kingdom, scholars from Ibn ʿAbd al-Wahhāb's family were once again in leading state positions.

Until today, the bond between the two families is very visible, especially in the legal system. For example, the current Grand Mufti ʿAbd al-ʿAzīz bin ʿAbd Allāh is a direct descendent of Ibn ʿAbd al-Wahhāb. However, whereas in the past, the scholarly discourse was dominated by members of the al-Shaykh family, the Saudi scholarly establishment today consists of members of many different Najdī families. Nabil Mouline called this the democratization of the Saudi Arabian clerical corps.[4] However, scholars from outside the Najd, especially from the Ḥijāz, remain underrepresented.[5]

This chapter explores how the Wahhābī tradition has developed in Saudi Arabia and how its key beliefs have redefined the authority and role of the schools of Islamic jurisprudence. We will put a special focus on how the Wahhābī and Salafī roots of the Saudi judiciary are reflected in the way legal reasoning is understood and how this relates to the jurists' understanding of pluralism in Islamic law.

2 Wahhābism and Salafism

2.1 *What Is Wahhābism?*

2.1.1 The Controversy Surrounding the Term Wahhābism

Ibn ʿAbd al-Wahhāb never used the term Wahhābism (*wahhābiyya*) to describe his movement. It is and was mostly a foreign appellation that was historically used by opponents of the movement. Later, the term continued to be used in a pejorative way. Muḥammad bin ʿAbd al-Laṭīf (d. 1921), one of the most

---

3 Mouline, *Clerics of Islam*, 69.

4 Ibid., 171.

5 According to Nabil Mouline, seventy-three percent of the Council of Senior Scholars' members between 1971 and 2010 were of Najdī origin. Mouline, *Clerics of Islam*, 181.

prominent members of the al-Shaykh family at his time, complained that, for him, the problem with the term Wahhābism did not lie in the association with Ibn ʿAbd al-Wahhāb, but in the fact that the term implied that the movement followed another authority than the Quran and the Sunna.[6] This line of thought is still very present. The Saudi-based Syrian scholar Ṣāliḥ al-Munajjid, one of the most influential Muslim voices today, argued that since the movement would clearly not constitute a new madhhab, only ignorant people would use the term Wahhābism.[7]

The movement's adherents call themselves by different names that reflect their focus on tawḥīd. Most importantly, they use the term *al-muwaḥḥidūn*, which can be translated as "monotheists".[8] However, since all Muslims understand themselves as monotheists, the term al-muwaḥḥidūn did not prove to be distinguishable. As a result, the movement's followers increasingly accepted being called Wahhābīs by others.[9] When Ibn Bāz (d. 1999) was asked about the term, he stated that, for him, Wahhābism was, in fact, an honourable and acceptable description because it was the name of the people who call for tawḥīd.[10] Ṣāliḥ al-Fawzān even replied in a fatwa that it would be an honour to be called a Wahhābī since Wahhābism was not more than the legitimate quest for tawḥīd.[11] Nevertheless, even though some scholars accept being called Wahhābīs, Saudi ʿulamāʾ usually do not refer to themselves as Wahhābīs, and many still consider the term a misnomer.[12]

The controversy about the term Wahhābism is reflected in the way Saudi kings referred to the movement. In 1929, King ʿAbd al-ʿAzīz forbade the use of the name and replaced it, mostly for political reasons, with the then still less contentious term "Salafism."[13] By that time, the movement had gotten a bad

6 ʿAbd al-Raḥmān bin Muḥammad bin Qāsim, *Al-Durar al-saniyya fī al-ajwiba al-najdiyya* (N.p, 1417/1996), 1:566.

7 Al-Munajjid's fatwa page islamqa.info is constantly ranked as one of the most visited websites on Islam worldwide. The fatwa can be accessed through the website, see bit.ly/2uBDTsS [last access: 28 January 2020].

8 ʿAbd Allāh bin Ṣāliḥ al-ʿUthaymīn, *Al-Shaykh Muḥammad bin ʿAbd al-Wahhāb: Ḥayātuhu wa-fikruhu* (Riyadh: Dār al-ʿUlūm, 1406/1986), 103.

9 Mouline, *Clerics of Islam*, 9.

10 An audio recording of the fatwa can be found on binbaz.org.sa, bit.ly/2RDOJYh [last access: 29 January 2020].

11 An audio recording of the fatwa can be found on YouTube, www.youtube.com/watch?time_continue=10&v=u2MeW1CN1A4&feature=emb_title [last access: 29 January 2023].

12 ʿAbd Allāh bin Muḥammad al-ʿAbd al-Laṭīf, *Daʿāwā al-munāwiʾīn li-daʿwat al-shaykh Muḥammad bin ʿAbd al-Wahhāb: ʿArḍ wa-naqḍ* (Riyadh: Dār Ṭayba li-l-Nashr wa-l-Tawzīʿ, 1409/1989), 76.

13 Mouline, *Clerics of Islam*, 9, 111.

image. Since the late nineteenth century, Ottoman propaganda and Western travellers had increasingly become aware of the movement and depicted them as bloodthirsty, ignorant, and fanatical Bedouins.[14]

Until today, Saudi leaders refrain from using the term Wahhābism when they talk about law and religion in Saudi Arabia. In his famous interview with TIME magazine in 2018, Crown Prince Muhammad bin Salman said that there was no such thing as Wahhābism in Saudi Arabia and stated that he would "need someone to explain to me what are the teachings of Wahhābism." Instead of describing a particular set of beliefs, Muhammad bin Salman argued that the term was first used by extremists to legitimize themselves by creating a link to Saudi Arabia, and second by Iran, which claimed that Saudi Arabia had invented a different school of Sunni Islam. Muhammad bin Salman insisted in the interview that Saudi Arabia encourages and includes all schools of Islam, the four major schools of Sunni Islam and the various schools of Shia Islam.[15] However, from an academic perspective, the teachings of Saudi ʿulamāʾ, as it will be shown presently, are undoubtedly influenced by the thought of Ibn ʿAbd al-Wahhāb and his followers.

2.1.2 The Teachings of Ibn ʿAbd al-Wahhāb

The Prophet Muḥammad had once said that Islam began as something strange and would become strange again.[16] Ibn ʿAbd al-Wahhāb was convinced that it was in his times, the late 1700s, that Islam had, due to deviations from the Prophet's original teachings, again turned into something strange.[17] He saw himself as one of the "renewers" (*mujaddidūn*, sing. *mujaddid*) of Islam, who according to a Prophetic hadith, appear at the turn of every century.[18]

Ibn ʿAbd al-Wahhāb is often described more as an activist than an intellectual. Although he was from a scholarly family, his writings are widely considered to lack originality. For instance, Nabil Mouline argued that Ibn ʿAbd al-Wahhāb did not change Ḥanbalī doctrine but only aimed to impose orthopraxy.[19] Mouline claimed that "[h]is writings are a near systematic reprise of the classic Ḥanbalī corpus, his main contribution being to render this generally

14 Ibid., 107.

15 The interview can be found on TIME magazine's website, time.com/5228006/mohammed-bin-salman-interview-transcript-full [last access: 30 January 2023].

16 Al-Tirmidhī, *Jāmiʿ al-Tirmidhī* (Riyadh: Bayt al-Afkār al-Dawliyya, 1424/2003), 426 (Nr. 2629).

17 Commins, *Wahhabi Mission*, 16.

18 Abū Dāwūd, *Sunan Abī Dāwūd* (Damascus: Dār al-Risāla al-ʿĀlamiyya, 1430/2009), 6:349 (Nr. 4291).

19 Mouline, *Clerics of Islam*, 62.

very elitist production accessible to a larger public."[20] Samira Haj criticized this common depiction of Ibn ʿAbd al-Wahhāb as a simple transmitter of Ḥanbalī thought as an oversimplification. She suggested that his originality lies not in the fact that he "invented" new ideas but in the way he referred to ideas that were already present in the Islamic tradition. Haj pointed out that Ibn ʿAbd al-Wahhāb did not just randomly pick quotes from medieval texts but that his thinking was expressed in the way he put together these ideas.[21]

In fact, Ibn ʿAbd al-Wahhāb's theological and legal opinions differ in many aspects from traditional Ḥanbalī thought. For example, he was quick to declare others, even prominent Muslims, to be unbelievers whenever they did not follow his understanding of tawḥīd.[22] Mainstream Ḥanbalīs, on the contrary, were very careful in doing so. Moreover, his stance against Sufi practices contradicted traditional Ḥanbalī doctrine, which was more tolerant.[23] These deviations from traditional Ḥanbalism led to fierce disputes between him and other Najdī and Ḥijāzī ʿulamāʾ, among them many Ḥanbalīs.

David Commins called the association with the supposedly strict Ḥanbalī school "one of the myths about the Wahhābī tradition."[24] He pointed out that the most distinctive aspect of Wahhābī thought is that for Ibn ʿAbd al-Wahhāb, the mere claim of practising tawḥīd is not sufficient. The true Muslim, Ibn ʿAbd al-Wahhāb demanded, has to refute any object of worship other than God.[25] From the Wahhābī perspective, whoever turns to holy men or saints for help or sacrifices animals for anybody other than God is an idolater (*mushrik*) and thus an unbeliever (*kāfir*). Consequently, Ibn ʿAbd al-Wahhāb's main aim was to fight popular practices that he considered idolatry (*shirk*), most importantly, the worshipping of tombs of saints.

Violence was a legitimate way for him to reach his goals. He justified the destruction of popular Sufi shrines, legitimized attacks on Muslims he considered idolaters, and had prisoners of war executed when they refused to adopt his understanding of Islam. One of the most problematic practices, in his opinion, was the prayer at the Prophet's tomb, which he considered a violation of tawḥīd. Until today, scholars in Ibn ʿAbd al-Wahhāb's tradition, like Ṣāliḥ al-ʿUṣaymī, a professor at Riyadh's Imām University, call for the destruction

---

20 Ibid., 67.

21 Haj, "Reordering Islamic Orthodoxy," 340.

22 Ibn ʿAbd al-Wahhāb even declared his own brother Sulaymān an unbeliever, because he was critical of Ibn ʿAbd al-Wahhāb's teachings, Commins, *Wahhabi Mission*, 22.

23 For example, one of Ibn ʿAbd al-Wahhāb's earliest critics, the Ḥanbalī scholar al-Ṭandatāwī, was a member of a Sufi ṭarīqa, see Samer Traboulsi, "An Early Refutation of Muḥammad ibn ʿAbd al-Wahhāb's Reformist Views," *Die Welt des Islams* 42, no. 3 (2002), 380.

24 Commins, *Wahhabi Mission*, 12.

25 Ibid., 7–10.

of the tomb. In 2005, al-ʿUṣaymī prompted the Saudi authorities to demolish the tomb's dome. However, the jurists are aware that the tomb's destruction is refused by many Muslims, especially outside of Saudi Arabia. Therefore, the king, al-ʿUṣaymī wrote, should wait for a good opportunity to destroy the tomb in order to avoid unrest (*fitna*) among the Islamic community.[26]

2.1.3 The Difference between Law and Creed in Ibn ʿAbd al-Wahhāb's Thought

When assessing Ibn ʿAbd al-Wahhāb's teachings, we have to differentiate between his creed (*ʿaqīda*) and his approach to jurisprudence (*fiqh*). Whereas the Ḥanbalī tradition remained important for Ibn ʿAbd al-Wahhāb's understanding of creed, he held that the individual believer was free to follow the school of his choice in jurisprudence.[27]

But Ibn ʿAbd al-Wahhāb's strict understanding of tawḥīd also has implications for the law.[28] For him, idolatry not only has negative implications for the relationship between an individual and God but for the whole Islamic community. He considered law to be one of the foundations of the Islamic community and looked at it through the lens of his understanding of tawḥīd. As a result of the unconditional submission to God, all human-created aspects and categories of the law lose their authority.[29]

Accordingly, Ibn ʿAbd al-Wahhāb was suspicious of fiqh and its methodology, whereas he emphasized the role of the revelation. This scepticism resulted in a profound critique of the religious establishment of his times. He accused them of blindly following (*taqlīd*) established opinions in jurisprudence. Ibn ʿAbd al-Wahhāb complained that the jurists took medieval legal opinions for granted and did not review whether they were actually in line with the Islamic revelation.[30] The scholars should again engage in the study of Quran and Sunna and re-evaluate their teachings. At the same time, he was cautious in his call for independent legal reasoning (*ijtihād*) and never explicitly referred to himself as a *mujtahid*, a scholar capable of independent legal reasoning.[31]

---

26 Ṣāliḥ Al-ʿUṣaymī, *Bidaʿ al-qubūr: Anwāʿuha wa-aḥkāmuha* (Riyadh: Dār al-Faḍīla, 1426/2005), 253; Today, the question whether the tomb of the Prophet should be destroyed is discussed in the context of siyāsa sharʿiyya. See, for example, Al-ʿUtaybī, *Maqālāt fī al-siyāsa al-sharʿiyya*, 81–83.

27 Mouline, *Clerics of Islam*, 65.

28 Haj, "Reordering Islamic Orthodoxy," 339.

29 Ibid., 343.

30 Ibid., 340.

31 Guido Steinberg, *Religion und Staat in Saudi-Arabien: Die wahhabitischen Gelehrten 1902–1953* (Würzburg: Egon Verlag, 2002), 313.

Even though many Najdī scholars refused his call, Ibn ʿAbd al-Wahhāb's bond with the Saudi rulers helped him to spread his message. By the nineteenth century, his reformist movement dominated the religious and legal life in the Najd. With the Saudi conquest of the Ḥijāz in the 1920s, his followers encountered another intellectual movement in Islam, which surprisingly shared many of their key beliefs: modernist Salafism.

2.2 *What Is Salafism?*

2.2.1 The Two Forms of Salafism

Like Wahhābism, Salafism (*salafiyya*) is a contentious term. Firstly, as Henri Lauzière pointed out, it describes not only one movement but very different understandings of Islam.[32] Lauzière even argued that the question "What is Salafism?" could not be answered due to the concept's controversial nature, both in the primary and the secondary literature.[33] Secondly, like Wahhābism, the term Salafism is mostly a foreign appellation, which is refused by the majority of the people who are called Salafists. Thirdly, due to the rise of Salafī jihadism, the term is increasingly linked with violence and terrorism.

Today, two main movements are commonly described as Salafī in Western literature: modernist Salafism and purist Salafism. Even though both movements are very different in their goals and beliefs, they share a focus on the first three generations of Muslims, the *salaf* (often translated as the "pious predecessors"), which traditionally play an essential role in the Islamic tradition. According to a well-known account, the Prophet said that the best people were those of his and the two following generations.[34]

2.2.2 Modernist Salafism

The Salafī movement started at the end of the nineteenth century, when Islamic scholars and activists, mostly from Egypt, engaged in a reinterpretation of the Islamic tradition. This movement is today known as the first salafiyya, or modernist Salafism. It is mostly associated with three scholars: Jamāl al-Dīn al-Afghānī (d. 1897), Muḥammad ʿAbduh (d. 1905), and Rashīd Riḍā (d. 1935). These Muslim intellectuals wanted to leave behind the rigid system of norms that Islam had, in their opinion, become and to renew Islam by thinking again like the salaf. For ʿAbduh, the salaf were not only the first three generations of Muslims, as it was commonly understood, but he used the term more broadly

32 See Lauzière, *Making of Salafism*, 2.

33 Ibid., 14.

34 Al-Bukhārī, *Ṣaḥīḥ al-Bukhārī* (Damascus: Dār Ibn Kathīr, 1423/2002), 1601 (Nr. 6428).

to describe the timeframe in which the fundamentals of Muslim thought were established. In his view, this period ended with the death of al-Ghazālī in 1111.[35]

The modernists questioned the authority of traditional Sunni teachings, which they considered backward and antiquated. Islamic teachings should be revived and brought in line with modernity,[36] which made some of their ideas radical at the time. In his famous book *The Liberation of the Woman* (*Taḥrīr al-marʾa*), Qāsim Amīn, a companion of Muḥammad ʿAbduh, even argued that the veil was not mandatory for women but a non-Islamic custom that was adopted by Islam and framed religiously.[37] Further, a strong sense of anticolonialism fueled the movement's desire to modernize Islam. Throughout the nineteenth century, European influence had risen in the Arab world, and secular ideas and laws spread in the region. The modernist Salafīs hoped that a reform of Islam could help to overcome the European domination of the region and restore the leading role of the Islamic community. To achieve the desired renewal, modernist Salafīs called to end the blind imitation (*taqlīd*) of established opinions in law and creed and advocated for a new interpretation (*ijtihād*) of the sources of Islam. Their goal was a more rational religion. However, from the perspective of the orthodoxy, this meant moving away from the revelation.

Even though ʿAbduh and his circle spoke of a revival of the salaf, they did not adopt the label salafiyya themselves.[38] For centuries, to follow the salaf was a common and favourable description for an Islamic scholar. However, this did not evoke adherence to a particular movement in Islam. Lauzière pointed out that Salafism as a conceptual construct was created after ʿAbduh's death in the early twentieth century by Western orientalists like Louis Massignon (d. 1962). Later, Islamic scholars absorbed the orientalists' concept and used it in their writings.[39]

---

35 Albert Hourani, *Arabic Thought in the Liberal Age, 1798–1939* (Cambridge: Cambridge University Press, 1983), 230.

36 I understand modernity as the set of technologies and modes of organization that originated in eighteenth- and nineteenth-century Europe.

37 Qāsim Amīn, *Taḥrīr al-marʾa* (Cairo: Mu'assasat al-Ḥindāwī, 2016), 39.

38 Frank Griffel, "What Do We Mean by 'Salafī'? Connecting Muḥammad ʿAbduh with Egypt's Nūr Party in Islam's Contemporary Intellectual History," *Die Welt des Islams* 55, no. 2 (2015), 202.

39 Henri Lauzière, "The Construction of Salafiyya: Reconsidering Salafism from the Perspective of Conceptual History," *International Journal of Middle East Studies* 42, no. 3 (2010), 370, 380–81.

From the 1920s onwards, many of the modernist Salafīs began to follow a more literalist approach to Islam. Most prominently, Rashīd Riḍā, one of ʿAbduh's closest companions, turned away from the speculative theology of ʿAbduh and started to sympathize with the Wahhābīs. In his writings, he tried to rehabilitate the Wahhābī movement's adherents who, as we have seen, had a reputation for being religious fanatics. When the Ottoman caliphate ended in 1924, Riḍā and others looked for new Islamic leadership and found it in the Saudi king ʿAbd al-ʿAzīz. Riḍā established close connections to the Wahhābī establishment in the kingdom, and many of his students started to teach at universities in the Ḥijāz and engaged in fierce debates with Wahhābī scholars.[40]

Although, at first glance, the Wahhābī tradition and modernist Salafism depart from different presumptions, their views are often surprisingly similar. For example, both reject superstitious beliefs, albeit for other reasons. Whereas the Wahhābīs regard superstitious beliefs as a violation of tawḥīd, modernist Salafīs dismiss them as irrational and primitive. Riḍā's students, many of whom followed their teacher's literalist understanding of Islam, differed from the Wahhābīs not so much in their creed but more in their approach to modernity.[41] Scholars from the Najd had a notorious reputation for their scepticism towards modern science. In the 1920s, many Wahhābīs still held that the earth was flat, and in 1966, Ibn Bāz famously claimed that the sun orbited the earth, contrary to established scientific evidence.[42]

2.2.3 Purist Salafism

The interaction between modernist Salafīs and traditional Wahhābīs led to a movement that is commonly described as the second salafiyya, or purist Salafism. It is important to note that in this context, my use of "purism" does not imply a normative claim but refers to these Salafīs' typical preoccupation with the unadulteratedness of Islamic teachings and practices.[43] From the 1970s on, purist Salafism almost entirely superseded modernist Salafism, and many of its concepts and ideas became part of mainstream Islam.[44] Both forms of Salafism share the idea that Islam must be reformed by focusing on the model of the Prophet and his early followers. However, in contrast to modernist reformers, purists not only want to use the first generations as a model

40 Lauzière, *Making of Salafism*, 60–94.

41 Ibid., 80.

42 ʿAbd al-ʿAzīz bin ʿAbd Allāh bin Bāz, *Al-Adilla al-naqliyya wa-l-ḥissiyya ʿalā imkān al-ṣuʿūd ilā al-kawākib wa-ʿalā jarayān al-shams wa-l-qamr wa-sukūn al-arḍ* (Riyadh: Maktabat al-Riyāḍ al-Ḥadītha, 1982).

43 See Lauzière, *Making of Salafism*, 4–6.

44 Ibid., 25.

for reform but aim to imitate them in any way possible. Instead of just rehabilitating their way of thinking, the salaf should become role models for every aspect of life.

Because of its focus on religious purity, purist Salafism does not seem to differ much from the Wahhābī tradition at first sight. This similarity has led scholars to question the originality of purist Salafism.[45] However, many famous twentieth-century Salafīs substantially disagreed with the more traditional Wahhābī doctrine. A good example is Muḥammad Nāṣir al-Dīn al-Albānī (d. 1999), one of the most prominent purist Salafīs. Originally from a working-class family in Damascus, al-Albānī soon became known for his strict emphasis on the Prophetic tradition. He developed a new methodology for the analysis of ḥadīth transmission by focusing on the transmitter's reliability. In 1961, Ibn Bāz invited him to Saudi Arabia, where al-Albānī taught at the University of Medina. Once in Saudi Arabia, his controversial views clashed with the Najdī establishment. This was not surprising since al-Albānī had declared the *miḥrāb* a forbidden innovation and claimed that Muslims could pray in a mosque with their shoes on.[46] When he published a book in which he argued against the veiling of women's faces, he had to leave Saudi Arabia.[47] However, despite his disputes with the Wahhābī establishment, al-Albānī gained a large following in Saudi Arabia. He and his followers were critical of the religious aristocracy of the Najdī Wahhābīs, who had built their own networks and developed their own tradition and canon of literature. Despite the opposition of part of the religious establishment, al-Albānī's opinions became prominent, and today he is considered a respectable scholar in Saudi Arabia and is regularly cited in legal literature.

The views of Saudi jurists today resemble more purist Salafism than traditional Wahhābism. Their approach to Islamic law reflects the influence that modernist Salafism had on Wahhābī thought throughout the second half of the twentieth century, as most Saudi scholars have moved away from anti-modern Wahhābī ideas. The vast majority today, as we will see in the next chapters, embrace modern technology and, to some extent, accept new social developments. Even though today purist Salafism is still associated with Saudi Arabia, its mission to spread a purist understanding of Islam outside the kingdom has been successful. Purist groups are now on the rise globally. This was

45 Nabile Mouline, for example, described contemporary Saudi scholars as Ḥanbali-Wahhābis, see Mouline, *Clerics of Islam*, 10.

46 Stephane Lacroix, "Al-Albani's Revolutionary Approach to Hadith," *ISIM Review* 21 (2008): 6.

47 Ibid., 7.

especially visible in Egypt when the purist Salafī Ḥizb al-Nūr (The Party of Light) became Egypt's second most popular political party after the revolution of February 2011.[48]

We have seen that the goal of purist Salafism is a revitalization of Islam by strictly following the model of the Prophet Muḥammad. Next, we will look in more detail at how this has influenced the ways in which Islamic law is conceptualized.

3 Law in Wahhābī and Salafī Thought

3.1 *School Coherency*

Modernist Salafīs were not so much interested in the technicalities of Islamic jurisprudence but concerned with the overall reformulation of the foundations of Islam. Even though many modernist Salafīs were trained Islamic scholars, they were not jurists in the narrow sense of the word. ʿAbduh, for example, was criticized for using the terms *qānūn* (usually understood as positive law) and *sharīʿa* interchangeably.[49] Even though at first sight, this seems to be a terminological question with little practical relevance, the use of the terms, as we have seen in the last chapter, has implications for the way the relationship between Islamic and positive law is understood.

Since the focus of purist Salafism is on the correct following of Islamic law, even minor questions of Islamic jurisprudence are given great importance. As a result, purist Salafīs focus much more on fiqh and ḥadīth than modernist Salafīs. The purists not only put a stronger emphasis on the law but also have a distinct understanding of fiqh. This is reflected in their approach to the schools of Islamic jurisprudence.[50]

Purist Salafīs claim to only follow the practices of the salaf.[51] Muslims should not cling to any of the legal schools but build their reasoning directly on

---

48 See Griffel, "What Do We Mean by 'Salafī'?", 186–220.

49 Leonard Wood, *Islamic Legal Revival: Reception of European Law and Transformations in Islamic Legal Thought in Egypt, 1875–1952* (Oxford: Oxford University Press, 2016), 60.

50 The rejection of the schools is one of the main criticisms that traditional scholars have made against Salafī 'ulamā'. The Syrian scholar Muḥammad Saʿīd Ramaḍān al-Būṭī, for example, wrote a book, in which he called the rejection of the schools (*al-lāmadhhabiya*) the most dangerous innovation that threatens Islamic law today. See Muḥammad Saʿīd Ramaḍān al-Būṭī, *Al-Lāmadhhabiyya: Akhṭar bidʿa tuhaddidu al-sharīʿa al-islāmiyya* (Damascus: Dār al-Fārābī, 1426/2005).

51 Lauzière, *Making of Salafism*, 8.

the primary sources. Purist Salafīs like Ibn Bāz argue that since the madhāhib and their institutionalization of dissent were created after the first generations of Muslims, they are generally not binding.[52]

Contemporary Salafī scholars usually distinguish between the "school of the salaf" (*madhhab al-salaf*) and the "method of the salaf" (*manhaj al-salaf*).[53] They prefer to speak of Salafism as a method (*manhaj*), since the notion of a school would imply that they follow a specific group or sect of Islam and not the pure teachings of the Quran and the Sunna. By calling Salafism a method, they thus prevent being accused of violating their own strict understanding of tawḥīd.

The purist Salafī approach to the madhāhib has its roots in the Ḥanbalī tradition. Like premodern Ḥanbalī scholars, contemporary Salafīs are traditionally much more interested in ḥadīth studies than in judicial reasoning.[54] Aḥmad bin Ḥanbal, the school's founder, considered himself more a ḥadīth scholar than a jurist and explicitly disapproved the institutionalization of the schools.[55] He even tried to avoid his views becoming authoritative by not allowing his students to write down his legal opinions.[56] Many scholars in his tradition nevertheless developed a madhhab thinking comparable to that prevailing in other schools. For jurists like Ibn Qudāma[57] (d. 1223), the opinions of earlier scholars became an essential point of reference.

The Saudi scholars' opposition against the madhāhib stems from another line of tradition in the Ḥanbalī school, most prominently from the thought of Ibn Taymiyya. Like Ibn Ḥanbal, Ibn Taymiyya was critical of clinging to a single school. In one of his fatwas, he stated:

> If a man follows Abū Ḥanīfa, Mālik, Shāfiʿī, or Aḥmad [bin Ḥanbal], and thinks that in some questions, another school would be preferable and follows it, [then] this might be better. This does not infringe on his

52 Recorded fatwa of Ibn Bāz. Available on binbaz.org.sa, bit.ly/3alNft9 [last access: 17 January 2023].

53 Lauzière, *Making of Salafism*, 225–26.

54 Griffel, "What Do We Mean by 'Salafī'?," 208.

55 Christopher Melchert, *Ahmad ibn Hanbal* (Oxford: Oneworld Publications, 2006), 79.

56 Christopher Melchert, *The Formation of the Sunni Schools of Law, 9th–10th Centuries* C.E. (Leiden: Brill, 1997), 14.

57 Here, and throughout the book, I am referring to Muwaffaq al-Dīn bin Qudāma al-Maqdisī, who is commonly known simply as Ibn Qudāma. There are, however, other great Ḥanbalī scholars stemming from the Qudāma lineage, including Ibn Qudāma's nephew ʿAbd al-Raḥmān bin Qudāma (d. 1283).

> religion, nor his integrity [*ʿadāla*], without question. It is even the most proper [way]. This is more affectionate towards God and His Prophet than to take the side of someone specific other than the Prophet.[58]

Even though the scepticism towards the schools predates modernity, it was in the wake of modernity that the critique of the legal schools became more popular, not only among Ibn ʿAbd al-Wahhāb and his followers in the Najd. One of the most famous voices against the legal schools was the Yemeni reformer al-Shawkānī (d. 1834), who advanced the idea that no madhhab should be followed in the Arab world.[59]

Even though Salafīs deny their binding authority, the schools continue to play an important practical role in Salafī jurisprudence, in particular as a tool to structure legal reasoning. Saʿd al-Shithrī, for example, contended that although the schools were not binding for the individual believer, they did offer a vehicle for education and the systematization of knowledge.[60]

In their legal reasoning on a specific issue, Saudi jurists almost always refer to all four schools. Usually, they present the established opinions in the schools before weighing (*tarjīḥ*) them by analyzing the presented arguments and the textual references to the revelation.

Another popular claim of Salafī scholars is that they would look beyond the four major schools of law. However, in fact, the only other school that is regularly referred to in Salafī jurisprudence is the almost extinct Ẓāhirī school. For example, Taqī al-Dīn al-Hilālī (d. 1987), an influential student of Rashīd Riḍā, admired the Ẓāhirī school for its devotion to a literalist approach and its refusal of taqlīd.[61]

The influence of Ibn Ḥazm, the most prominent Ẓāhirī today, is very visible in the Saudi legal discourse. Even though he is rarely cited in court decisions, Saudi scholars often think of him and the Ẓāhirīs as the fifth school of jurisprudence. One example of this is the debate on the maximum length of pregnancy. Whereas premodern scholars of all four major schools held that women could be pregnant for two or four years or even longer, Ibn Ḥazm criticized the jurists for relying on unreliable reports about prolonged pregnancies and maintained that the maximum length of pregnancy was one year.[62] Although

58 Ibn Taymiyya, *Majmūʿat al-fatāwā*, 22:248.

59 Griffel, "What Do We Mean by 'Salafī'?," 205.

60 Saʿd al-Shithrī emphasized this in a TV interview, which is available on YouTube, www.youtube.com/watch?v=P-TP5To7pbs, min 3 [last access: 29 January 2023].

61 Lauzière, *Making of Salafism*, 158.

62 Ibn Ḥazm, *Al-Muḥallā bi-l-athār* (Beirut: Dār al-Kutub al-ʿIlmiyya, 1425/2003), 10:133. For the debate on the maximum length of pregnancy see Dominik Krell, "Saudi Arabia," in

this still exceeds the actual average length of pregnancy, many Saudi jurists today refer to Ibn Ḥazm in order to bring their legal reasoning in line with modern science.[63]

3.2 *The Acceptance of Normative Pluralism*

The Salafī critique of the schools' binding authority breaks with traditional understandings of authority in Islamic jurisprudence. Without the limitation to the established schools, diverse opinions can stand side by side. This leads to what I call the normative pluralism in Salafī jurisprudence: a multitude of equally recognized but possibly contradicting legal opinions. Normative pluralism should not be confused with legal pluralism. Whereas legal pluralism describes the parallel existence of several normative systems,[64] normative pluralism refers to a variety of accepted norms that can be found in a single normative system.

The roots of the jurists' acceptance of normative pluralism lie in the foundations of Islamic jurisprudence. According to a popular narration, the Prophet Muḥammad said that the disagreement (*ikhtilāf*) in his community was a mercy of God.[65] Finally, the respect for normative pluralism also derives from the fundamental Islamic principle that no human should stand between the believer and God.[66]

Regarding law and legal reasoning, this entails two important aspects: Firstly, human legal reasoning cannot be absolute. "The respect for normative pluralism (*ikhtilāf*)," as Baber Johansen pointed out, "is possible only because the fiqh scholars conceive an ontological difference between the knowledge as revealed by God in Koranic texts, the Prophet's praxis, or the community's consensus on the one hand, and the knowledge which human beings acquire through their own reasoning."[67] Human reasoning can thus never reach the

---

Filiation and the Protection of Parentless Children: Towards a Social Definition of the Family in Muslim Jurisdictions, ed. Nadjma Yassari, Lena-Maria Möller, and Marie-Claude Najm (The Hague: T.M.C. Asser, 2019), 304–308.

63 We will discuss the debate on the maximum length of pregnancy in more detail in Chapter 7.

64 See John Griffiths, "What is Legal Pluralism?" *Journal of Legal Pluralism* 24 (1986): 2.

65 Today, some scholars question the authenticity of this ḥadīth. Al-Albānī, for example, noted that whenever scholars in the past attempted to link the ḥadīth to a reliable chain of transmitters (*isnād*), they were unable to do so. Muḥammad Nāṣir al-Dīn al-Albānī, *Silsilat al-aḥādīth al-ḍaʿīfa wa-al-mawduʿa* (Riyadh: Maktabat al-Maʿārif, 1412/1992), 1:141.

66 Wael Hallaq, *Sharīʿa: Theory, Practice, Transformations* (Cambridge: Cambridge University Press, 2009), 78–83.

67 Baber Johansen, *Contingency in a Sacred Law: Legal and Ethical Norms in the Muslim Fiqh* (Leiden: Brill, 1999), 65–66.

level of "true" knowledge, which is restricted to God, whereas the Islamic community's consensus (*ijmāʿ*) is located somewhere between human and Godly knowledge. Although the consensus stems from human efforts, it has been raised to the level of "true" knowledge, since the Prophet, among other things, declared that his followers would never agree on the wrong.[68] As a result, all legal reasoning is necessarily subjective.[69]

Secondly, the immediacy between the believer and God hinders the development of an Islamic clergy that, similar to the Catholic Church, could elaborate binding interpretations for all Muslims based only on its structural religious authority. The idea that all human action and reasoning is contingent thus forms the basis of Islamic jurisprudence and the institution of the schools.[70] Some Islamic scholars have even argued that contradicting legal opinions should not only be respected, provided that they are derived through the methods of Islamic jurisprudence, but that every legal question has many equally correct answers. If God had wanted the jurists to be united, they claimed, he would have sent them clear textual evidence.[71]

Although the normative pluralism of Islamic legal thinking is acknowledged by Western scholars of Islamic law, purist Salafīs or Wahhābīs are often excluded. For example, in an influential article on the Salafī movement, Quintan Wiktorowicz claimed that by focusing on the strict following of the Quran and the Sunna, Salafīs "eliminate the biases of human subjectivity and self-interest, thereby allowing them to identify the singular truth of God's commands." Consequently, he asserted that, "from this perspective, there is only one legitimate religious interpretation; Islamic pluralism does not exist."[72] Wiktorowicz concluded that, in practice, purist Salafī jurisprudence does nothing more than to "narrowly rel[y] on the Quran and authentic (sound or verifiable) hadiths."[73]

---

68 Ibn Mājah, *Sunan Ibn Mājah* (Cairo: Dār Iḥyāʾ al-Kutub al-ʿArabiyya, n.d.), 2:1303 (Nr. 3950). For an overview of the concept of consensus in Islamic law see Mairaj Syed, Ijmāʿ, in *The Oxford Handbook of Islamic Law*, ed. Anver Emon and Ahmed Rumee (Oxford: Oxford University Press, 2018), 271–98.

69 See Norbert Oberauer, "Wahrheitssuche und 'Mut zur Hölle': Zum Problem juristischen Entscheidens im Islam," in *Religion und Entscheiden: Historische und kulturwissenschaftliche Perspektiven*, ed. Wolfram Drews, Ulrich Pfister, and Martina Wagner-Egelhaaf (Baden-Baden: Ergon, 2018), 151.

70 See also Johansen, *Contingency*, 65–66.

71 Khaled Abou El Fadl, *Speaking in God's Name: Islamic Law, Authority, and Women* (London: Oneworld Publications, 2001), 306.

72 Quintan Wiktorowicz, "Anatomy of the Salafi Movement," *Studies in Conflict & Terrorism* 29 (2006): 207.

73 Ibid., 209.

While Wiktorowicz' assessment might be accurate for Salafī creed, where there is, as we have seen, less space for pluralism, it is less convincing when it comes to the law. Legal reasoning in Saudi Arabia, which he considered the origin and promotor of Salafī beliefs and jurisprudence,[74] is much more complex. In fact, the Saudi scholars' dismissal of school coherency makes them much more open to normative pluralism in law than is widely imagined. The general acceptance of plural legal opinions not only exists in practice, as we will see in the upcoming chapters, it is also openly admitted by Saudi ʿulamāʾ.

Ibn Bāz acknowledged the advantages of normative pluralism in one of his fatwas. When asked about the soundness of the Prophet's account that pluralism was a mercy of God, he replied:

> This is not true, it is not a word of the Prophet, but it is from some of the second generation of Muslims [*tābiʿūn*]. The Prophet did not say this. Some of the tābiʿūn said: I saw the companions [*aṣḥāb*] of the Prophet disagree, only for God's mercy. This means: The mujtahid looks into it and considers the textual evidence [*dalīl*]. In the pluralism [*ikhtilāf*] of the scholars [*ʿulamāʾ*] lie benefits [*maṣāliḥ*] for the Muslims, even though consent is preferable and better. In consent lies mercy and blessing, as God says: "They will not cease to differ, except whom your Lord has given mercy" [Hūd 118–19]. Mercy is within unity. However, if there is a question on which there is disagreement between the scholars, the jurist has to look into the textual evidence [*dalīl*] and has to undertake *ijtihād* by weighing between [the opinions] that are based on the evidence. He must not be lenient in this matter and not careless, but look into the evidence of the sharīʿa, and what he considers preponderant is what should be worked with, no matter if there are two, three, or four opinions on this question, he studies the textual evidence in the verses [of the Quran] and the accounts [of the Prophet] with open eyes. He stays away from personal affection [*hawa*] and fanaticism [*taʿaṣṣub*].[75]

Here, Ibn Bāz presented the ideal type of Salafī legal reasoning, whereby normative pluralism is considered necessary and beneficial. At first, all opinions should be considered, no matter from which school they originate. The work of the jurist now lies in verifying the opinions that are presented by the schools.

74 Ibid., 221.

75 A transcript of the audio recording of the fatwa can be found on binbaz.org.sa, bit.ly/2yRBHyY [last access: 21 April 2023].

Wiktorowicz was right when he argued that Salafī jurisprudence was particularly strongly connected to the revelation. However, this does not mean that the acceptance of normative pluralism inherent in Islamic law is abolished. Instead, it serves as a map for the jurist in his search for the opinion that he finds is most in accordance with the primary sources. Normative pluralism thus lies at the heart of the Salafī concept of law; it is the starting point for the jurist's ijtihād.

4 The Debate on Ijtihād

4.1 *What Is Ijtihād?*

Whilst ijtihād is understood, both in Western scholarship and in Islamic legal writings, very broadly as the jurist's effort to find a solution to a particular legal question,[76] its nature remains one of the most controversial topics in Islamic jurisprudence. To better understand what the term means in the Saudi context, we have to keep in mind that ijtihād refers to two different levels of legal interpretation: the "basic" level and the "particular" level.[77] The basic level consists of debates over fundamental concepts of Islamic jurisprudence, whereas the particular level comprises discussions on specific rulings inside each school. Since it is often unclear to which level of ijtihād an author is referring, the unreflected use of the term has, as Montgomery Watt pointed out, led to many misunderstandings.[78]

At the center of the controversy surrounding ijtihād lies the idea of the closing of the "gate to ijtihād" (*bāb al-ijtihād*).[79] Western scholars, most famously Joseph Schacht, forwarded the idea that Islamic jurists around the ninth century started to feel that all essential questions in Islam had been answered by their predecessors and concluded that all that was left for them to do was the mere application and interpretation of the established doctrine.[80] This was the time when the gate of ijtihād was supposedly closed and the age of taqlīd

76 See for example ʿAbd Allāh bin Muḥammad Āl Khunayn, *Tawṣīf al-aqḍiya fī al-sharīʿa al-islāmiyya* (Riyadh: Dār Ibn al-Farḥūn, 1434/2014), 1:353.

77 This division was introduced by Montgomery Watt. See Montgomery Watt, "The Closing of the Door of iğtihād," *Orientalia Hispanica* 1 (1974): 678.

78 Ibid., 678.

79 For a more detailed discussion of the different perspectives on the closure of the gate of ijtihād see Shaista Ali-Karamali and Fiona Dunne, "The Ijtihad Controversy," *Arab Law Quarterly* 9, no. 3 (1994).

80 Joseph Schacht, *An Introduction to Islamic Law* (Oxford: Clarendon, 1982), 70–71. Others date the assumed closure of the gate of ijtihād to the fourteenth century. See Count Léon

(commonly translated as "imitation") began, in which the existing corpus of jurisprudence was supposed to be accepted and replicated.[81]

The underlying assumption of this narrative is that Islamic law became static and thus unavailable for new interpretations, a notion that was, as we have seen, very present among modernist Islamic scholars in the late nineteenth century. The idea that there was no innovation in Islamic law after a certain time period has, among other things, its roots in the epistemology of premodern Islamic law. As Bernhard Weiss pointed out, premodern Muslim jurists never considered themselves to be *inventing* rules. Instead, their exercise of premodern ijtihād meant articulating what had already been decided by God but remained concealed to humans.[82]

But the closure of the gate of ijtihād was largely a myth: Wael Hallaq showed that ijtihād was prevalent in Islamic legal theory as well as in the jurists' practice throughout time and was considered a crucial element of Islamic law.[83] However, even though Hallaq was the first to emphasize that the closure of the gate of ijtihād was more theory than actual practice, earlier writers were also aware of this. Schacht himself, for example, stated that later Islamic jurists were in practice not less creative than their predecessors.[84]

Premodern jurists supporting taqlīd were often reacting to practical demands. Sherman Jackson showed that some jurists viewed taqlīd positively as a tool to stabilize the schools' inner coherence, which helped secure their authority.[85] Similarly, Muhammad Fadel suggested seeing taqlīd as a way to standardize Islamic law. He argued that taqlīd is "best understood as an expression of the desire for regular and predictable legal outcomes,"[86] similar to European notions of the rule of law.

With the advent of modernity and the influence of new epistemologies on Islamic scholars, the prevailing understanding of ijtihād changed. Aria Nakissa argued that premodern Islamic jurisprudence was based on a linguistic

---

Ostrorog, *The Angora Reform: Three Lectures Delivered at the Centenary Celebrations of University College* (London: University of London Press, 1927), 31.

81 Schacht, *Introduction to Islamic Law*, 71.

82 Weiss, "Interpretation in Islamic Law," 200. Like Schacht and later Hallaq, Weiss concluded that the gate of ijtihād was never fully closed despite the jurists' reluctancy to engage in ijtihād.

83 Wael Hallaq, "Was the Gate of Ijtihad Closed?," *International Journal of Middle East Studies* 16, no. 1 (1984): 4.

84 Schacht, *Introduction to Islamic Law*, 73.

85 Sherman Jackson, *Islamic Law and the State: The Constitutional Jurisprudence of Shihāb al-Dīn al-Qarāfī* (Leiden: Brill, 1996), 227.

86 Mohammad Fadel, "The Social Logic of Taqlīd and the Rise of the Mukhtaṣar," *Islamic Law and Society* 3, no. 2 (1996), 197.

conception of knowledge and should, therefore, "more accurately [be] understood as being similar to language."[87] According to Nakissa, premodern Muslim jurists held that "just as there is no progress or creativity in grammar, there is none in law."[88] Premodern Islamic education, Nakissa asserted, combined the teaching of law with that of language. Both areas, the ʿulamāʾ believed, involved the mastery of a specific corpus of rules. An Islamic scholar's proficiency was not judged according to his production of original works but his mastery of the already established rules. However, this is not to say that Muslim jurists did not acknowledge that the law was developing. When circumstances changed or new legal questions arose, they used the established methodology of Islamic jurisprudence to develop an answer.[89] Yet, for them, the task of a jurist was not to change the doctrine.

Beginning in the nineteenth century, the foundations of legal training changed. Natural science, with its strong belief in progress, introduced the idea that legal knowledge could be advanced.[90] This meant that legal reasoning was not anymore about adopting established rulings to changing circumstances but about the introduction of new concepts. A successful jurist now formulated new ideas based on his original thinking. Nakissa concluded that this change of epistemes led to the conception in Western oriental literature and modernist Islamic writings that premodern Islamic law lacked dynamism and innovation.[91]

At this time, ijtihād became associated with law reform. Muslim reformers used established terms like ijtihād to frame their efforts within the tradition of Islamic jurisprudence. The South Asian intellectual and politician Muhammad Iqbal (d. 1938), for instance, understood ijtihād as a thoroughgoing rethinking of the corpus of Islamic jurisprudence.[92] Ijtihād was now not anymore restricted to technical legal questions but signified the fundamental re-evaluation of Islam, most notably in the fields of education, authority, and the state.

Today, this notion of ijtihād is still very present among Muslim reformers. However, at the same time, the term continues to have many different meanings. While many associate ijtihād with Islamic reform, it is also used as a legal

---

87 Aria Nakissa, "An Epistemic Shift in Islamic Law: Educational Reform at al-Azhar and Dār al-ʿUlūm," *Islamic Law and Society* 21 (2014), 246.

88 Ibid., 212.

89 Ibid., 223.

90 Ibid., 213.

91 Ibid., 244.

92 Muhammad Qasim Zaman, "Evolving Conceptions of Ijtihād in Modern South Asia," Islamic Studies 49, no. 1 (2010): 15.

technical term, both in contemporary Islamic jurisprudence and positive law. In most Arab countries, the word is also used to describe the secular courts' legal reasoning. For instance, decisions of the Syrian High Court (Maḥkamat al-Naqḍ) are usually called *ijtihādāt*.[93] Furthermore, ijtihād is today not anymore limited to Islamic scholars. In Egypt, the constitutional court explicitly granted the legislator the right to undertake ijtihād in disputed questions of Islamic jurisprudence.[94]

4.2 *Ijtihād in the Saudi Context*

When Saudi scholars write or speak about ijtihād, their understanding of the term resembles Nakissa's description of premodern Islamic jurisprudence. While Saudi jurists acknowledge that the law has to be adapted to modern circumstances, they avoid giving the impression that they create new rulings. This is coherent with the Salafī idea that any kind of innovation (*bidaʿ*) in Islam should be rejected.

For Ibn Khunayn, for instance, ijtihād is not more than the simple application of Islamic legal methodology through the scholar's legal reasoning. Consequently, in his view, it is and was possible at any time to undertake ijtihād.[95] However, whereas other scholars held that the scope to undertake ijtihād narrowed over the centuries, Ibn Khunayn argued that ijtihād was, in fact, much easier today. In early Islam, the Quran and the Sunna were not yet wholly compiled, and the basic methodology of Islamic jurisprudence was not yet developed. Thus, the deduction of rules from the sources, Ibn Khunayn claimed, was much more complicated than today.[96] He quoted the medieval Ḥanbalī scholar Ibn Ḥamdān (d. 1296), who wrote that already in his times, in the thirteenth century, ijtihād had become much easier to master than in earlier periods due to the availability of literature.[97]

93 See for example Maḥmūd Zakī Shams, *Ijtihādāt al-hay'a al-ʿāmma li-maḥkamat al-naqḍ* (Damascus: Maṭbaʿat al-Dāwūdī, 2008).

94 Kilian Bälz, "The Secular Reconstruction of Islamic Law: The Egyptian Supreme Constitutional Court and the 'Battle over the Veil' in State-Run Schools," in *Legal Pluralism in the Arab World*, ed. Baudouin Dupret, Maurits Berger, and Laila al-Zwaini (The Hague: Kluwer Law International, 1999), 237.

95 Āl Khunayn, *Tawṣīf al-aqḍiya*, 1:361.

96 Ibid.

97 However, the jurists of his times, Ibn Ḥamdān complained, neglected their responsibilities and had "little ambition and languid desire" for ijtihād, since they had become "satisfied with imitation (*taqlīd*), had no need for substantiated labor, [and] were running away from [their] burden," see Ibn Ḥamdān, *Ṣifat al-fatwā wa-l-muftī wa-l-mustaftī* (Damascus: Al-Maktab al-Islāmī, 1380/1960), 17.

Since the corpus of Islamic jurisprudence and its sources can be easily accessed today, Ibn Khunayn demanded that judges and scholars should undertake ijtihād in their work and not rely on taqlīd. Most importantly, Ibn Khunayn called upon the ʿulamāʾ to address new legal questions (*nawāzil*) that are raised by modern life. Although this resembles the modernists' call to bring Islamic law in line with modernity, Ibn Khunayn did not question the established methodology of Islamic jurisprudence but wanted to adapt the law by using the traditional corpus of Islamic jurisprudence. Especially in the context of new legal questions, Ibn Khunayn emphasised that ijtihād could also be undertaken collectively by a group of scholars (*ijtihād jamāʿī*).[98]

Ibn Khunayn's approach is a good example of contemporary Saudi legal methodology. Contrary to the extreme social conservatism that dominated the Wahhābī tradition, Ibn Khunayn is generally open to new technical and social developments, provided they are in line with the basic tenets of Islamic law. On the other hand, he emphasized the importance of premodern Islamic legal methodology and its strict adherence. For him, the revitalization of Islamic law through ijtihād signifies the correct application of the established teachings, which, in his view, have been neglected for a long time. When we later turn to Saudi case law, we will see that even though the judges follow a grammar-like application of the law similar to Ibn Khunayn, their critical attitude towards the schools leads to surprising results that often resemble the opinions of modernist scholars.

4.3 *Who Is a Mujtahid?*

Despite their scepticism towards taqlīd, Saudi scholars do not allow everyone to undertake ijtihād. Due to the importance of legal methodology, they restrict the right to ijtihād to people formally trained in Islamic jurisprudence. For instance, Saʿd al-Shithrī contended that it was forbidden for people not trained in the principles of Islamic jurisprudence (*uṣūl al-fiqh*) to give a ruling, even if they present the textual evidence in the revelation (*dalīl*) for their decision.[99] Al-Shithrī followed a very narrow understanding of ijtihād. For example, whereas most scholars hold that the determination of the qibla before prayer by a lay Muslim would already constitute a form of ijtihād, al-Shithrī did not consider this an ijtihād. He maintained that only a ruling that was given by trained ʿulamāʾ who have reached the level of a mujtahid could be considered

---

98 Āl Khunayn, *Tawṣīf al-aqḍiya*, 1:362.

99 See Saʿd bin Nāṣir al-Shithrī, *Sharḥ al-waraqāt fī uṣūl al-fiqh* (Riyadh: Dār Kunūz Ishbīliyā, 1425/2004), 185.

an ijtihād, such as, for example, the determination of the qibla by a trained scholar.[100]

The question of who is a mujtahid, namely a jurist who is allowed to undertake ijtihād, was intensively debated by premodern Islamic scholars. The majority opinion in Islamic jurisprudence, including in the Ḥanbalī school, requires a judge to be a mujtahid in all fields of the law.[101] As we have seen, the Salafī tradition gives particular importance to ijtihād, and it is thus not surprising that Saudi scholars, too, generally require a judge to be a mujtahid.

However, to be called or to call oneself a mujtahid implies that one is in the line of the great scholars of Islam, a claim that could be seen as presumptuous. This difficulty is nicely illustrated by a statement made by Ibn Khunayn during an interview in August 2018. After we had talked for over an hour about more detailed aspects of Islamic law, I asked him whether he would allow a personal question. "Please, go on", he replied. "Are you a mujtahid?," I asked. Ibn Khunayn laughed and said no. "Not even within the school?" He smiled and said, "Maybe within the school, maybe."[102] This did not come as a surprise to me since during an earlier meeting, Ibn Khunayn had already made fun of a first-instance judge who did not want to accept the appeal courts' comments on his judgements because he claimed to be a mujtahid.[103] Although Ibn Khunayn's statement could be dismissed as false modesty, his comments show that the office of a judge does not automatically mean that someone is recognised as a mujtahid.

The question of how to appoint judges if there are no or only a few scholars available that are widely considered mujtahids was already debated by premodern jurists. In order to come up with a pragmatic solution, some ʿulamāʾ argued that exceptions from the general rule could be made under certain circumstances. For instance, the sixteenth-century Ḥanbalī jurist al-Ḥajjāwī (d. 1560) stated,

> There are ten requirements for judgeship: [a judge] has to be mature, sane, and male, free, […], a mujtahid, if only in the school of his Imām, in case of necessity, picked [according to his] eloquence and care, or a *muqallid* [a scholar only able to undertake taqlīd].[104]

---

100 Al-Shithrī emphasized this in the second episode of his lecture series Manhaj al-ijtihād wa-l-taqlīd. The lecture series is available on YouTube, see www.youtube.com/watch?v=-vQHLeKV4oo&t=192s, min 3 [last access: 21 April 2023].

101 ʿAbd al-ʿAzīz bin ʿAbd al-Raḥmān al-Mashʿal, "Sharṭ al-ijtihād fī man yalī al-qaḍāʾ," *Majallat al-ʿAdl* 34 (1430/2009): 114.

102 Interview with Ibn Khunayn in his house in Riyadh, 1.8.2018.

103 Interview with Ibn Khunayn in his house in Riyadh, 24.4.2018.

104 Al-Ḥajjāwī, *Al-iqnāʿ* (Beirut: Dār al-Maʿrifa, n.d.), 4:398.

In Saudi Arabia, jurists have developed a similar solution for the scarcity of mujtahids. Muḥammad al-Zuḥaylī, a renowned Syrian scholar with links to Saudi Arabia, wrote in 1982 that although the premodern scholars considered the capability to undertake ijtihād a requirement to become a judge, the Saudi king would only be obliged to appoint the best available person as a judge. Al-Zuḥaylī traced this opinion back to Aḥmad bin Ḥanbal.[105] In 2009, ʿAbd al-ʿAzīz al-Mashʿal, a professor at the Imām University in Riyadh, argued in a similar fashion that a non-mujtahid could work as a judge in case no mujtahid is available.[106] He referred to the Ḥanbalī jurist Ibn Mufliḥ (d. 1362), who stated that from his perspective, the ʿulamāʾ agreed on this compromise.[107]

To cope with the scarcity of mujtahids, the majority of premodern scholars accepted that a judge is only a mujtahid in some areas of the law or in one of the schools.[108] The schools developed sophisticated hierarchies of jurists, with several ranks between a mujtahid who is not restricted to any school (*mujtahid muṭlaq*) and a muqallid. These hierarchies are supposed to regulate the limits of a scholar's competences.[109] While the details vary from school to school, the general idea is that a jurist can be a mujtahid in only one of the schools if he studied the schools' authoritative scholars, learnt their rulings, and mastered their way of legal reasoning.[110] Alternatively, a scholar can be a mujtahid only, for example, in inheritance law, provided that he has extensively studied that area, but would remain a muqallid in all other areas of the law.

This division of mujtahids allows Saudi scholars to uphold the requirement that a judge should be a mujtahid, at least to some degree. Saʿd al-Shithrī held that this division of ijtihād was necessary today because of the high degree of specialization in contemporary Islamic jurisprudence.[111] Due to the complexity

105 Muḥammad bin Muṣṭafā al-Zuḥaylī, *Al-Tanẓīm al-qaḍāʾī fī fiqh al-islāmī wa-taṭbīquhu fī al-Mamlaka al-ʿArabiyya al-Saʿūdiyya* (Damascus: Dār al-Fikr, 1402/1982), 60.

106 Al-Mashʿal, "Sharṭ al-ijtihād," 126.

107 Ibn Mufliḥ, al-Mardāwī, and al-Baʿlī, *Kitāb al-Furūʿ wa-maʿhu taṣḥīḥ al-furūʿ wa-ḥāshiyyat Ibn Qaldas* (Beirut: Muʾassasat al-Risāla, 1424/2003), 11:104–6.

108 The majority of Ḥanafī scholars, however, did not require the judge to be a mujtahid, provided that he can consult a mujtahid if needed. See al-Mashʿal, "Sharṭ al-ijtihād," 114–15.

109 See Mohammad Fadel, "The Social Logic of Taqlīd and the Rise of the Mukhtaṣar," *Islamic Law and Society* 3, no. 2 (1996): 200.

110 For more details, see Norman Calder's analysis of al-Nawawī's Typology of Muftis. Norman Calder, "Al-Nawawī's Typology of Muftīs and Its Significance for a General Theory of Islamic Law," *Islamic Law and Society* 3, no. 2 (1996): 145.

111 Second episode of al-Shithrī's lecture series Manhaj al-ijtihād wa-l-taqlīd. The lecture series is available on YouTube, see www.youtube.com/watch?v=-vQHLeKV4oo&t=192s, min 7 [last access: 29 October 2022].

of today's life, jurists could no longer have in-depth knowledge of all areas of the law.

Ultimately, the question of whether a judge must be a mujtahid muṭlaq, a mujtahid in only one school, or not a mujtahid at all, is largely symbolic.[112] The Saudi king simply has to appoint the most qualified person as judge, whether he is recognised as a mujtahid or not. Although most of Saudi jurists do not consider themselves to be mujtahids, we will see in the course of the next chapters that Saudi judges of all levels of experience and knowledge undertake ijtihād, even beyond school boundaries.

5 The Saudi Judiciary and the Ḥanbalī School

5.1 *The Role of the Schools in Early Twentieth-Century Saudi Arabia*

Although Ibn ʿAbd al-Wahhāb rejected their binding authority, he did not completely refuse the four major schools of law.[113] Later Najdī scholars were even less critical of the schools, and some openly followed Ḥanbalī law. In 1926, Ibn Bulayhid, one of the most influential Najdī scholars of his times, wrote that although people in the Najd were Salafī in creed, they followed Ḥanbalī law.[114] The predominance of Ḥanbalī law can also be seen in the education of Najdī scholars. The former Grand Mufti Muḥammad bin Ibrāhīm (d. 1969), for example, was educated in Islamic law by primarily studying al-Ḥajjāwī's *Ẓād al-mustaqniʿ*, an abridgement of the classical Ḥanbalī compendium *Al-Muqniʿ* by Ibn Qudāma.[115] From the early twentieth century onwards, the Saudi judiciary gradually opened itself to other schools of law. In 1927, King ʿAbd al-ʿAzīz proclaimed,

112 Historians of Islamic Law have made similar observations in premodern jurisprudence. Muhammad Fadel argues that the primary function of the hierarchy of jurists was the regulation of communication to a non-legal audience. See Fadel, "Social Logic of Taqlīd," 200.

113 Commins, *Wahhabi Mission*, 20.

114 Lauzière, *Making of Salafism*, 93.

115 Additionally, he was tutored by three local Najdī scholars and studied the creed of Ibn ʿAbd al-Wahhāb with his uncle ʿAbd Allāh bin ʿAbd al-Laṭīf Āl al-Shaykh. See Muḥammad bin ʿAbd al-Raḥmān al-Qāsim, ed., *Fatāwā wa-rasāʾil samāḥat al-shaykh Muḥammad bin Ibrāhīm bin ʿAbd al-Laṭīf Āl al-Shaykh* (Mecca: Maṭbaʿat al-Ḥukūma bi-Makka Mukarrama, 1399/1979), 1:10.

> The sharīʿa court is not limited to a particular school of law but decides according to what the court endorses from any of the schools. There is no difference between one school and the other.[116]

Seven years later, in 1934, the king issued a similar statement:

> We are not limited to one school. When we find strong textual evidence (*dalīl*) in one of the four schools, we refer to it and stick to it. However, if we do not find strong proof, we use the opinion of Imām Aḥmad.[117]

In 1937, King ʿAbd al-ʿAzīz wrote in the spirit of Ibn ʿAbd al-Wahhāb that he was not against the schools as such but only against following a single school of jurisprudence.[118]

In practice, however, the Saudi judiciary still had to follow the Ḥanbalī opinion in most questions. On 10 September 1928, the Highest Judicial Authority (al-Hayʾa al-Qaḍāʾiyya) circulated their decision that "the judiciary must apply the followed opinion (*al-muftā bihi*) in the school of Imām Aḥmad bin Ḥanbal, considering the ease of consulting the school's books."[119] However, if "the judges find that the application [of the Ḥanbalī opinion] is inconvenient (*mashaqqa*) and contradicts the public interest (*maṣlaḥat al-ʿumūm*), it is looked at the remaining schools [and considered] what suits the interests (*maṣlaḥa*)."

The decree by the Highest Judicial Authority listed two books by the seventeenth-century scholar Manṣūr al-Bahūtī (d. 1641),[120] which judges had to use to determine the correct Ḥanbalī opinion. Both books by al-Bahūtī are commentaries on handbooks (*mukhtaṣarāt*, sing. *mukhtaṣar*) of Ḥanbalī doctrine, the first on al-Futūḥī's (d. 1564) *Muntahā al-irādāt*, and the second on al-Ḥajjāwī's (d. 1560) *Al-Iqnāʿ*. The decree further stipulated that if the two books disagree, the judge has to follow the opinion found in al-Bahūtī's

116 The proclamation is printed in Muḥammad bin Barrāk al-Fawzān, *Al-Tanẓīm al-qaḍāʾī al-jadīd fī al-Mamlaka al-ʿArabiyya al-Saʿūdiyya* (Riyadh: Maktabat al-Qānūn al-Iqtiṣād, 1431/2010), 58.

117 Printed in Ibid., 58.

118 ʿAbd al-Raḥmān bin Muḥammad Ibn Qāsim, *Al-Durar al-saniyya fī al-ajwiba al-najdiyya* (N.p, 1417/1996), 14:401–2.

119 The decree is printed in Al-Fawzān, *Al-tanẓīm al-qaḍāʾī*, 62–64.

120 Little is known about al-Bahūtī, except that he was one of the last great representatives of the Ḥanbalī school in Egypt. Henri Laoust described al-Bahūtī's works as "devoid of any great originality on the part of the author." However, his works remain among the most cited books in Saudi jurisprudential writings. See the article "al-Bahūtī" in the *Encyclopedia of Islam, Second Edition*. Available online: dx.doi.org/10.1163/1573-3912_islam_SIM_1079 [last access: 24 June 2022].

commentary of the *Muntahā*. In case the judge did not have access to any of the two books, he could also use another commentary by al-Ḥajjāwī (*Ẓād al-mustaqniʿ*) as well as the today lesser-known *Dalīl al-ṭālib* by al-Karmī (d. 1624).[121] Only if the judge could not find a ruling on the issue in the mentioned Ḥanbalī books was he allowed to turn to books from other schools. However, the availability of books at the time must have limited the extensive use of any non-Ḥanbalī opinions, since even Ḥanbalī books were scarce, especially in the Najd. It is reported that before 1926, even Ibn Qudāma's *Al-Mughnī*, one of the most authoritative books in the Ḥanbalī school, could not be found as a complete copy in the whole Najd.[122]

The decree thus not only bound the judges in most questions to the Ḥanbalī school but even to certain books inside the school. In 2012, Ḥasan bin Muḥammad Safar, a lecturer in siyāsa sharʿiyya from Jeddah, argued that the decree was intended as an alternative to codification, an issue that, as we will see in Chapter 7, was debated at that time.[123] What is rather certain is that the decree did not constitute a significant rupture in the courts' workings, as the majority of judges seemed to have accepted the decision. This is illustrated by later decisions of appeal courts that revoked court decisions on the grounds that they had been issued contrary to the mainstream opinion in the Ḥanbalī school.[124]

In 1936, the Saudi-Lebanese diplomate Fu'ād Ḥamza (d. 1951) observed that judges used, in addition to the two commentaries by al-Bahūtī, four other books in their everyday practice: the *Iqnāʿ* by al-Hajjāwī, the *Muntahā al-irādāt* by al-Futūḥī (which both form the basis of al-Bahūtī's commentaries mentioned in the 1928 decree), the *Mughnī* by Ibn Qudāma and the *Sharḥ al-kabīr* by Ibn Qudāma's nephew, ʿAbd al-Raḥmān bin Qudāma (d. 1283).[125]

5.2 *Are Judges Still Bound to the Ḥanbalī School?*

Whether and, if so, to what extent the 1928 decree still applies, and Saudi judges are bound to the Ḥanbalī school is still debated among Saudi scholars.

---

121 At the time of the decree, however, the *Dalīl al-ṭālib* was discussed and used in education. See Steinberg, *Religion und Staat*, 113.

122 Ibid., 320.

123 See, for example, Ḥasan bin Muḥammad Safar, "Taqnīn aḥkām al-sharīʿa fī al-tajruba al-islāmiyya," *Majallat al-Qaḍā'iyya* 3 (1433/2012): 106.

124 Muḥammad bin Ibrāhīm al-Saʿīdī, "Ishkāliyat al-taqnīn wa-l-tadwīn," in *Al-Niẓām al-ʿadl fī al-Saʿūdiyya*, ed. Muḥammad bin Saʿūd al-Bashr and Manṣūr bin ʿAbd al-Raḥmān al-Ḥaydarī (Riyadh: Markaz al-Fikr al-ʿĀlamī, 1436/2010), 300.

125 Fu'ād Ḥamza, *Al-Bilād al-ʿarabiyya al-saʿūdiyya* (Riyadh: Maktabat al-Naṣr al-Ḥadītha, 1355/1968), 197.

In 2000, members of the Council of Senior Scholars mentioned a case that supposedly occurred in 1967 in Riyadh. According to the Council's members, the Riyadh Court of Appeal (at the time called Hay'at al-Tamyīz) overruled a decision for being contrary to Ḥanbalī doctrine, and Muḥammad bin Ibrāhīm, at the time Grand Mufti, apparently backed this decision with a fatwa.[126] In another case, to which the Council's members referred, the appeal court argued that the first instance judge was a muqallid and, therefore, a verdict issued by him that deviates from his school could be overruled.[127]

The common understanding in the Saudi judiciary today is that the judges gradually moved away from the Ḥanbalī School in the decades after the 1928 decree.[128] Muḥammad bin Ibrāhīm al-Saʿīdī, a professor at the Umm al-Qurā University in Mecca, argued that the judges felt the need to adapt the law to the economic and social changes in Saudi Arabia and saw themselves as obliged to undertake ijtihād outside the Ḥanbalī school whenever they felt capable of doing so.[129] Similarly, Ḥamd al-Khuḍayrī, a well-known judge at the Riyadh Court of Appeal and author of a book on Saudi court practice, claimed that the inclusion of non-Ḥanbalī opinions was a natural and necessary process in order to adapt the law to the changing needs and demands of the Saudi people.[130] For others, the opening towards other schools is a result of the Salafī understanding of Islamic law. Qays Āl Mubārak, for instance, a member of the Council of Senior Scholars, held that judges departed from Ḥanbalī teachings whenever they found that it contradicted the textual evidence in the revelation or saw a benefit in following another school in a particular legal question.[131]

Due to the scarcity of historical sources, the reasons for the inclusion of non-Ḥanbalī teachings are difficult to assess. However, as we will see in the coming chapters, the application of non-Ḥanbalī opinions in Saudi court practice is a reality today. Yet, at the same time, late Ḥanbalism still plays an important role in the everyday work of Saudi judges. This is reflected in the judges' use of fiqh books and manuals.

---

126 Al-Amāna al-ʿĀmma li-Hay'at Kibār al-ʿUlamā' (ed.), *Abḥāth Hay'at Kibār al-ʿUlamā'* (Riyadh: Hay'at Kibār al-ʿUlamā', 1434/2013), 3:248.

127 Ibid., 249.

128 See also Vogel, *Saudi Business Law*, 78.

129 Al-Saʿīdī, "Ishkāliyat al-taqnīn wa-l-tadwīn," 301.

130 Interview with Ḥamd al-Khuḍayrī in his office at the Appeal Court in Riyadh, 25 July 2018.

131 Qays bin Muḥammad Āl Mubārak, "Al-Madhhab al-qaḍā'ī fī al-Saʿūdiyya," in *Al-Niẓām al-ʿadl fī al-Saʿūdiyya*, ed. Muḥammad bin Saʿūd al-Bashr and Manṣūr bin ʿAbd al-Raḥmān al-Ḥaydarī (Riyadh: Markaz al-Fikr al-ʿĀlamī, 1436/2010), 284.

5.3 *The Judges' Use of Ḥanbalī Literature*

The books of the Ḥanbalī school still remain important in Saudi court practice, especially those mentioned by Fu'ād Ḥamza in 1936. To give an example, al-Bahūtī was still the most cited scholar in the law of sales (*bayʿa*), according to the published court judgements of the hijrī year 1434 (2012/2013). Thirty-one percent of all references to fiqh literature were made to his books *Kashshāf al-qināʿ*, *Al-Rawḍ al-murbiʿ* and *Sharḥ al-muntahā*. Twenty percent were references to books by Ibn Qudāma, and fourteen percent to books by Ibn Taymiyya and his student Ibn al-Qayyim. The rise of the influence of Ibn Taymiyya and Ibn al-Qayyim in Saudi court practice thus seems to be one of the most significant changes that occurred between the 1930s and 2010s.

The published court judgements from the hijrī year 1435 (2013/2014) paint a similar picture. According to a list made by the collection's editors, al-Bahūtī's *Kashshāf al-qināʿ* and Ibn Qudāma's *Al-Mughnī* were by far the most used books. Even though they mostly consulted Ḥanbalī books, the judges additionally referred to a huge variety of books from all madhāhib in their judgements. In the 1,153 published court decision, Saudi judges referred to sixty-three different fiqh books, of which the large majority were written by premodern jurists. Only nine books (14%) by nineteenth- and twentieth-century jurists were cited, most of them written by Najdī scholars. Thirty-two books (52%) were premodern works from the Ḥanbalī tradition, twelve books (19%) stem from the Mālikī school, five books (8%) from the Shāfiʿī school, and only three books (5%) were written by Ḥanafī jurists. One judge (2%) cited Ibn Ḥazm, the most famous proponent of the Ẓāhirī school. The popularity of Mālikī books is surprising, especially compared to the limited use of works by nineteenth- and twentieth-century scholars.[132]

In their everyday practice, Saudi judges very rarely consult many books to find the proper ruling for every single case. The huge workload, I heard from Saudi judges, made extensive research in every case impossible. Furthermore, as we will see in more detail in Chapter 5, the judges have agreed among themselves to apply the same ruling in many disputed questions in Islamic jurisprudence.

When I visited Saudi courts in the summer of 2018, it was surprising how few books could be seen, especially in the appeal court judges' offices. Appeal court judge Ḥamd al-Khuḍayrī, for example, only had a copy of the first compilation of Saudi court judgements and an old edition of Ibn Qudāma's *Al-Mughnī*

132 Nevertheless, as we will see in Chapters 6 and 7, the reliance on premodern books does not mean that contemporary views in Islamic jurisprudence have no influence on Saudi court practice.

in his office.[133] Al-Khuḍayrī's colleague Muḥammad Jār Allāh explained that he did not use any legal books in his daily practice at court.[134] On an average day, there was simply no time to consult them. Thus, the judges' everyday work is, to some extent, detached from the detailed debates in Islamic jurisprudence. In difficult cases, however, Jār Allāh said that he took the files home and conducted research in his private library.[135] Many lawyers work similarly. For example, one lawyer from Riyadh explained that there was no need for extensive use of fiqh books in his daily practice. However, in difficult questions, he consulted the published court decisions and sometimes also premodern fiqh books.[136]

None of the published decisions cited Ibn ʿAbd al-Wahhāb's writings, which is not surprising, given that explicit references to Ibn ʿAbd al-Wahhāb in the Saudi legal discourse are rare. If scholars make a reference to Ibn ʿAbd al-Wahhāb, it is in preambles or introductions to books or fatwa collections. For instance, on a rare occasion, the Council of Senior Scholars mentioned Ibn ʿAbd al-Wahhāb in the introduction to their influential decision on codification, but they only briefly referred to his call for tawḥīd and did not further engage with his ideas.[137]

6 Conclusion

Acceptance of pluralism in Islamic law might be one of the last things that come to mind when one thinks about contemporary Salafism. Yet, normative pluralism and the critique of the schools' authority is one of the main aspects in which the Salafīs' strict focus on the revelation and their refusal of any interference between humans and God is reflected in the law. When deciding on a legal question, the ideal Salafī scholar considers all opinions in the schools and, through his ijtihād, determines the correct one for the individual case.

133 Visit of the Riyadh Court of Appeal, 25 July 2018.
134 Appeal court judges usually do not quote fiqh literature in their comments on the first instance judges' decisions.
135 Interview with Muḥammad Jār Allāh in his office at the Riyadh Court of Appeal, 31 July 2018.
136 Interview with Manṣūr al-Dhufayrī at his law firm's offices, 13 May 2018.
137 Al-Amāna al-ʿĀmma li-Hayʾat Kibār al-ʿUlamāʾ (ed.) *Abḥāth Hayʾat Kibār al-ʿUlamāʾ*, 3:232.

In practice, however, Saudi judges are more pragmatic. Although they consult books from all madhāhib in some challenging legal questions, in most judgments, the judges only refer to a handful of classic Ḥanbalī books.[138] Nevertheless, legal flexibility remains one of the fundamental concerns of Saudi scholars and judges when they think about the law.

138 This gap is well illustrated by a conversation that I had with five lawyers of a mid-sized law firm in Riyadh. All of them were very familiar with Islamic family law, were confident in their work, and represented clients at the local court. After I had asked some more detailed questions on Islamic family law, I became interested in the way the young lawyers use legal literature. They insisted that fiqh books only played a minor role in their daily practice. However, the most senior of them explained that in some rare cases she consulted Ibn Qudāma's *Al-Mughnī*. I wanted to know more about her use of books and asked what role the fatwas of Muḥammad bin Ibrāhīm played in their work. She hesitated and looked at her colleagues, who started to debate who the shaykh was. It became evident that the young lawyers had heard the name, but never actually read his works. Then, the senior lawyer turned to me with a smile and said, "of course we use the books of Muḥammad bin Ibrāhīm!".

CHAPTER 3

The Dilemma of Codified Law

1 Introduction

In Saudi Arabia, the codification of Islamic law is commonly understood as a power struggle between traditionalists, who want to preserve the "original" sharīʿa, and progressives, who aim to implement a European-style legal system. However, as Guido Steinberg rightly pointed out, scholarship on Saudi ʿulamāʾ tends to neglect religious and legal understandings that drive the Saudi scholarly discourse and to explain the scholars' actions with their economic interests.[1]

This chapter explores the debate on codification from the perspective of the Saudi jurists' own understanding of the Islamic legal tradition. Looking at the debate from the perspective of the ʿulamāʾ will allow us to see beyond the power struggle between the king and the jurists.

In the last thirty years, the discourse of the ʿulamāʾ, and in particular of those that work in the Saudi legal system, largely focused on theoretical problems.[2] It will be those detailed and complex arguments forwarded by ʿulamāʾ who specialized in Islamic legal theory to which we will pay special attention. In order to illustrate how the Saudi jurists' scepticism is often driven by general

1 Steinberg emphasized that it is equally problematic to only focus on the scholars' discourse without considering the social and political context. Steinberg, *Religion und Staat*, 17. Frank Vogel's analysis of the debate on codification is a notable exception. While he also focuses on the relationship between the king and the ʿulamāʾ, he also looks very closely at the jurists' arguments. Vogel found that the arguments on codification at the time of his research were sterile, since they were stuck in the old rhetoric between opponents and supporters of codification. The debate, he wrote, was dominated by quotations of premodern scholars, especially of Ibn Taymiyya. Today, as we will see, Saudi jurists present original arguments related to codification. Moreover, as we have already seen in our discussion of Ibn ʿAbd al-Wahhāb's thought, a new way of using premodern legal writings can also constitute an original legal argument. See Vogel, *Islamic Law and Legal System*, 309–62.

2 Vogel stated that very few extensive public statements by Saudi ʿulamāʾ opposing codification could be found at the time of his research in the 1980s and '90s. As we will see in this chapter, the situation has changed. Today, Saudi ʿulamāʾ do not hesitate to speak or write about codification. I will mainly draw on these newer, much more differentiated views. See ibid., 337.

© DOMINIK KRELL, 2025 | DOI:10.1163/9789004726314_005

considerations of the nature of law, parallels will be drawn between Islamic and European notions of codification.[3]

2 The Codification of Islamic Law

2.1 *The Different Forms of Codification*

Codification describes two different concepts: firstly, it can be understood more broadly as any form of written law. Such codes are not bound to a specific epistemology but simply record rulings on certain legal questions. Thereby, they do not aim to form a comprehensive system of rules. Such forms of codification have been known since the Bronze Age, when several codes, most famously the Code of Hammurabi, laid down the Babylonian king's law.

Secondly, codification can be understood as a systematized comprehensive system of rules. This understanding originates in enlightenment rationalism, which called for a comprehensive restructuring of the law.[4] The first code that tried to systematize the law in a comprehensive way was the Bavarian Civil Code from 1756.[5] New codifications soon spread all over Europe, most notably the Allgemeine Preußische Landrecht from 1794 and the French Code Civil from 1804.

If we understand codification simply as any form of written law, we can see that Islamic jurists discussed the issue since early Islam. The most famous attempt to introduce a written code was in 757, when Ibn Muqaffaʿ, a Persian bureaucrat who had converted to Islam, wrote a letter to the Abbasid caliph al-Manṣūr. In the letter, he criticized that court judgements differed between the cities of the caliphate and sometimes even between courts in the same city. Ibn Muqaffaʿ suggested reviewing the different opinions in the schools

3 Although the epistemological foundations of European legal theory fundamentally differ from those of the Islamic tradition, the jurists' arguments for and against codification are surprisingly similar. I am fully aware that such an approach is a risky endeavour and largely ignores the social and historical context in which these European debates took place. However, the goal is not to give a full portrait of European legal thought but to understand that ideas presented in the Saudi legal discourse are not unique to Saudi Arabia or Islamic law.

4 Pio Caroni, *Gesetz und Gesetzbuch: Beiträge zu einer Kodifikationsgeschichte* (Basel: Helbing & Lichtenhahn, 2003), 126.

5 Reinhard Zimmermann, "Codification: The Civilian Experience Reconsidered on the Eve of a Common European Sales Law," *European Review of Contract Law* 8, no. 4 (2012): 372.

and compiling them in a single book. The caliph, however, did not follow Ibn Muqaffaʿ's proposition.[6]

Later, one of the Abbasid caliphs[7] told Mālik, the founder of the eponymous legal school, that he intended to send a copy of Mālik's most famous legal treatise, the *Muwaṭṭaʾ*, to all judges in the caliphate and planned to force the judges to apply it. Mālik is said to have refused the caliph's plan because he held that every town and every people have their own view of the law and therefore should apply the laws that they choose and believe in.[8] Mālik's famous refusal of codification was one of the main reasons why codified law only played a minor role in subsequent fiqh debates.

Codifications that systematized the law were introduced to the Arab world in the nineteenth century. From the 1840s onward, codification became an essential element of legal reform in the Ottoman Empire. As Avi Rubin pointed out, the Ottoman Empire thereby followed a global trend towards systematic and comprehensive law codes.[9] Over the subsequent decades, codification in most parts of the Arab world went hand in hand with a loss of influence of Islamic law. French law became more and more of a role model for new legislation, especially in commercial and criminal law. Eventually, only the area of "personal status" (*al-aḥwāl al-shakhṣiyya*), a newly formed category that included family law, inheritance law, and the law of Islamic endowments (*awqāf*), remained under the realm of the sharīʿa.[10] As Talal Asad argued, the restriction of Islamic law to matters of personal status was fundamental for the process of secularization in the Middle East. By limiting religious law to the private sphere, a space for the modern secular nation-state was created.[11]

In the course of the twentieth century, and especially after the Second World War, the vast majority of the newly founded Arab nation-states also codified this last remaining area. However, this did not wipe away traditional Islamic jurisprudence. Egypt, for example, still has no single family code, and in most

---

6 Muḥammad Kurd ʿAlī, *Rasāʾil al-bulaghāʾ* (Cairo: Dār al-Kutub al-ʿArabiyya al-Kubrā, 1331/1913), 125.

7 There is some dispute over the Abbasid caliph's name, because several versions of the story exist. See Muḥammad bin ʿAbd al-ʿAzīz al-Fāyiz, *Taqnīn al-aḥkām al-qaḍāʾiyya* (n.p., 1431/2010), 25–26.

8 Ibn ʿAbd al-Barr, *Al-Intiqāʾ fī faḍāʾil al-thalātha al-aʾimma al-fuqahāʾ* (Cairo: Maktabat al-Quds, 1350/1931), 41.

9 Avi Rubin, "Modernity as a Code: The Ottoman Empire and the Global Movement of Codification," *Journal of the Economic and Social History of the Orient* 59 (2016): 828–56.

10 J.N.D. Anderson, "Codification in the Muslim World: Some Reflections," *RabelsZ* 30, no. 2 (1966): 245.

11 Asad, *Formations of the Secular*, 255.

Arab countries, judges turn to Islamic jurisprudence whenever the code is silent on a legal matter. In such cases, courts in Iraq, for instance, have to follow the opinion in Islamic jurisprudence that they consider most in line with the intention of the codified law.[12] Until 2022, Saudi Arabia remained the only country in the Arab world without a comprehensive codification of Islamic law.

2.2 *The Implications of Codification for Islamic Law*

If and in what ways codification changed Islamic law has been subject to intensive debate in Western scholarship on Islamic law. Wael Hallaq famously argued that the codification of Islamic law irrevocably altered the nature of the sharīʿa. "Traditional" Islamic law, as he called it, was thereby transformed into state law.[13] Hallaq wrote that "[i]n the Islamic context, the adoption of codification has an added significance since it represents potently efficacious modus operandi through which the law was refashioned in structured ways."[14] The traditional means of Islamic jurisprudence, he claimed, and most importantly, the epistemology of premodern law, were no longer used. For Hallaq, codification is not merely a pragmatic decision but a conscious choice to limit the powers of judges. Normative pluralism, a fundamental principle of premodern Islamic law, Hallaq held, was abolished by codes that aimed to create uniformity.[15]

Furthermore, many observers argue that codification most significantly changed the position of the ʿulamāʾ, the architects of the "traditional" law. Western literature commonly understands Islamic law as jurists' law.[16] By codifying the law, stateless Islamic law was transformed into statutory law and thus came under the control of the state. Rudolph Peters argued that this transformation of Islamic law could explain the religious scholars' loss of influence in the legal realm in most Muslim countries. The traditional jurists lost, as Peters put it, their position as "exclusive guardians of the law."[17]

---

12 Lauan al-Khazail and Dominik Krell, "Die Wirksamkeit von Minderjährigen- und Zwangsehen nach syrischem und irakischem Familienrecht," *Das Standesamt* 73 (2020), 12.

13 Wael Hallaq, "Can the Shariʿa Be Restored?" in *Islamic Law and the Challenges of Modernity*, ed. Yvonne Yazbeck Haddad and Barbara Freyer Stowasser (New York: AltaMira, 2004), 22–23.

14 Ibid., 23.

15 Hallaq, *Sharīʿa: Theory, Practice, Transformations*, 368–69.

16 This understanding of Islamic law was most importantly shaped by Joseph Schacht, see Schacht, *Introduction to Islamic Law*, 5.

17 Rudolph Peters, "From Jurists' Law to Statute Law or What Happens When the Shari'a is Codified," *Mediterranean Politics* 7, no. 3 (2007): 93.

Similarly, Aharon Layish contended that codified Islamic law was detached from orthodox sharīʿa. Codification could even be seen as a form of secularization of the law. Like Peters, Layish held that codification put Islamic law under the legislative authority of the state and transformed it into statutory law, and that, as a result, the ʿulamāʾ lost control over the application of Islamic law.[18]

Much of the literature on codification focuses on the state's role and therefore rarely considers internal developments in Islamic jurisprudence. Anver Emon pointed out that Western scholarship on Islamic law understands codification mostly as an ideology of statecraft and associates it with the coercive force of an executive.[19] Undoubtedly, the role of the ʿulamāʾ changed over the course of the nineteenth and twentieth centuries in many countries. Emon argued that the focus on the scholars' power led to the common understanding in Western literature that codification constituted a rupture in Islamic legal history.[20] Furthermore, he criticized that the different forms of codification and their epistemological foundations are often not distinguished. Yet, the effects a codification has on jurisprudence largely depend on the code's structure.

Most Western scholars focus on the developments in the Ottoman Empire during the nineteenth century. However, it is questionable whether and to what extent conclusions that are drawn from those historical discourses can be generalized. Earlier codifications took place in the context of the colonial project, whereas the legal discourse today is influenced by globalization and modern capitalism. Nevertheless, the literature on codification in the nineteenth century still frames our understanding of the codification of Islamic law today.

2.3 *Contemporary Muslim Perspectives on Codification*

Today, most Islamic jurists outside of Saudi Arabia do not see a tension between "traditional" and codified Islamic law, and most of them support at least some form of codification.[21] This includes not only modernist reformers but also more traditional ʿulamāʾ. For example, the Syrian jurist Wahba al-Zuḥaylī (d. 2015), a moderate but conservative thinker, criticized the opposition of Saudi ʿulamāʾ to codification in his widely read book "The Efforts to Codify Islamic Jurisprudence" (*Juhūd taqnīn al-fiqh al-islāmī*):

---

18 Aharon Layish, "The Transformation of the Sharīʿa from Jurists' Law to Statutory Law in the Contemporary Muslim World," *Die Welt des Islams* 44, no. 1 (2004): 91–92.

19 Anver Emon, "Codification and Islamic Law: The Ideology Behind a Tragic Narrative," *Middle East Law and Governance* 8 (2016): 275–309.

20 Ibid., 293.

21 See Nāṣir bin ʿAbd Allāh al-Maymān, *Al-Nawāzil al-sharʿiyya* (Dammam: Dār Ibn Jawzī, 1430/2009), 90; and ʿAbd al-Barr Zakī, *Taqnīn al-fiqh al-islāmī: Al-Mabdaʾ wa-l-manhaj wa-al-taṭbīq* (Qatar: Idārat Iḥyāʾ al-Turāth al-Islāmī, 1407/1986), 56.

> Some ʿulamāʾ hold that there is no need for the codification of Islamic jurisprudence because the rulings [*aḥkām*] can be found in the books and these are Arabic books in Arabic script. However, this view cannot be accepted because the fiqh in the old books is known [only] to a small group, and these are specialists. Yet, [even] for most university professors, judges, and others like them, it is difficult to go back to these books since their structure is different from contemporary publications. And there are a lot of legal opinions in them. The researcher needs to read a lot in order to know the preponderant [*rājiḥ*] view. Perhaps a view is preferable according to one book, but [this] varies from another [view] in a different book. The understanding can vary, and it happens in some countries[22] that the judges' decisions differ in one question according to each judge's interpretation [*ijtihād*], knowledge and expertise.[23]

Al-Zuḥaylī regarded codification as a way to make Islamic law more understandable and approachable. For him, codification is not the demise of Islamic law but a way to uphold its authority and a requisite for legal security, which he considers mandatory in the context of today's life.[24] His brother, Muḥammad al-Zuḥaylī, a respected scholar in his own right, even called the codification of Islamic law the newest development in Islamic jurisprudence (*aḥdath taṭawwur li-l-fiqh al-islāmī*).[25]

Similarly, the famous Egyptian jurist Muḥammad Abū Zaḥra (d. 1974) considered codification the only way to defend the application of Islamic law today.[26] For Yūsuf al-Qaraḍāwī (d. 2022), one of the most influential contemporary Islamic intellectuals, codification was a means to renew Islamic law. According to al-Qaraḍāwī, codification should not be limited to one school of Islamic jurisprudence but should be based on comparative studies of different schools to find the opinions that best suit the needs of our times. In order to do this, al-Qaraḍāwī argued, a new generation of ʿulamāʾ were needed who could connect the Islamic legal tradition to modern jurisprudence.[27]

---

22 The context leaves no doubt that he is referring to Saudi Arabia.

23 Wahba al-Zuḥaylī, *Juhūd taqnīn al-fiqh al-islāmī* (Beirut: Muʾassasat al-Risāla, 1408/1987), 50.

24 Ibid., 29.

25 Lecture by Muḥammad al-Zuḥaylī on the schools of Islamic jurisprudence and their influence on the flexibility of codified law. Available on YouTube: www.youtube.com/watch?v=aW_FWsdFOsA, min 5 [last access: 21 August 2022].

26 See Abū Zahra's introduction to ʿAbd al-Raḥmān bin ʿAbd al-ʿAzīz al-Qāsim, *Al-Islām wa-taqnīn al-aḥkām* (Riyadh: Dār al-Maʿārifa al-Saʿūdiyya, 1977), Nūn.

27 Yūsuf al-Qaraḍāwī, *Madkhal li-dirāsat al-sharīʿa al-islāmiyya* (Beirut: Muʾassasat al-Risāla, 1414/1993), 263.

These contemporary ʿulamāʾ, of course, operate in the context of legal systems that have largely abandoned Islamic law. Many of their arguments are directed at the general public to defend Islamic law from further loss of influence. However, what becomes clear is that contemporary Islamic scholars outside Saudi Arabia generally do not consider codification a separation of "traditional sharīʿa" and modern law.

3 The Problem of Binding Rules

3.1 *Islamic Law as State Law?*

We have seen that Western literature on Islamic law usually associates codification with the relationship between the state and the law. By codifying the law, Hallaq and others argued, uncodified Islamic law would be transformed into a new category, namely state law.

Saudi ʿulamāʾ generally follow a different understanding of codification: even if the state codifies the law, this does not change the law's nature. A codification of Islamic law would become, as former appeal court judge Muḥammad al-Fāyiz framed it, a "new text of fiqh" (*naṣṣ fiqhī jadīd*).[28] Hence, it would not introduce something new but merely rephrase the law.[29] For al-Fāyiz, who is a supporter of codification, it is, most importantly, a tool to present Islamic law to a wider public. In an interview, he stated,

> What is sharīʿa? Is there a single book? When it is said, the Quran and the Sunna, there are many schools and views. What is sharīʿa? When we have a code of the school of sunna and jamāʿa, which stems from a meeting of some ʿulamāʾ and is based [on Islamic jurisprudence], we can tell the rest of the world and the Muslims: this is the sharīʿa.[30]

---

28 Interview with Muḥammad bin ʿAbd al-ʿAzīz al-Fāyiz in an episode of the TV program al-Barnāmij Midād titled "Taqnīn al-fiqh," available on YouTube: www.youtube.com/watch?v=fJfIuDAhxMk, min 43 [last access: 12 March 2023].

29 This view is by no means unique to Saudi scholars. The influential nineteenth-century German scholar Friedrich Carl von Savigny, whose ideas we will discuss later in this chapter, wrote in 1831 that he considered "the code as the exposition of the aggregate existing law, with exclusive validity conferred by the state itself." Friedrich Carl von Savigny, *Of the Vocation of Our Age for Legislation and Jurisprudence* (London: Littlewood, 1831), 27.

30 Interview with Muḥammad bin ʿAbd al-ʿAzīz al-Fāyiz in an episode of the TV programme al-Barnāmij Midād titled "Taqnīn al-fiqh," available on YouTube: www.youtube.com/watch?v=fJfIuDAhxMk, min 44 [last access: 12 March 2023].

Similarly, Nāṣir al-Maymān, a trained jurist and member of the Shūrā Council (Majlis al-Shūrā),[31] complained that jurists from other countries always requested to see the Saudi laws, which left him in an uncomfortable position.[32] The lack of codification, he maintained, hindered the inclusion of the sharīʿa into international law. Moreover, it was difficult for comparative legal studies at foreign universities to include Saudi law.[33] Ḥamd al-Khuḍayrī, a judge at the Riyadh Court of Appeal, held that the codification of Islamic law would open a way for foreign NGOs to understand the judiciary and help to correct wrong ideas about the Saudi legal system.[34]

Interestingly, the same argument is made the other way around. ʿAbd Allāh al-ʿAsaylān, a judge at the General Court in Riyadh, argued that, because of the judges' similar education, there was a broad consensus among them on what the law is. He pointed to the fact that all Saudi universities, and especially the Higher Judicial Institute, share a curriculum. A codification of Islamic law, he asserted, would thus only express what is already practiced, and is therefore unnecessary.[35]

References to the role of the state are hard to find in the jurists' discourse. The state is not seen as the lawgiver but, following the doctrine of siyāsa sharʿiyya, as the enforcer of the law as determined by the ʿulamāʾ.[36] At least in theory, the king and the scholars are imagined to be working hand in hand. For instance, the decision of the Council of Senior Scholars on codification emphasized the king's good intentions when he planned to codify Islamic law.[37]

31 *Shūrā* (consultation) has its roots in early Islam. The Prophet encouraged leaders to consult with those affected by their decisions, and subsequent Islamic leaders often followed his example. In addition to consulting the king, the Saudi Shūrā Council also has limited powers to enact some laws. In the context of the legal system, however, the Shūrā Council is of little importance. See Joseph Kéchichian, *Legal and Political Reforms in Saʿudi Arabia* (London: Routledge, 2013), 114.

32 Undated lecture by Nāṣir bin ʿAbd Allāh al-Maymān on the codification of Islamic law, available on YouTube: www.youtube.com/watch?v=LR6-EaA3OYI&t=942s, min 15 [last access: 24 April 2023].

33 Ibid., min. 18.

34 Interview with Ḥamd al-Khuḍayrī in his office at the Appeal Court in Riyadh, 25 July 2018.

35 Interview with ʿAbd Allāh al-ʿAsaylān in a hotel in Riyadh, 23 July 2018.

36 However, this does not mean that the state is not seen as a lawgiver in other areas of the law. As we have discussed in Chapter 2, the Saudi Basic Law generally acknowledges the separation of state power into a legislative, an executive, and a judicial branch.

37 Al-Amāna al-ʿĀmma li-Hayʾat Kibār al-ʿUlamāʾ (ed.), *Abḥāth Hayʾat Kibār al-ʿUlamāʾ*, 3:232.

3.2 *Codification as a Matter of School Coherency*

Since Saudi jurists consider codification a mere reformulation of the law, they discuss the issue in the context of the much older problem of whether a judge could be forced to follow a specific opinion. Bakr Abū Zayd (d. 2008), a former member of the Council of Senior Scholars, summed up the debate as follows:

> Codification is actually a literary work [*taʾlīf*]. The mistake is to give up the terminology of the sharīʿa. If this language is taken away, among the bad consequences is the separation of the views [on this matter] from the established truths and meanings in sharīʿa jurisprudence and its rulings.
>
> No matter if it is called codification [*taqnīn*], compilation [*tadwīn*], or books [*taʾālīf*], this is a wrong description. The field of the dispute is limited to the question of whether the restriction [*ilzām*] [to a specific opinion] is allowed or forbidden.[38]

Saʿd al-ʿUtaybī, a well-known professor of siyāsa sharʿiyya, held that the discourse on codification was about the theological and legal roots (*judhūr ʿaqadiyya wa-fiqhiyya*) of Islam.[39] Since Islamic creed demands that humans judge according to Islamic law, every Islamic codification has to be based on the primary sources of Islamic law. The legal aspects of the debate, on the other hand, are about an "area of controversy in Islamic jurisprudence, namely the ruling on the restriction of the judge – who is responsible for dispensing justice – in matters of ijtihād".[40]

The reference to the question of madhhab restriction enables the jurists to connect their discourse to the older debate on school coherency. Many Saudi scholars discuss Ibn Taymiyya's legal reasoning, who, as we have seen in the last chapter, generally opposed the strict following of a single school of jurisprudence. Consequentially, Ibn Taymiyya was also against forcing the judge to adjudicate according to one single madhhab.[41]

In this regard, Ibn Taymiyya's opinion is very much in line with mainstream Islamic jurisprudence. All schools, except the Ḥanafīs and some Mālikīs, oppose any restriction of the judge to one particular madhhab.[42] For the majority, as we have seen in the last chapter, the judge should be a mujtahid. Ibn Qudāma,

---

38 Bakr bin ʿAbd Allāh Abū Zayd, *Fiqh al-nawāzil* (Riyadh: Muʾassasat al-Risāla, 1416/1996), 1:11.

39 Al-ʿUtaybī, *Maqālāt fī al-siyāsa al-sharʿiyya*, 15.

40 Ibid., 16.

41 Ibn Taymiyya, *Majmūʿat al-fatāwā*, 31:73.

42 Muḥammad Ḥamdī, *Al-Mutūn al-fiqhiyya wa-ṣilatuha bi-taqnīn al-fiqh* (Jeddah: Dār al-Bilād li-l-Ṭabāʿa wa-l-Nashr, 1421/2000), 411–16.

for instance, wrote that a judge is obliged to dispense justice, and since "justice cannot be found in one school,"[43] any restriction to only one school or a particular opinion in the school would be void. The situation changes slightly when the judge is a muqallid. In this case, Ḥanafī scholars allowed the ruler to restrict the adjudication of the judge to a single school and sometimes even to a particular opinion in the school.[44]

3.3 *Individual Justice and Codified Law*

However, Saudi jurists do not only rephrase the opinions of older generations of scholars. Some, mostly specialists in the judiciary, discuss the problem of madhhab restriction and its relationship to different forms of codified law in greater detail.

Saudi jurists generally distinguish between the codification (*taqnīn*) and the compilation (*tadwīn*) of Islamic law. For Saudi scholars, compilation describes the arrangement of legal information in the form of numbered articles and paragraphs. The main difference between codification and compilation is the binding effect. Whereas a compilation is never binding, a codification must always be coercive. This distinction is by no means unique to Islamic law or to Saudi scholars but is also common among European jurists.[45]

Ibn Khunayn demands that the two different levels should be kept in mind while discussing the codification of Islamic law. For Ibn Khunayn, codification itself does not contradict the nature of Islamic law, but only some aspects of a binding law code are problematic. Most importantly, he is concerned with the interpretative flexibility in disputed questions in Islamic jurisprudence. He explained the problem of codification as follows:

> Codification [*taqnīn*] has two meanings:
>
> The first [is]: the arrangement of the material in the form of numbered paragraphs that are divided into chapters. This is a form of text that is not concerning. However, the writer has to state the textual evidence [*dalīl*] and the underlying cause [*taʿlīl*] [of a ruling].
>
> The second [is]: the enforcement of this codified material. There are [several] forms:

---

43 Ibn Qudāma, *Al-Mughnī* (Beirut: Dār ʿĀlam al-Kutub, 1417/1997), 14:91.

44 Ibn ʿĀbidīn, *Radd al-muḥtār ʿalā al-darr al-mukhtār* (Beirut: Dār ʿĀlam al-Kutub, 1423/2003), 8:98.

45 Damiano Canale, "The Many Faces of the Codification of Law in Modern Continental Europe," in *A History of the Philosophy of Law in the Civil Law World, 1600–1900*, ed. Damiano Canale, Paolo Grossi, and Hasso Hofmann (New York: Springer, 2009), 136.

> The first form: What the Quran and the Sunna state, and when there is a consensus [*ijmāʿ*] on a ruling, like: the ḥadd [punishment] for a married or a virgin [person], the ḥadd [punishment] for false accusation, and other questions of human interaction, marriage, inheritance, and the like. This is binding, and it is not possible to deviate from that.
>
> The second form: the general principles of Islamic jurisprudence [*qawāʿid al-fiqhiyya*], like "no harm should be inflicted or reciprocated" [*lā ḍarar wa-lā ḍirār*] … and many other legal principles. These are binding … and if there is uncertainty, this belongs to the fourth form.
>
> The third form: procedural rulings, like the Code of Procedure, [the rules on] founding companies, the ways to prove a crime, and other forms of procedural statutes [*anẓima*]. As long as it is derived from the foundations [*uṣūl*] of the law, it is binding.
>
> The fourth form: rulings on specific issues, like rulings on sales, rents, marriage, and other areas of ijtihād, [in which] the jurists interact with the revelation. This is the area where the question of being bound [to a rule] has to be seen.[46]

The opponents of codification argue that a codified law would bind the judge to rigid rules, which would hinder them in their primary aim: the achievement of justice. To bridge the gap between individual justice and binding law, some Saudi jurists propose different forms of codification that, if introduced, could provide for the necessary flexibility.

Al-Fāyiz, for example, argued that the ideal law code should include the option for the judge to depart from the codified law or, under certain circumstances, even allows the judge to establish a new ruling. However, al-Fāyiz only granted the judge this right if three requirements are met: Firstly, the judge's legal reasoning has to follow the general principles (*qawāʿid*) laid down in the written law. Secondly, the judge must base his verdict on the sources of Islamic law. And thirdly, the decision has to be reviewed by the High Court. A legal code that under these conditions allows for exceptions from the binding law would benefit from all the advantages of a codification while avoiding its negative consequences.[47]

The idea that the judge can depart from established legal norms in exceptional cases originates in Islamic law's acknowledgement of normative pluralism and is commonly invoked by Saudi jurists. It is referred to in the 1928

46 ʿAbd Allāh bin Muḥammad Āl Khunayn, "Muqābila maʿ ṣāḥib al-faḍīla al-shaykh ʿAbd Allāh bin Muḥammad bin Saʿd Āl Khunayn," *Al-Majalla* 1086 (6–12.9.1421/3–9.12.2000).

47 Al-Fāyiz, *Taqnīn al-aḥkām al-qaḍāʾiyya*, 140.

decision by the Higher Judicial Authority that we discussed in the last chapter and, as will be shown in the next chapter, the same idea is brought up in the context of the concept of the prevailing practice at court. Thus, the discourse on codification revolves mainly around the concept of normative pluralism, which is considered the pivotal element of Islamic law. Therefore, diverging court judgements in similar cases are considered a natural part of the Islamic legal tradition. For example, al-Fāyiz argued,

> There are many who demand a binding codification and call it necessary to end the differences between judicial decisions in similar or perhaps identical cases. It is said that this divergence is a form of injustice [*ẓulm*] and points to the lack of continuity and the loss of rights since the basis of human rights is that a person knows his rights. When a person does not know his rights, then how can he demand his rights and how can he organize his legal actions, how can it be accepted today that there are two conflicting rulings [*ḥukmān*] on a contract, a divorce, or a crime etc.
>
> The correct answer to this question is that pluralism [*ikhtilāf*] was present at the time of the pious forebears [*salaf*]. This is proven, for example, by the stories of Fārūq [the epithet of ʿUmar bin al-Khaṭṭāb] about the [case of the] distribution of the estate. He deprived the brothers of their inheritance,[48] and when they came to him after he had judged differently in a second case, he told them, "This is what I judge, and that is what I judged."[49]

The normative pluralism inherent in the Islamic legal tradition, al-Fāyiz explained, allows for the consideration of the peculiarities of the case, especially in family law:

> A binding codification clashes with the benefits it brings because it restricts the judge in his discretionary power to consider the best interests in family law. Like, to declare that a woman has violated her marital duties [*tanshīz*], contrary to the Ḥanbalī School, or to accept the utterance [*lafẓ*] in the dissolution [*firqa*] of the marriage, contrary to the Shāfiʿī

48 According to Ibn al-Qayyim, ʿUmar bin al-Khaṭṭāb was confronted with a dispute regarding the inheritance of a deceased woman, who had full brothers and half-brothers from her mother's side. He divided the estate equally between the half-brothers and full brothers. In an earlier judgement, however, he had given the inheritance only to the half-brothers from her mother's side. Ibn al-Qayyim, *Iʿlām al-muwaqqiʿīn ʿan rabb al-ʿālamīn* (Beirut: Dār al-Kutub al-ʿIlmiyya, 1425/2004), 83–84.

49 Al-Fāyiz, *Taqnīn al-aḥkām al-qaḍāʾiyya*, 121.

> School, or to accept the triple major irrevocable divorce [*ṭalāq*] according to the four schools,[50] or [to determine] the age of the child [*maḥḍūn*] [in custody cases] and the role of the remarriage of the mother, opposing all four schools in this question.[51] It is not in the interests of the parents or the child that the judge is bound to one single view in these questions.[52]

Like other Saudi jurists, al-Fāyiz hoped to thereby establish justice on a case-to-case basis and considered legal reasoning beyond school boundaries necessary for a just solution of the case. In other words, he followed an interest-based approach, whereby the law itself is not just or unjust. Instead, justice largely depends on the interests of the parties, at least in family law. Similarly, ʿAṭiya bin Muḥammad Sālim (d. 1999), a former appeal court judge as well, argued for an individual interpretation of justice:

> From the perspective of judicial methodology, everyone who practices [as a judge] knows that every case has its special circumstances. He knows what is appropriate for this case and not for the other case. There begins the alleviation or aggravation according to the case … So, if we introduce, for example, a criminal code and force the judge to apply it to every criminal case that looks similar, but differs in the circumstances and motives, this does not establish justice.[53]

This tension between abstract rules and individual justice is not unique to Islamic law or to Saudi ʿulamāʾ.[54] European legal scholars have extensively debated this issue since the nineteenth century. Although the social, political, and epistemological context in Europe is, of course, very different, the underlying dilemma remains the same. For example, the French philosopher Jacques

---

50 See Chapter 7 for a detailed discussion of the debate on triple ṭalāq.

51 See Chapter 6 for a detailed discussion of Saudi court practice in custody cases.

52 Al-Fāyiz, *Taqnīn al-aḥkām al-qaḍāʾiyya*, 135.

53 Interview with ʿAṭiya bin Muḥammad Sālim, printed in Muḥammad al-Majdhūn, *ʿUlamāʾ wa mufakkirūn ʿarraftuhum* (Riyadh: Dār al-Shawāf, 1992), 2:213.

54 It is important to note that there has been no substantial influence of European legal theory on Saudi Islamic scholars. This is in contrast to many other Arab countries, where Islamic scholars were directly reacting to developments in European jurisprudence. As Leonard Wood showed, Egyptian legal discourse in the nineteenth and early twentieth centuries was deeply influenced by earlier European debates on codification. See Wood, *Islamic Legal Revival*, esp. Section II.

Derrida (d. 2004) claimed that justice "exceed[ed] law and calculation."[55] Justice, contrary to the calculation of written law, was incalculable and indeterminable in an abstract rule. Derrida wrote,

> To be just, the decision of a judge, for example, must not only follow a rule of law or a general law but must also assume it, approve it, confirm its value, by a reinstituting act of interpretation, as if ultimately nothing previously existed of the law, as if the judge himself invented the law in every case. No exercise of justice as law can be just unless there is a "fresh judgement".... Each case is other, each decision is different and requires an absolutely unique interpretation, which no existing, coded rule can or ought to guarantee absolutely.[56]

For Derrida, a law code can even contradict justice since the calculation that lies at its heart might hinder the judge's "fresh judgement." A similar view was forwarded in early twentieth-century Germany, when legal scholars became increasingly critical of the formalistic legal reasoning of nineteenth-century pandectism. The German *Freirechtsschule*, one of the most important legal movements in twentieth-century Europe, argued that judges should not only look at the law but consider the social context of the case and search for individual justice. Ernst Fuchs (d. 1929), one of the most prominent advocates of the Freirechtsschule, described the movement as follows:

> The Freirechtsschule shifts the emphasis of jurisprudence away from mere bookishness to an observation of the needs and to experience. Hence, its focus is on the in-depth exploration of the legal facts and the peculiarities of the case, as well as on weighing up the opposing interests.[57]

Although the jurists of the Freirechtsschule were not against written laws per se, they criticized how mainstream legal reasoning at their time was bound to abstract legal rules that were derived from Roman law. In a similar fashion,

---

55 Jacques Derrida, The "Mystical Foundation of Authority," in *Deconstruction and the Possibility of Justice*, ed. Drucilla Cornell, Michel Rosenfeld, and David Carlson (New York: Routledge, 1992), 28.

56 Ibid., 23.

57 Ernst Fuchs, *Was will die Freirechtsschule* (Rudolstadt: Greifenverlag, 1929), 12–13.

Ibn Khunayn criticized that law should be more than mere calculation and instead explore the peculiarities of the case:

> [Codification] kills the spirit [*rūḥ*] of the judge's ijtihād. He cannot consider the specifics [*khuṣūṣiya*] of the case. Instead, this forces him to handle it like mathematics [*riyāḍiya*] without consideration of the specifics of the case. This is wrong because it restricts the view [*naẓr*] of the judge to the codified articles and does not open his view to other things that are not in the codification, [but it] would perhaps be better and more reasonable to solve the specifics of the case. The mistake gets worse when the judge applies the codified law. From the point of view of Islamic law [*naẓr al-sharʿ*], this is far away from what is desired.[58]

In addition to the inflexibility of the law when it comes to individual cases, Saudi ʿulamāʾ argue that a written law would not be flexible enough to react to social changes. To make their case, Ibn Khunayn and others referred to the German scholar Carl Friedrich von Savigny (d. 1861), one of the most important opponents of codification in Europe.

3.4 *Carl Friedrich von Savigny and Saudi ʿUlamāʾ*

Saudi judges generally see Islamic law as a living tradition that must serve the needs of the Islamic community today. Legal change is considered necessary to adapt Islamic law to the questions of our times. Codification, on the other hand, is equated with inflexibility and standstill. When I asked Ibn Khunayn about his view on codification, he immediately referred to von Savigny.[59] This was undoubtedly inspired by the fact that I was a German lawyer; however, in an interview published in 2000, he had already mentioned von Savigny and his opposition to codification.[60]

Von Savigny was one of the most influential European jurists of the nineteenth century. His works profoundly influenced jurisprudence in all of Europe, South America, and even parts of Asia.[61] His main criticism was that codified law was not flexible enough to adapt to the ever-changing circumstances of human life.[62] He held that there was an "organic connection of law with the

58 Āl Khunayn, "Muqābila maʿ ṣāḥib al-faḍīla".

59 Interview with Ibn Khunayn in his home in Riyadh, 24 April 2018.

60 Āl Khunayn, "Muqābila maʿ ṣāḥib al-faḍīla".

61 See Joachim Rückert and Thomas Duve, *Savigny international* (Frankfurt am Main: Klostermann, 2015).

62 Von Savigny, *Vocation of Our Age*. Von Savigny argued against his contemporary Friedrich Justus Thibaut (d. 1840), who advocated for a unified German law code. The discussion

being and character of the people," which was "also manifested in the progress of the times."[63] For von Savigny, law at no point reaches a moment of absolute cessation.[64] Instead, it was the jurist's task to listen to the spirit of the people, the *Volksgeist*, and translate it into law.

Ibn Khunayn took up von Savigny's argument and claimed that codified Islamic law would be too static to keep pace with the changing living circumstances in Saudi Arabia today. He argued that if circumstances changed, the state could not react as fast as the jurists and adapt the law to new conditions. The discrepancy between society's needs and the written law would eventually result in unjust court decisions.[65] ʿAbd al-Raḥmān bin Saʿd al-Shithrī, a younger scholar with strong ties to leading Saudi ʿulamāʾ, used a similar argument. In his book on the permissibility of codification, he wrote,

> Codification poses a restriction to rulings that are open to ijtihād. It blocks legal change [*taghayyur al-fatwā*] [that is necessary to adapt] to the change over time. [There is] a principle of Islamic law [*qāʿida sharʿiyya*]: the law changes with the change over time and the change of circumstances.[66]

Later in his book, Al-Shithrī referred to von Savigny and cited the writings of the Jordanian Islamic scholar ʿUmar al-Ashqar (d. 2012) on the opposition against codification in Europe. Nevertheless, al-Shithrī is more hesitant than Ibn Khunayn to explicitly use a foreign jurist like von Savigny in his argument. He emphasized that Islamic jurisprudence alone sufficiently proved the inadmissibility of codification but that some people prefered to follow worldly opinions such as von Savigny's argument instead of turning to God, the Prophet, and the ʿulamāʾ.[67]

Since von Savigny's books are not translated into Arabic, the jurists' references to the German scholar remain superficial.[68] Ibn Khunayn explained that

---

on the codification of German law in the nineteenth century later became known as the "codification dispute" (*Kodifikationsstreit*) and eventually ended with the enactment of the German civil code in 1900.

63 Ibid., 27.

64 Ibid.

65 Interview with Ibn Khunayn in his home in Riyadh, 24 April 2018.

66 ʿAbd al-Raḥmān bin Saʿd al-Shithrī, *Taqnīn al-aḥkām al-sharīʿa: Tārīkhuhu wa-ḥukmuhu* (Riyadh: Dār al-Tawḥīd li-l-Nashr, 1435/2014), 51.

67 Al-Shithrī, *Taqnīn al-aḥkām al-sharīʿa*, 61.

68 For a more detailed discussion of Savigny's theory of legislation in English, see Karl Mollnau, "The Contributions of Savigny to the Theory of Legislation," *American Journal of Comparative Law* 37, no. 1 (1989).

it was the language barrier that prevents him from a more in-depth study of European legal theory.[69]

The nineteenth-century German scholar and contemporary Saudi ʿulamāʾ pursue a similar aim: Von Savigny focused on the historical growth of the law over the centuries because his goal was the revitalization of Roman law. He wanted to show that Roman law could be suitable for the nineteenth century.[70] Likewise, Saudi ʿulamāʾ fear that a law code that is not continuously adjusted to new legal phenomena would strengthen the critique that Islamic law is not suitable for the modern age.

3.5 *The Bond between the Judge and the Law*

Islamic law's acceptance of normative pluralism empowers the judge. At the same time, judgeship is traditionally considered a dangerous endeavour, especially in early Islam.[71] According to a famous account of the Prophet Muḥammad, of three judges, one will be in heaven and two in hell. The first, who is in heaven, knew the law and judged accordingly; the second knew the law but deviated from it and went to hell, as well as the third, the ignorant judge, who judged nevertheless.[72] There are several famous reports of pre-modern Islamic scholars who tried to escape forced judgeship. Abū Ḥanīfa, for instance, allegedly preferred prison to an appointment as a judge.[73]

The notion of judgeship as a dangerous profession is still present in the Saudi legal discourse. ʿAbd Allāh al-ʿAsaylān, a judge at the General Court in Riyadh, considered theoretical fiqh debates to be of little relevance for his daily practice. However, when asked about the risks of being an Islamic judge, he expressed his fear of being punished on the day of judgement for his decisions in court.[74] The before-mentioned account of the Prophet is regularly cited in lectures by Saudi scholars to emphasize the great responsibility of being a

69 Since only a few works of European legal theory have been translated into Arabic, Saudi jurists largely rely on secondary literature in Arabic.

70 Benjamin Lahusen, *Alles Recht geht vom Volksgeist aus* (Berlin: Nicolai, 2013), 8–9.

71 See for example Ibn Qudāma, *Al-Mughnī*, 14:6. Later jurists took a more optimistic stance towards the dangers of judgeship. Since the fate of a knowledgeable judge who simply is mistaken remains unclear in the Prophetic account of the three judges, they argue that a judge can get to heaven as long as he is knowledgeable and attentive. See Norbert Oberauer, "Wahrheitssuche," 148.

72 Abū Dāwūd, *Sunan Abī Dāwūd* (Damascus: Dār al-Risāla al-ʿĀlamiyya, 1430/2009), 5:426 (Nr. 3573).

73 Al-Dhahabī, *Siyar aʿlām al-nubalāʾ* (Beirut: Muʾassasat al-Risāla, 1409/1988), 6:401.

74 Interview with ʿAbd Allāh al-ʿAsaylān in a hotel in Riyadh, 23 July 2018.

judge.[75] The judge's metaphysical accountability for his decisions results in a profound connection between the judge and the law. Against this background, some Saudi jurists fear that the codification of Islamic law would disturb this link. With the introduction of binding law, they assert, the judge would become detached from his own judgement.

To better understand the Saudi jurists' fears, we should briefly look at the general understanding of the role of a judge in jurisdictions with a tradition of codified law enacted by a parliament. Very broadly speaking, the dominant idea in civil law democracies is that laws are an expression of the will of the people, mediated by an elected assembly, with the judiciary being the mere interpreter and applier of the law. It is the parliament, not the judge, that is supposed to create the law. This idea was most radically followed in France after the revolution of 1789 when judges were not even allowed to interpret the written law but had instead to consult the government every time the law was silent or unclear.[76] The judges' own views did not matter. Whether they approved the law or not, they were nevertheless bound to apply it. Generally speaking, judges were often met with suspicion, as is illustrated by the remarks of eighteenth-century Italian jurist Cesare Beccaria (d. 1794), one of the most prominent critics of the idea of judicial interpretation. In 1764, he warned against giving power to the judges:

> Every person has his own point of view, and at different times, every person has a different one. The spirit of the law, therefore, would be the upshot of good or bad logic on the part of the judge and of the state of his digestion, and would depend on the turbulence of his emotions, on the weakness of the aggrieved party, on the judge's relations with the plaintiff and on all those tiny pressures which, to the wavering mind of man, change the appearance of every object.[77]

Ideally, the law should be independent of the person of the judge. Extreme positions, like Beccaria's, were criticized by others as being too technical and

75 This notion of the dangers of judgeship has also been observed in other contemporary legal systems. For example, Morgan Clarke reported that similar ideas are expressed in present-day Lebanon. Morgan Clarke, "The Judge as Tragic Hero," *American Ethnologist* 39, no. 1 (2012): 110.

76 Article 12 of the "Décret des 16–24 août 1790 sur l'organisation judiciare". See Mathias Gläser, *Lehre und Rechtsprechung im französischen Zivilrecht des 19. Jahrhunderts* (Frankfurt am Main: Vittorio Klostermann, 1996), 4.

77 Cesare Beccaria, *An Essay on Crimes and Punishments* (Albany: W. O. Little & Co, 1872), 22–23.

mechanical. Judges, some European jurists complained particularly in the nineteenth century, resembled slot machines, in which you drop the facts and costs, and it spews out the decision, including the opinion.[78] The metaphor of the judge as a slot machine was later made famous by the German sociologist Max Weber.[79] The Saudi jurist Bakr Abū Zayd used the same image when he warned against the codification of Islamic law:

> To undertake ijtihād is one of the requirements for judges. A binding codification bans ijtihād for a legal opinion or an opinion's strength. Then, the judge starts to resemble a machine [*āla*].[80]

Given the judge's personal responsibility for his decision, Saudi jurists are especially concerned that a codification would restrain the judge from following his understanding of Islamic law. In his fatwa on codification, Ibn ʿUthaymīn, for instance, argued that such a process would mean that a judge would have to decide based on someone else's legal opinion. No legal code issued by the ruler (*walī al-amr*) should interfere with the judges' legal reasoning.[81]

The Council of Senior Scholars considered this break of the personal connection between the judge and the law a forbidden innovation in Islam, an argument that illustrates the scholars' Salafī background. In their decision on the permissibility of codification, they argued:

> 1. To force the judges to decide according to what is called the preponderant [*rājiḥ*] [opinion] by those who choose it requires the judges to decide differently from what they believe, if only in some questions. This is not allowed and is different from what was practised at the time of the Prophet, the rightly guided caliphs, and some of the pious predecessors [*al-salaf al-ṣāliḥ*]. …[82]
> 2. To force the judge to decide according to what is called the preponderant opinion is restricting them. It detaches them in their judgement from the Quran, the Sunna, and the heritage of the Islamic fiqh. It damages

78 Regina Ogorek, *Richterkönig oder Subsumtionsautomat? Zur Justiztheorie im 19. Jahrhundert* (Frankfurt am Main: Vittorio Klostermann, 1986), 40.

79 Weber referred to this idea in his seminal work *Economy and Society*, see Max Weber, *Economy and Society* (Berkeley: University of California Press, 1978), 886.

80 Bakr bin ʿAbd Allāh Abū Zayd, *Fiqh al-nawāzil* (Riyadh: Muʾassasat al-Risāla, 1416/1996), 1:89.

81 Muḥammad bin Ṣāliḥ Ibn ʿUthaymīn, *Izālat al-sitār ʿan al-jawāb al-mukhtār li-hadāyat al-muḥtār* (N.p.: n.d.), 85.

82 Here, the Council recounted the story of Mālik and the Abbasid caliph discussed earlier.

> this wealth, which is the best heritage that we inherited from the pious predecessors.[83]

Hence, from the Council's point of view, the disruption of the personal relationship between the judge and the law, not the text as such, constitutes a break with the Islamic legal tradition.

4 New Understandings of Legal Certainty

4.1 *Normative Pluralism as a Liability*

Max Weber famously argued that capitalism required a high degree of legal rationality.[84] Weber held that a rational legal system relied on formal and generalized rules that transcended the case in question. A legal system that prioritized the individual case over general rules, on the other hand, was irrational.[85] Weber maintained that it was also because of the rationality of European law that capitalism came into being in Europe and not in other parts of the world.

In Weber's view, the focus on the individual case in the Islamic legal tradition makes Islamic law the antithesis of rational law.[86] He called Islamic adjudication *Kadijustiz*, a term he had borrowed from the German scholar of Islam Richard Schmidt.[87] For Weber, the main characteristic of Kadijustiz is the absence of abstract rational rules for decision-making.[88] As Islamic adjudication was guided by revelation and not intellect, it was irrational. Therefore, the adjudication by an Islamic judge was necessarily subjective and rule-free.[89] Wherever Kadijustiz was predominant, Weber argued, capitalism was hindered because of the lack of formal rules and abstract principles.

Weber's depiction of Islamic law has been criticized by many scholars of Islamic law, who point to the sophisticated discourses in Islamic jurisprudence and its high degree of formality.[90] Yet, the Saudi government, but also many

---

83 Al-Amāna al-ʿĀmma li-Hayʾat Kibār al-ʿUlamāʾ (ed.), *Abḥāth hayʾat kibār al-ʿulamāʾ*, 3:234.

84 Max Weber, *Wirtschaft und Gesellschaft* (Tübingen: Mohr Siebeck, 2010), 3:619.

85 David Trubek, "Max Weber on Law and the Rise of Capitalism," *Wisconsin Law Review* 720 (1972): 730.

86 Bryan Turner, *Weber and Islam* (London: Routledge, 1998), 111.

87 Johansen, *Contingency in a Sacred Law*, 48.

88 Weber, *Wirtschaft und Gesellschaft*, 2:571.

89 Ibid., 572.

90 See, for example, David Powers, "Kadijustiz or Qāḍī-Justice? A Paternity Dispute from Fourteenth-Century Morocco," *Islamic Law and Society* 1, no. 3 (1994): 365–66.

ʿulamāʾ and lawyers, believe that the acceptance of normative pluralism and the resulting legal uncertainty poses a risk to the economic development of the kingdom. They share Weber's belief that abstract, general, and transparent laws are a precondition for economic development.

For example, Usāma al-Qaḥtāni, a trained Islamic scholar and influential lawyer, expressed his frustration that the existing normative pluralism made it fairly impossible to assess the chances and risks of any given case, especially in commercial issues.[91] Generally, lawyers are among the most vivid supporters of a codification since many of them are not educated in Islamic jurisprudence and, therefore, especially struggle to comprehend the judges' legal reasoning. Judges, too, criticized the divergence of court judgements that results from the acceptance of normative pluralism. For example, Muḥammad Jār Allāh, a senior judge at the Riyadh Court of Appeal, who mostly deals with family law, complained that even with his expertise, he could not predict the outcome of other courts' judgements. The different chambers at his court, he explained, still differed in their views on several crucial legal questions.[92]

But most importantly, it was the Ministry of Justice that considered diverging court judgements one of the main problems of the Saudi judiciary. Bashār al-Mufadda, a trained judge, teacher at the Higher Judicial Institute (Maʿhad al-ʿĀlī li-l-Qaḍāʾ) and vice president of the Ministry of Justice's Research Center (Markaz al-Buḥūth), argued in 2018 that court decisions in Saudi Arabia largely depend on the first letter of the plaintiff's name. Differences in legal interpretations, al-Mufadda admitted, exist in every legal system, even in those with codified law, since the interpretation of a written rule may differ. However, in his view, the situation in Saudi Arabia cannot be compared to the problem of contradicting court decisions in other legal systems. Not only does the interpretation of a rule differ in the Saudi judiciary, but the law itself is not clearly determined. He gave the example of crossing a red streetlight. In other legal systems, he explained, one would ask whether crossing a red light violates the law. In Saudi Arabia, on the other hand, the discussion would start with the question of whether it is the green or the red light that allows you to cross the street in the first place.[93]

Other Saudi scholars doubt that it is even possible to positively know whether court decisions diverge in similar cases. ʿAbd al-Raḥmān bin Saʿd al-Shithrī, for example, held that every court decision is deeply connected

91 Interview with Usāma al-Qaḥṭānī in his office in Riyadh, 15 May 2018.

92 Interview with Muḥammad Jār Allāh in his office at the Riyadh Court of Appeal, 31 July 2018.

93 Interview with Bashār al-Mufadda in the Ministry of Justice, 8 May 2018.

to the circumstances and characteristics of the case. Hence, it is difficult for everyone except the judge to see whether the applied law actually differs since only the judge knows the specifics of the case.[94] Other 'ulamā' claim that uncertainty is not a particularity of Islamic law but exists in all legal systems. For example, the Council of Senior Scholars argued,

> The judges' verdicts differ even in the civil courts of countries, in which they judge according to positive law that has been compiled in the structure of articles and arranged by numbers. Inconsistency and mistakes happen. Some of them are appealed and annulled by the appeal court. The laws and the obligation to [follow them] do not prevent inconsistency and mistakes [but] accuse the judges.[95]

However, for the majority of scholars and judges, normative pluralism increasingly becomes a burden. This has resulted in a shift of opinions on codification.

4.2 *Shifting Opinions on Codification*

In the past, not only the Council of Senior Scholars opposed codification, but, as Frank Vogel wrote based on his fieldwork in the 1980s, the great majority of Saudi scholars.[96] In his 2014 book on codification, 'Abd al-Raḥmān bin Sa'd al-Shithrī listed many names of famous Saudi scholars that have expressed their rejection of codification, either in personal conversations with al-Shithrī or in their writings.[97] A closer look at the names, however, reveals that most of these scholars are now in their seventies and eighties and thus represent an older generation of Saudi jurists.

Today, the stance towards codification is changing, particularly among younger jurists. According to al-'Utaybī, the number of supporters of codification grew after the introduction of the Basic Law of Governance (al-Niẓām al-Asāsī li-l-Ḥukm) in 1992, since the law ensured that the Saudi king was now formally bound to follow and apply the sharī'a.[98] Therefore, scholars could be sure that a codification would not include non-Islamic positive law. Former appeal court judge Al-Fāyiz also saw a changing attitude towards codification and estimated that the majority of Saudi judges today support some form of

94 'Abd al-Raḥmān bin Sa'd al-Shithrī, *Ḥukm taqnīn al-sharī'a al-islāmiyya* (Riyadh: Dār al-Ṣamī'ī li-l-Nashr wa-l-Tawzī', 1428/2007), 27.

95 Al-Amāna al-'Āmma li-Hay'at Kibār al-'Ulamā' (ed.), *Abḥāth hay'at kibār al-'ulamā'*, 3:236.

96 Vogel, *Islamic Law and Legal System*, 340.

97 Al-Shithrī, *Taqnīn al-aḥkām al-sharī'a*, 60.

98 Al-'Utaybī, *Maqālāt fī al-siyāsa al-shar'iyya*, 17.

codification.[99] Even jurists who do not favor codification generally admit that siyāsa sharʿiyya generally grants the king the right to codify Islamic law.

The changing attitudes towards codification reflect a change of generations in the Saudi judiciary and a loss of authority of more senior scholars. Today, many Saudi jurists demand the codification of Islamic law for the same reasons as jurists in other Islamic countries: they hope to establish legal security, create a more transparent legal system, and thereby uphold the authority of Islamic law.

5 Conclusion

Opponents of the codification of Islamic law view the restriction to a single opinion in Islamic jurisprudence as the main problem of codified law. They fear that a binding codification will conflict with their understanding of legal flexibility and normative pluralism. The jurists believe that a codification cannot be adapted to the individual case and changing social circumstances in the same way as the judges' interpretation of Islamic law. The chapter has also shown that the arguments of Saudi jurists are not specifically 'Islamic,' as jurists in European history grappled with very similar problems.

Saudi jurists do not view codified law as state law in the way it is understood in common and civil law system. Hence, the jurists' debate on codification does not center around the role of the state but focuses on how justice can be achieved through rules. As a consequence, Saudi jurists do not consider the codification of Islamic law a turning point in the history of Islamic legal systems. For them, it is not a break with the tradition but rather the next step in adapting the Islamic legal tradition to the challenges of modernity.

The absence of a codification of Islamic law, and hence of a restriction to a particular legal opinion, put the individual Saudi judge in a powerful position. To balance individual ijtihād and legal certainty, Saudi ʿulamāʾ and the Ministry of Justice developed a new understanding of legal precedent and judicial appeal, which will be discussed in the next chapter.

99 Written correspondence with Muḥammad bin ʿAbd al-ʿAzīz al-Fāyiz, 4 October 2017. Frank Vogel made similar observations. Vogel, *Saudi Business Law*, 34.

CHAPTER 4

Narrowing the Gate of Ijtihād

1 Introduction

Codified law is not the only way judges can be restricted in their legal reasoning. Common law systems, for instance, rely more on legal precedents than on codified law. Usually, legal precedents are defined by high-ranking courts and enforced by the appeal court system.

In premodern Islamic law, both legal precedent and appeal courts played a minor role. Much more important were the schools: they structured legal reasoning and education. However, as we have seen in Chapter 3, premodern ʿulamāʾ agreed that a judge has to be a mujtahid, which theoretically allowed him to choose between the schools' opinions. Yet, in some situations, premodern scholars feared the resulting inconsistency in the courts' adjudication. Overshadowed by the debate on ijtihād and largely ignored by Western scholarship, they developed the idea of a prevailing practice of the court (*mā jarā ʿalayhi al-ʿamal*, or *mā jarā bihi al-ʿamal*) as a mechanism to ensure the consistency of court decisions.

This chapter explores how Saudi ʿulamāʾ revitalized the concept of the prevailing practice and reinterpreted the position of judicial review in Islamic jurisprudence in order to unify court decisions in the absence of a binding codified law. It shows how the reference to the premodern notion that judges should jointly follow a specific opinion in Islamic jurisprudence allowed them to establish a system that resembled the concept of legal precedent in common law systems.

The question of legal precedent and judicial appeal has implications far beyond the technicalities of procedural law but determines how political power is established. Appeal courts can facilitate the hierarchical control of centralizing regimes and can thereby ensure political loyalty, which is especially important for Islamic political and religious institutions with their traditionally weak hierarchy.[1] Understanding how law is unified through appeal

1 Martin Shapiro, "Islam and Appeal," *California Law Review* 68, no. 2 (1980): 350; David Powers convincingly showed that Martin Shapiro, who is not a scholar of Islamic law by training, was to some extent misinformed by older scholarship on judicial review in Islamic law and thus exaggerated its limitations. Although many of his claims have lost their validity, his main argument regarding the political power of appeal mechanisms, I think, remains convincing. See David Powers, "On Judicial Review in Islamic Law," *Law & Society Review* 25, no. 2 (1992).

DOI:10.1163/9789004726314_006

courts and legal precedents can thus tell us a lot about the relationship between power, authority, and the law in Saudi Arabia and how it changed through codification.

2 The Institutionalization of the Prevailing Practice

2.1 *The Concept's Origins and Its Development*

2.1.1 The Two Meanings of the Prevailing Practice in Premodern Jurisprudence

Saudi ʿulamāʾ referred to premodern jurists when developing their understanding of the prevailing practice. In Islamic jurisprudence, the concept of the prevailing practice is mostly associated exclusively with the Mālikī School.[2] The underlying idea, however, is more or less recognized in all schools of Islamic jurisprudence.[3] Whereas the Mālikīs discussed the concept explicitly, it is less visible in other schools, which use various names to describe the same idea.[4] The Ḥanafīs, for example, called it, among other things, "what we choose" (*bihi naʾkhudh*) or simply "the practice" (*al-ʿamal*[5]).[6] Yet, it is important to note that the jurists did not always carefully distinguish between the prevailing practice at court and the prevailing opinions in their fatwas.

The concept of a prevailing practice is employed in two different but interconnected ways: the first is the institutionalized departure from the predominant (*rājiḥ*) view in the school. Especially scholars in the Mālikī tradition held that a judge should under certain circumstances follow the prevailing practice in his area or at his court, even if it is based on a weak (*ḍaʿīf*) opinion.[7] Thereby, the scholars wanted to adjust the law to particular local developments, for instance, a spreading disease or a war. To establish a new prevailing practice, the leading scholars of a specific area had to come together and choose a minority opinion that would be more suitable to the circumstances. Once the said situation ended, the judges had to return to the predominant view in the school.

---

2 See, for example, ʿAbd al-ʿAzīz bin Saʿd al-Dughayther, "Ḥujjiyyat al-sawābiq al-qaḍāʾiyya," *Majallat al-ʿAdl* 34 (1428/2007): 184.

3 ʿĀṣim bin ʿAbd Allāh al-Mutawwaʿ, *Al-ʿUdūl ʿalā al-qawl al-rājiḥ fī al-futyā wa-l-qaḍāʾ* (Riyadh: Dār al-Maymān, 1439/2018), 424.

4 Ibid., 387.

5 This should not be confused with the practice of the people of Medina (*ʿamal ahl al-Madina*), which is considered a source of the law in the Mālikī school.

6 Al-Mutawwaʿ, *Al-ʿUdūl ʿalā al-qawl al-rājiḥ*, 403.

7 Schacht, *Introduction to Islamic Law*, 62.

This understanding of the prevailing practice is also recognized in the other schools. There too, the predominant opinion could be abandoned for more general considerations. For example, when discussing whether a woman could file a lawsuit against her absent husband, the sixteenth-century Ḥanafī jurist Ibn Nujaym (d. 1563) wrote,

> According to the school, her evidence is not considered because [this would] be a trial against an absentee. According to Zufar,[8] the evidence is heard …, [and] this is what is practiced. It is one of the six questions in which Zufar's opinion is followed because of the needs of the people [*li-ḥājat al-nās*].[9]

Likewise, the Ḥanafī scholar al-Ḥaṣkafī (d. 1677) stated that, in contrast to the common opinion in the Ḥanafī school, an alleged thief could be tortured. He wrote that "this is what suits the people, and what is practiced since in theft there is only in the rarest occasions a witness testimony."[10] In a similar way, the fifteenth-century Ḥanbalī scholar al-Mardāwī (d. 1480) argued for the permissibility of selling copies of the Quran, contrary to the opinion of Aḥmad bin Ḥanbal and leading Ḥanbalī scholars like Ibn Qudāma: "This is what is practiced (*ʿalayhi al-ʿamal*), and nothing else suits the people (*lā yasaʿu al-nās ghayruhu*)."[11]

The concept is also used in a different sense, which was of more importance for Saudi scholars: some premodern ʿulamāʾ also called the usually applied rules at a given time and place in history the prevailing practice. This understanding seemed to have been particularly common among Ḥanbalī scholars. Ibn Mufliḥ (d. 1362), for instance, referred to the notion of the prevailing practice when he stated that in the limited partnership agreement (*sharikat al-ʿinān*),[12] the partners do not have to give each other explicit permission (*idhn ṣarīḥ*)

8 Most likely, Ibn Nujaym was referring to Zufar bin al-Hudhayl (d. 774), a student of Abū Ḥanīfa and one of the most prominent early Ḥanafī scholars.

9 Ibn Nujaym *Al-Baḥr al-rāʾiq sharḥ kanz al-daqāʾiq* (Beirut: Dār al-Kutub al-ʿIlmiyya, 1434/2013), 4:334.

10 Cited in Ibn ʿĀbidīn, *Radd al-muḥtār*, 6:146.

11 Ibn Mufliḥ, al-Mardāwī, and al-Baʿlī, *Kitāb al-Furūʿ*, 6:136.

12 In a sharikat al-ʿinān, the partners agree to share their capital in order to generate profit. In contrast to the sharikat al-mufāwada, the other important form of limited partnership in Islamic law, the partners' assets in a sharikat al-ʿinān can be unequal and the partners can freely agree on the distribution of responsibilities and the partnerships' profits. While all schools accept the general idea of a sharikat al-ʿinān, they considerably differ on important details. See Norbert Oberauer, *Islamisches Wirtschafts- und Vertragsrecht: Eine Einführung* (Ergon: Würzburg, 2017), 201–6.

to dispose of each other's property: "This is the practice (*al-maʿmūl ʿalayhi*) among my companions."[13]

2.1.2 The Saudi Jurists' Use of the Prevailing Practice

In the early twentieth century, Saudi scholars extended the concept's scope in order to unify the judges' ijtihād, which was increasingly decoupled from the Ḥanbalī tradition.[14] Whereas premodern scholars only sporadically referred to the prevailing practice on a matter, Saudi jurists applied the concept more broadly. Muḥammad bin Ibrāhīm Āl al-Shaykh (d. 1969) emphasized that "no [judge] should decide [*yuftī*] differently from the usually used opinion [*mā ʿalayhi al-fatwā*] in all courts throughout the kingdom".[15] Although low-ranking judges were not bound to a single madhhab, Muḥammad bin Ibrāhīm obliged them to follow the prevailing opinion in the Saudi legal discourse.

On one occasion, for example, Muḥammad bin Ibrāhīm was asked whether three ṭalāq uttered at the same time should be counted as one or three ṭalāq utterances, a classical problem in Islamic jurisprudence. He replied that, contrary to Ibn Taymiyya's popular opinion, the practice in Saudi courts was to count each utterance as a separate ṭalāq.[16] In a later letter, Muḥammad bin Ibrāhīm criticized a judge at the court in Mecca who claimed that the three ṭalāq should be counted as one. There was no need for the judge, Muḥammad bin Ibrāhīm wrote, to deviate from the prevailing view in the kingdom.[17] In yet another letter, he demanded that a judge should follow what is usually practiced at his court (*mā ʿalayhi al-ʿamal*), when he determines the compensation for injuries (*arūsh al-jirāḥāt*).[18] In doing so, Muḥammad bin Ibrāhīm acted, as we will see in more detail, as an appeal instance, similar to supreme courts in contemporary legal systems. Thus, it must be assumed that the letters had a significant impact on court practice at the time. However, Muḥammad bin Ibrāhīm did not develop a comprehensive theory of the prevailing practice. This is probably a result of his education in Ḥanbalī jurisprudence, whose proponents largely neglected to theorize the concept.[19]

---

13 Ibn Mufliḥ, al-Mardāwī, and al-Baʿlī, *Kitāb al-Furūʿ*, 7:106.

14 The relationship between the contemporary Saudi understanding and premodern ideas of the prevailing practice is complicated. Ibn Khunayn, for instance, considered the concept of the prevailing practice a natural part of the Ḥanbalī tradition. Interview with Ibn Khunayn in his home in Riyadh, 24 April 2018.

15 Al-Qāsim, *Fatāwā wa-rasāʾil*, 11:30.

16 Ibid.

17 Ibid., 37.

18 Ibid., 413.

19 Al-Mutawwaʿ, *Al-ʿUdūl ʿalā al-qawl al-rājiḥ*, 424.

Today, the prevailing practice has become the main guideline for ijtihād in most questions. In his commentary on the Saudi procedural code, Ibn Khunayn wrote,

> The practice in the courts of the kingdom [is]: it is used what Quran and Sunna state. However, in disputed questions of ijtihād, the prevailing practice (*maʿmūl bihi*) is chosen by the court, then the dominant (*mashhūr*) view in the Ḥanbalī school.[20]

The maʿmūl bihi thus became the main point of reference for the judges' application of Islamic law, while the Ḥanbalī school merely served as fallback option whenever the prevailing practice cannot be determined.

2.2 *Prevailing Practice and Legal Precedent*

2.2.1 The Differences between the Prevailing Practice and Legal Precedent

Important questions remain: Who defines the prevailing practice? And how is it developing? When asked what constitutes the maʿmūl bihi, Ibn Khunayn explained that the term would just be another way to refer to judicial precedents (*sawābiq qaḍāʾiyya*). The recognition of precedent in the form of the maʿmūl bihi was similar to the concept of legal precedent in Anglo-American legal systems. He emphasized that the concept of the maʿmūl bihi was not borrowed from other legal systems but derived from the Islamic tradition.[21]

However, in detail, Ibn Khunayn saw considerable differences between the way the two concepts worked:[22] for him, judicial precedent represents every court decision on a legal question that has not yet been decided on by any court nor addressed by the ʿulamāʾ.[23] In other words, whenever contemporary or premodern Islamic jurists have addressed an issue, a court decision on that issue, even the first one, could not be considered a legal precedent. Thus,

---

20 ʿAbd Allāh bin Muḥammad Āl Khunayn, *Al-Kāshif fī sharḥ niẓām al-murāfaʿāt al-sharʿiyya al-saʿūdī* (Riyadh: Dār Ibn Farḥūn, 1433/2012), 1:15.

21 Interview with Ibn Khunayn in his home in Riyadh, 24 April 2018.

22 It was only when I asked more detailed questions in a second meeting that Ibn Khunayn told me that he had used the equation of the maʿmūl bihi with judicial precedent to introduce me to the topic. He then referred me to an article on legal precedent that he had written a couple of years before for a conference at the Imām University in Riyadh.

23 ʿAbd Allāh bin Muḥammad Āl Khunayn, "Working paper for the conference 'al-Sawābiq al-Qaḍāʾiyya wa-l-Iʿtimād ʿalayha fī al-Qaḍāʾ' [Legal precedents and the reliance on them in the judiciary] at the Imām Muḥammad bin Saʿūd Islamic University in Riyadh on the 20.11.1434/25.9.2013" (1434/2013), 5.

Ibn Khunayn's understanding of what constitutes a legal precedent is much broader than in the Anglo-American tradition, where only court decisions, not jurisprudential writings, can constitute precedents. Likewise, he defines the prevailing practice as rulings that are not only established by the courts but also by ʿulamāʾ outside the judiciary.[24]

Ibn Khunayn held that one of the main differences between the two concepts in the context of Islamic law is that only court decisions form a legal precedent, whereas the Islamic legal discourse as a whole defines the prevailing practice. Legal precedents in Islamic law, he argued, are not binding, whereas the judges have to respect the prevailing practice.

Likewise, Muḥammad bin Ibrāhīm maintained that judges are bound to the prevailing practice as a whole, not to individual previous court judgements by the same or another court. In one of his letters, he emphasized that a decision could not be based on another court's judgement.[25] Nonetheless, in another letter, he stressed that earlier court decisions should not be ignored since they constitute an essential source for the judges. He wrote,

> The [importance of] knowledge of earlier court judgements: it is to build upon them and to be enlightened by them. For the most part, the preceding [*sābiq*] is preferable to the subsequent [*lāḥiq*].[26]

2.2.2 The Prevailing Practice as the Sum of Past Court Decisions

Despite these differences, the maʿmūl bihi is still mostly associated with past court decisions in the contemporary Saudi legal discourse. Appeal court judge Ḥamd al-Khuḍayrī, for instance, the author of a handbook on Saudi court practice, explained that the maʿmūl bihi could be determined by looking at the higher courts' decisions. The appeal system produces a constant stream of new judgements, most notably of the appeal courts' decisions, that are circulated among the judges and become de-facto binding for them.[27]

Other jurists have greater difficulties defining the concept of maʿmūl bihi. ʿAbd Allāh al-ʿAsaylān, a judge at the General Court in Riyadh, for example,

24 Ibn Khunayn's concept of the prevailing practice encompasses the two understandings in the Islamic legal tradition that we discussed earlier. Firstly, the systematic and institutional application of a generally refused (*marjūḥ*) minority opinion and secondly, the unified application of what at the time is considered the preponderant (*rājiḥ*) view. See Ibid., 12–13.

25 Al-Qāsim, *Fatāwā wa-rasāʾil*, 7:277.

26 Ibid., 333.

27 Interview with Ḥamd al-Khuḍayrī in his office at the Riyadh Court of Appeal, 25 July 2018.

stated that in his everyday practice, the maʿmūl bi-hi was formed informally. Al-ʿAsaylān compared this with the training under a particular shaykh: a student listening to his teacher repeatedly absorbs the teacher's opinions and often refrains from questioning them. The same happens, al-ʿAsaylān explained, in his interaction with the appeal court. If the appeal court judges are dissatisfied with his judgments, they note their criticism in the file and refer the case back to him. Through reading the appeal court judges' feedback on his verdicts, he absorbs their opinions and slowly adjusts his practice accordingly.[28] For al-ʿAsaylān, the development of the maʿmūl bihi is thus a subconscious process through which his understanding of the correct opinion is shaped.

It is difficult to assess at what point the idea of the maʿmūl bihi became fully recognized in the Saudi judiciary. During Frank Vogel's research in the 1980s, his interview partners did not mention the maʿmūl bihi.[29] On the other hand, the senior appeal court judges I spoke with claimed that the concept of the maʿmūl bihi was already present when they joined the judiciary.

The importance of the concept certainly increased when court decisions started to become publicly available. Although the published decisions were never binding for the judges, they slowly influenced the workings of the legal system. For instance, the head of a law firm in Riyadh, which mostly focuses on family and criminal law, stressed the importance of the compilations of court judgements as one of the most crucial resources in his daily work. Like lawyers in other legal systems, he now regularly used case-law to build his argument. When he tried to refer to case law before the court decisions were officially published, he had to rely on his personal contacts with other lawyers, which was only possible to a limited extent.[30]

Others, like the former appeal court judge Muḥammad al-Fāyiz, claimed that the publication of case-law had not influenced the way Saudi judges decide. Al-Fāyiz argued that court decisions are only one of the many sources that judges use in their decision-making process.[31] Until today, Saudi judges rarely base their decisions explicitly on published court judgements. However, it is very likely that the published court judgements have made it easier to grasp the maʿmūl bihi and thus strengthened the concept of the prevailing practice.

28 Interview with ʿAbd Allāh al-ʿAsaylān in a hotel in Riyadh, 23 July 2018.

29 Personal conversation with Frank Vogel at a conference in Tampere, Finland, 7 June 2018.

30 Interview with Manṣūr al-Dhufayrī in his law firm in Riyadh, 13 May 2018.

31 Written correspondence with Muḥammad bin ʿAbd al-ʿAzīz al-Fāyiz, 27 September 2017.

2.3 *The Formalization of the Prevailing Practice*

2.3.1 The Prevailing Practice in the 1975 Code of the Judiciary

From the 1970s onwards, the king's codes (*anẓima*) slowly incorporated the prevailing practice. In doing so, they combined the fiqh concept with Anglo-American understandings of legal precedent. As a result, the differences between a system of legal precedents and the ʿulamāʾ's conceptualization of the prevailing practice gradually blurred. It was the 1975 Code of the Judiciary (Niẓām al-Qaḍāʾ) that first introduced the idea of a prevailing practice into statutory law. It obliges the chambers of the appeal court to follow their own precedents, unless the courts' general assembly allows them to decide otherwise. Article 14 of the code stipulated,

> If one of the chambers of the court deviates from its former ijtihād or the former ijtihād of another chamber of the court while reviewing a case, the case is brought to the General Assembly [al-Hayʾa al-ʿĀmma] of the appeal court [Maḥkamat al-Tamyīz].[32]

Furthermore, the code gave the Higher Judicial Council the power to formulate general principles (*mabādiʾ ʿāmma*), whenever the minister of justice considered this necessary.[33] Moreover, the code specified that a research unit should be established in the Ministry of Justice, whose task would be to collect legal principles that were established by decisions of the appeal court and the Higher Judicial Council.[34] The members of the research unit should check whether these principles would still be just, considering the changing living circumstances in the kingdom, and then send them to the Higher Judicial Council.[35] At the time, these new mechanisms had little practical importance, and for more than forty years, no such principles were published.

2.3.2 The 2007 Reform of the Code of the Judiciary

In 2007, a new Code of the Judiciary was issued that extended the binding force of legal precedents. Now, the code did not refer to ijtihād but used the more general term "principles" (*mabādiʾ*), an expression that is rarely used in the writings of the ʿulamāʾ. The High Court (Maḥkama ʿUlyā), which was established in 2000, defined a legal principle as,

---

32 Article 14 of the 1395/1975 Code of the Judiciary.

33 Article 8 Nr. 1 of the 1395/1975 Code of the Judiciary; The code is printed in al-Fawzān, *Al-Tanẓīm al-qaḍāʾī al-jadīd fī al-Mamlaka al-ʿArabiyya al-Saʿūdiyya* (Riyadh: Maktabat al-Qānūn al-Iqtiṣād, 1431/2010).

34 Article 89 of the 1395/1975 Code of the Judiciary.

35 Article 89 h) of the 1395/1975 Code of the Judiciary.

> The general procedural or substantive rule which the High Court has established, and which is observed in the handling of cases and the issuing of verdicts and decisions.[36]

The new code revised the old Article 14, extended it, and adapted it to the new terminology. It now states,

> If one of the High Court's chambers – in a case that it is reviewing – deviates from a legal principle [*mabdaʾ*] to which the chamber or another chamber at the same court has referred in an earlier case, or if one of the appeal court's chambers deviates from a principle, which was established by a chamber of the High Court, the issue is brought to the High Court's president, who refers it to the High Court's general assembly [al-Hayʾa al-ʿĀmma] to decide.[37]

At first sight, both the old and the new versions of Article 14 seem to install a system of legal precedent. However, despite the explicit regulations of Article 14, legal precedents are still not considered binding.[38] ʿAbd al-ʿAzīz al-Dughayther, a lawyer who regularly publishes on legal theory, wrote in a 2007 article in the Ministry of Justice's law journal that Saudi courts still followed Muḥammad bin Ibrāhīm's fatwas on this issue. Therefore, a decision could not be appealed on the grounds that it deviates from a legal precedent.[39] As we will see when we turn to case-law in Chapters 6 and 7, this is still true, as Saudi appeal courts rarely revoke judgements based explicitly on a legal precedent.

Ibn Khunayn argued that also the new regulation in Article 14 expresses the concept of the prevailing practice. For him, the High Court is the administrator of the prevailing practice. The court, Ibn Khunayn maintained, does not only decide the case, but its judgements summarize the practice of the lower courts and condense it into abstract principles. Through this process, the prevailing practice becomes formally binding for the judges, with the High Court becoming the administrator of the prevailing practice.[40]

---

36 Markaz al-Buḥūth, *Al-Mabādiʾ wa-l-qarārāt al-ṣādira min al-Hayʾa al-Qaḍāʾiyya al-ʿUlyā wa-l-Hayʾa al-Dāʾima wa-l-ʿĀmma bi-Majlis al-Qaḍāʾ al-ʿĀlā wa-l-Maḥkama al-ʿUlyā min ʿām 1391 ilā ʿām 1437* (Riyadh: Markaz al-Buḥūth, 1438/2017), 33 (Principle 1).

37 Article 14 of the 1428/2007 Code of the Judiciary.

38 Generally, Saudi scholars rarely refer to Article 14. ʿĀṣim al-Mutawwaʿ is a notable exception. He sees Article 14 as proof that the prevailing practice, in the way earlier scholars understood it, is recognized by the Code of the Judiciary. Al-Mutawwaʿ, *Al-ʿUdūl ʿalā al-qawl al-rājiḥ*, 421.

39 Al-Dughayther, "Ḥujjiyyat al-sawābiq al-qaḍāʾiyya," *Majallat al-ʿAdl* 34, 196.

40 Āl Khunayn, "Working Paper," 15.

2.3.3 The 2018 Publishing of the "Legal Principles"

In January 2018, the research unit at the Ministry of Justice published a compilation of 2,323 "legal principles and decisions" (*mabādiʾ wa-qarārāt*).[41] The unit extracted the grounds for the decisions from all judgements of the higher judicial institutions in the kingdom since the year 1971 and condensed them into principles, which mostly consist of only one short sentence. Arranged by numbers, the compilation of principles resembles a modern law code.

A few months before the principles were published, the minister of justice at the time, Walīd al-Samaʿānī, emphasized in a TV interview that the legal principles were not binding for the judges.[42] Manṣūr al-Ḥaydarī, who at the time was the head of the Ministry's research unit, held that at least the decisions of the High Court were binding, whereas other judgements would merely serve as guidance for the judges.[43] This is surprising since Article 14 of the Code of the Judiciary does not make such a distinction. In the introduction of the compilation, al-Ḥaydarī wrote that the principles could, in fact, be called the prevailing practice (*mā jarā ʿalayhi al-ʿamal*) in Saudi courts.[44]

2.4 *Legal Flexibility*

2.4.1 Exceptions from the Prevailing Practice in Premodern Jurisprudence

The ʿulamāʾ's respect for normative pluralism is also reflected in their understanding of the prevailing practice. If a judge concludes that the prevailing practice is not suitable for the case in question, he is allowed to exceptionally follow another opinion. This individual departure from the prevailing practice should not be confused with the institutionalized application of a minority opinion discussed earlier.

Since medieval times, the ʿulamāʾ have debated whether judges could be allowed to depart from the practice in exceptional cases. This debate occurred under the more general question of whether a scholar could depart from the preponderant opinion (*ʿudūl ʿalā al-qawl al-rājiḥ*), although some jurists explicitly distinguished between *iftāʾ* and *qaḍāʾ* in their discussion.[45] In the Saudi legal discourse, a clear distinction between iftāʾ and qaḍāʾ is often missing and ideas and concepts discussed under the question of iftāʾ are used in debates on the judiciary.

---

41 Markaz al-Buḥūth, *Al-Mabādiʾ wa-l-qarārāt al-ṣādira min al-Hayʾa al-Qaḍāʾiyya al-ʿUlyā wa-l-Hayʾa al-Dāʾima wa-l-ʿĀmma bi-Majlis al-Qaḍāʾ al-ʿĀlā wa-l-Maḥkama al-ʿUlyā min ʿām 1391 ilā ʿām 1437* (Riyadh: Markaz al-Buḥūth, 1438/2017).

42 The video was sent to me by the former judge and lawyer Salmān al-Muhaynī.

43 Interview with Manṣūr al-Ḥaydarī in the Ministry of Justice in Riyadh, 8 May 2018.

44 Markaz al-Buḥūth, *Al-Mabādiʾ wa-l-qarārāt*, 14.

45 See al-Mutawwaʿ, *Al-ʿUdūl ʿalā al-qawl al-rājiḥ*, 435.

Some scholars completely rejected the idea of a departure from the preponderant opinion, most prominently the Mālikīs al-Shāṭibī (d. 1388) and al-Māzirī (d. 1141). Others argued that not everyone had the right to deviate from the preponderant opinion. The Mālikī uṣūl al-fiqh scholar al-Shinqīṭī (d. 1817), for instance, maintained that only a layperson could deviate from the preponderant opinion when necessary, but not a mufti or a judge.[46] Al-Qarāfī (d. 1285), one of the great Mālikī scholars of Mamlūk Egypt, held that only a muqallid, and not a mujtahid, could deviate from the preponderant opinion. This, al-Qarāfī argued, provided the muqallid with more legal flexibility.[47]

The majority of scholars, however, allowed a judge or a mufti to depart from the preponderant opinion or practice when necessary.[48] The Shāfiʿī jurist al-Subkī (d. 1355), for example, stated,

> It is permissible that the mufti chooses a rejected opinion [*qawl marjūḥ*] when he seeks religious benefit [*maṣlaḥa dīniyya*].[49]

Ibn Taymiyya, too, argued in one of his fatwas as follows:

> To do something rejected [*marjūḥ*] can be preferable [*arjaḥ*] to achieve the preponderant benefit [*maṣlaḥa rājiḥa*]. Similarly, to depart from the preponderant [*rājiḥ*] [opinion] can sometimes be preferable for the preponderant benefit.[50]

However, the jurists firmly emphasized that judges should only depart from the preponderant opinion in exceptional cases. Ibn al-Qayyim even considered the unnecessary use of a marjūḥ opinion "a most grievous sin" (*akbar al-kabāʾir*).[51]

Saudi ʿulamāʾ agree with the majority of their predecessors. Muḥammad bin Ibrāhīm, for instance, referred to Ibn Taymiyya's fatwa and commented,

46 Al-Shinqīṭī, *Nashr al-bunūd ʿalā marāqī al-saʿūd* (UAE: Ṣundūq Iḥyāʾ al-Turāth al-Islāmī, n.d.), 2:276.

47 Al-Qarāfī, *Al-Iḥkām fī tamyīz al-fatāwā ʿan al-aḥkām* (Beirut: Dār al-Bashāʾir al-Islāmiyya, 1416/1995), 92. However, the majority of the jurists seem to hold that only a mujtahid and not a muqallid could deviate from the preponderance opinion.

48 See Āl Khunayn, *Tawṣīf al-aqḍiya*, 1:395–97.

49 The quote is printed in ibid., 401.

50 Ibn Taymiyya, *Majmūʿat al-fatāwā*, 34:198.

51 Ibn al-Qayyim, *Iʿlām al-muwaqqiʿīn*, 835.

> If there is a need, it is possible to use the marjūḥ opinion considering the benefit [*maṣlaḥa*]. Generally, this is not used in all cases, but necessity must be proportionally [*al-ḍarūra tuqaddar bi-qadarihā*[52]].[53]

2.4.2 The Possibility to Diverge from the Prevailing Practice in the Saudi Judiciary

Today, the idea of diverging from the prevailing practice is well established in the Saudi judiciary. For example, Ibn Khunayn wrote in his commentary on the procedural code,

> Exceptionally, it is allowed to turn to the non-mashhūr if the established requirements are met in this case and if the judge states the grounds.[54]

The departure from the prevailing practice is not just a theoretical possibility: in their decisions, judges occasionally follow other opinions when they find that the prevailing practice would lead to unjust results. However, the judges are required to do it consciously and transparently. Muḥammad bin Ibrāhīm demanded the judges explicitly substantiate their reasons for deviating from the prevailing practice.[55]

ʿĀṣim bin ʿAbd Allāh al-Mutawwaʿ, a former Saudi judge and the author of a book on the subject, claimed that the departure from the prevailing practice is most visible in the decisions of the kingdom's highest courts, which frequently follow other opinions.[56] Most of the published decisions in which the High Court departs from the prevailing practice deal with criminal law.[57] In 2000, the Higher Judicial Council even went so far as to establish the departure from the prevailing practice as a legal principle:

52 Muḥammad bin Ibrāhīm is referring to a well-known principle of Islamic jurisprudence (*qāʿida fiqhiyya*). For a comprehensive explanation of the principle, see Luqman Zakariyah, *Legal Maxims in Islamic Criminal Law: Theory and Applications* (Leiden: Brill, 2015), 151.

53 Al-Qāsim, *Fatāwā wa-rasāʾil*, 11:272.

54 ʿAbd Allāh bin Muḥammad Āl Khunayn, *Al-Kāshif fī sharḥ niẓām al-murāfaʿāt al-sharʿiyya al-saʿūdī* (Riyadh: Dār Ibn Farḥūn, 1433/2012), 1:15.

55 Al-Qāsim, *Fatāwā wa-rasāʾil*, 2:16.

56 Al-Mutawwaʿ, *Al-ʿUdūl ʿalā al-qawl al-rājiḥ*, 640.

57 These decisions of the High Court are listed in ibid., 149.

> If the Council decides on a legal issue that it has decided on before and [now] holds that the [former] opinion is not appropriate to apply in this [case], then it is not bound to follow the former [decision].[58]

However, the judges must remain within the discursive boundaries of Islamic jurisprudence and as the Higher Judicial Council emphasized, every departure from the prevailing practice must be based on the Islamic revelation.[59] Ibn Khunayn went one step further and even demanded that the marjūḥ opinion in the particular case should be more in line with the revelation than the prevailing opinion.[60] Hence, the chosen marjūḥ opinion has, in any case, to be acknowledged as a legitimate minority opinion in Islamic jurisprudence.[61]

Until now, we have seen how Saudi jurists developed a new understanding of the prevailing practice that differs from earlier conceptualizations. A similar development can be witnessed when we look at the jurists' views on appeal courts, which, besides the prevailing practice, are the most essential institution that establishes legal security in the kingdom.

3 The Extension of the Appeal Court System

3.1 *Judicial Review in Premodern Islamic Jurisprudence*

According to a well-known principle (*qāʿida*) of Islamic jurisprudence, an ijtihād cannot be abrogated by any later ijtihād (*al-ijtihād la yanquḍu bi-mithlihi*), whether by the same person or by another. This general principle has led some Western scholars of Islam to conclude that Islamic law prohibits judicial review.[62]

However, Islamic scholars also refer to accounts of the Prophet and ʿUmar bin al-Khaṭṭāb, which express a more liberal stance towards judicial review. In his famous letter to Abū Mūsā al-Ashʿarī, ʿUmar allowed judges to review their former decisions, because he held that reviewing a decision is better than insisting on the wrong opinion.[63] Moreover, the Prophet himself apparently revoked a judgement by ʿAlī bin Abī Ṭālib.[64]

58 Markaz al-Buḥūth, *Al-Mabādiʾ wa-l-qarārāt*, 486 (Principle 1923).
59 Ibid., 485 (Principle 1918).
60 Āl Khunayn, *Tawṣīf al-aqḍiya*, 1:403–4.
61 Al-Mutawwaʿ, *Al-ʿUdūl ʿalā al-qawl al-rājiḥ*, 144.
62 For an overview of the scholarship on judicial appeal in Islamic law, see Powers, "On Judicial Review," 316.
63 Ibn al-Qayyim, *Iʿlām al-muwaqqiʿīn*, 69–70.
64 Shaʿīshaʿ, *Al-Tanẓīm al-qaḍāʾī al-jadīd*, 430.

The ʿulamāʾ disagreed on whether and to what extent judicial review should be permitted in an Islamic legal system. The majority of ʿulamāʾ agreed that as long as the judge's ijtihād is valid, it cannot be touched. From their perspective, judicial review is only possible when the judge's ijtihād is invalid.[65] Yet, if the judge's legal reasoning does not contradict the Quran and the Sunna and respects the consensus of the jurists (*ijmāʿ*) on the issue in question, his ijtihād can only lose its validity when it was derived through an incorrect process.[66] This would be the case when, for example, the judge was unfit or made major procedural mistakes, like issuing a verdict although no lawsuit was filed.[67] On the other side, scholars from the today largely extinct Ẓāhirī school, and most importantly their founder Dāwūd al-Ẓāhirī (d. 909), argued that a judge's verdict can be overturned by another judge, whenever he thinks that the decision is incorrect.[68]

Again, the limitation of judicial review roots in the ʿulamāʾ's acceptance of normative pluralism. The jurists argued that since nobody except God knows the correct ruling, it is impossible for others to assess whether a decision is wrong as long as the correct procedure of ijtihād is followed. Hence, provided the judge operates inside the discursive structures of Islamic jurisprudence and follows due process, his decision has to be respected.

3.2 *Contemporary Saudi Views on Judicial Appeal*

Contemporary ʿulamāʾ still debate to what extent judicial review can be in accordance with Islamic law. Muḥammad al-Zuḥaylī, for instance, a Syrian jurist with close ties to Saudi Arabia, argued that Islamic law does not allow for second-instance courts. However, he only referred to appeal courts that deal with the facts of the case. Courts that review the mere application of the law, Muḥammad al-Zuḥaylī held, are in accordance with Islamic law, as they assist the ruler in supervising the judiciary.[69] Fādī Shaʿīshaʿ, an assistant professor at Qaṣīm University, maintained that appeal courts could be installed as long as they operate within the boundaries set by the ʿulamāʾ.[70]

The vast majority of Saudi jurists today consider judicial appeal a natural part of the Saudi legal system. Ibn Khunayn did not even see any difference

---

65 Some scholars even argued that judicial appeal is not allowed, even if the judge's mistake is apparent. See ibid., 432.

66 See Muḥammad bin Muṣṭafā al-Zuḥaylī, *Al-Qawāʿid al-fiqhiyya wa-taṭbiqātuhu fī al-madhāhib al-arbaʿa* (Damascus: Dār al-Fikr, 1427/2006), 394.

67 Shaʿīshaʿ, *Al-Tanẓīm al-qaḍāʾī al-jadīd*, 434.

68 Cited in ibid., 432.

69 Al-Zuḥaylī, *Al-Tanẓīm al-qaḍāʾī*, 99.

70 Shaʿīshaʿ, *Al-Tanẓīm al-qaḍāʾī al-jadīd*, 434–35.

between the conception of judicial appeal in premodern Islamic law and the appeal court structure in Saudi Arabia today.[71] When asked about the aforementioned principle that an ijtihād cannot be revoked by any later ijtihād, Ibn Khunayn acknowledged the limited ways to withdraw an ijtihād. However, at the same time, he explained that all other accounts in the tradition equally show that judicial appeal is possible.[72]

For other jurists, the principle of the ijtihād's firmness does not stay in the way of judicial appeal at all. Salmān al-Muhaynī, a former judge at the General Court in Riyadh, argued that the first instance judge's decision together with the decision of the appeal court form one single ijtihād. The principle of the limited revocation of ijtihād only applies after the appeal court has finalized its decision. Hence, the concept of judicial appeal in Islamic law, he claimed, resembles the concept of *res iudicata* in Western legal systems.[73]

The Council of Senior Scholars also considered appeal courts to be in line with Islamic legal doctrine. In their decision on the permissibility of codification, the Council's members even called for the establishment of more appeal courts. Appeal courts, the Council's members argued, could point the lower-ranking judges to the shortcomings of their judgements. Furthermore, more appeal courts would help to end discrepancies between the first instance judges' decisions.[74]

3.3 *The Development of Judicial Review in Saudi Arabia*

3.3.1 Judicial Review in the Early Twentieth Century

It was mainly the resistance of an older generation of Najdī scholars that long prevented Saudi Arabia from establishing an extensive appeal court system comparable to other countries in the region.[75] After recapturing the Ḥijāz, King ʿAbd al-ʿAzīz installed a supervising court (Maḥkamat al-Murāqaba al-Qaḍāʾiyya) in 1927, which had the power to overturn the general courts' judgements.[76] However, a judge could, at least in theory, defend his opinion if he provided textual evidence (*dalīl*) for his view.[77]

71 ʿAbd Allāh bin Muḥammad Āl Khunayn, *Al-Kāshif fī sharḥ niẓām al-murāfaʿāt al-sharʿiyya al-saʿūdī* (Riyadh: Dār Ibn Farḥūn, 1433/2012), 2:191.

72 Interview with Ibn Khunayn in his home in Riyadh, 24 April 2018.

73 Interview with Salmān al-Muhaynī in his law firm in Riyadh, 15 May 2018.

74 Al-Amāna al-ʿĀmma li-Hayʾat Kibār al-ʿUlamāʾ, *Abḥāth hayʾat kibār al-ʿulamāʾ*, 3:238.

75 For an overview of the Saudi judiciary at the beginning of the twentieth century see Steinberg, *Religion und Staat*, 343–95.

76 Āl Khunayn, *Al-Kāshif*, 2:192.

77 Saudi judges long refused to state the grounds for their verdicts. By 2019, the Ministry of Justice still urged judges to make their legal reasoning more transparent.

Whereas ʿulamāʾ in the Ḥijāz were familiar with appeal courts from Ottoman times, in central Arabia, and especially in the Najd, local scholars refused to implement the king's judicial reforms.[78] Since no appeal courts existed, the only way for the parties to appeal a judgement was to turn to the local governor, who, according to siyāsa sharʿiyya, supervised the judges and make them aware of potential flaws in their decisions.[79]

3.3.2 The Role of Muḥammad bin Ibrāhīm Āl al-Shaykh

At the same time, an alternative system of judicial review slowly developed. Informal ways of appeal were already known in medieval Islamic legal systems. David Powers, for example, showed how in the Marinid dynasty of medieval Northern Africa, the chief judge of the capital city reviewed judgements issued by local and provincial judges.[80]

Similarly, respected Najdī scholars long served as informal appeal courts, most importantly, Muḥammad bin Ibrāhīm Āl al-Shaykh. His student Muḥammad bin ʿAbd al-Raḥmān al-Qāsim wrote that Muḥammad bin Ibrāhīm "appealed judgements that needed reviewing and that he reviewed what was assigned to him by the rulers (*wulāt al-umūr*)".[81] In 1953, King Saʿūd nominated Muḥammad bin Ibrāhīm Grand Mufti of Saudi Arabia, thereby making him the primary authority for the judges in the Najd.[82] Two years later, he was appointed to supervise the courts in the central and eastern provinces of the kingdom as well,[83] whereas in the Ḥijāz and other areas in western Arabia, another member of the Āl al-Shaykh family, ʿAbd Allāh bin Ḥasan,[84] oversaw the courts.[85] When ʿAbd Allāh bin Ḥasan died in 1958, Muḥammad bin Ibrāhīm also became responsible for the courts in western Saudi Arabia.[86] Eventually, he was appointed "head of the judiciary" (*raʾīs al-qaḍāʾ*), an honorary title that is still used when Saudi jurists refer to him today.

---

78 ʿAbd al-Malik bin Aḥmad Āl al-Shaykh, *Taṭawwur idārat al-qaḍāʾ fī al-Mamlaka al-ʿArabiyya al-Saʿūdiyya* (Riyadh: N.p, 1431/2010), 54.

79 Ibid., 64. Based on the writings of Harry St. John Philby, Guido Steinberg argued that the review of court decisions was even the prime task of the local rulers at that time. Steinberg, *Religion und Staat*, 356.

80 Powers, "On Judicial Review."

81 Al-Qāsim, *Fatāwā wa-rasāʾil*, 1:19–20.

82 Āl al-Shaykh, *Taṭawwur idārat al-qaḍāʾ*, 66.

83 Al-Qāsim, *Fatāwā wa-rasāʾil*, 1:20.

84 For information on ʿAbd Allāh bin Ḥasan, see Commins, *Wahhabi Mission*, 93.

85 Āl al-Shaykh, *Taṭawwur idārat al-qaḍāʾ*, 66.

86 Al-Qāsim, *Fatāwā wa-rasāʾil*, 1:20.

Muḥammad bin Ibrāhīm's powers exceeded that of an appeal court today. In addition to supervizing the courts, he was, among other things, also responsible for the appointment of schoolteachers and imāms and controlled the Committee for the Promotion of Virtue (Hay'at al-Amr bi-l-Maʿrūf), a government institution that enforced the ʿulamā''s understanding of Islamic morality in the public sphere.[87]

Al-Qāsim's collection of Muḥammad bin Ibrāhīm's letters and fatwas allows insights into his work as an informal appeal court. Accordingly, Muḥammad bin Ibrāhīm was regularly contacted by judges, court presidents, high-ranking government officials, and even the Royal Court (Dīwān al-Malikī) to review court judgements or policy decisions on their accordance with Islamic law.[88] Most cases were sent to him by government officials like the mayor of Riyadh. Following the doctrine of siyāsa sharʿiyya, the officials considered themselves the guarantors of the judiciary.

Muḥammad bin Ibrāhīm not only reviewed court decisions but also advised the courts on general questions of Islamic jurisprudence. For example, in one case, the president of the court in Abhā asked Muḥammad bin Ibrāhīm to provide him with legal opinions (*kalām al-ʿulamā'*) on how to deal with the withdrawal of a confession of illicit sexual intercourse (*zinā*).[89] Furthermore, Muḥammad bin Ibrāhīm was also contacted by individual judges and asked about the correct ruling in their cases. One judge from Riyadh, for instance, asked him about the validity of a will (*waṣīya*) that benefited only his sons' male children but not his daughters' sons.[90]

The style of many of his letters resembled that of Saudi appeal court judgements today, since, like present-day Saudi appeal courts, Muḥammad bin Ibrāhīm was very careful with his recommendations and corrections.[91]

---

87 The Committee was commonly known as the Saudi "religious police." Āl al-Shaykh, *Taṭawwur idārat al-qaḍā'*, 67–68.

88 One letter, for example, is addressed to Crown Prince Fayṣal, who later became one of the most important kings in Saudi history. The crown prince had asked the shaykh whether it was allowed to execute a person accused of producing alcohol. See Al-Qāsim, *Fatāwā wa-rasā'il*, 12:69–70.

89 Ibid., 12:51.

90 Ibid., 9:228–29. In general, testators are expected to treat their children and grandchildren (*awlād*) equally. However, for Saudi jurists, this often does not include grandchildren from the daughter's side (*awlād al-banāt*).

91 In his published letters, I did not come across any evidence that Muḥammad bin Ibrāhīm annulled decisions by first instance courts.

3.3.3 The Formalization of Judicial Review

From the 1960s on, the Saudi government, step by step, formalised the appeal system. Muḥammad bin Ibrāhīm supported the king's judicial reforms. In a letter from 1958, he wrote that the planned reforms were not only in accordance with Islamic law but even required from an Islamic standpoint since they would protect the people's rights.[92]

Soon, committees of scholars were established in the Najd to oversee the courts; however, they were not competent to overturn judgements, but whenever the committee and the first instance judge disagreed, Muḥammad bin Ibrāhīm could review the case.[93] For instance, in 1963, Muḥammad bin Ibrāhīm decided on the punishment for two individuals accused of insulting each other, which was disputed between the supervizing committee and the first instance judge.[94]

In 1966, the first government guidelines were issued that regulated the ways court judgements could be revoked.[95] Subsequently, the Higher Judicial Council and the Ministry of Justice were established, and Muḥammad bin Ibrāhīm became their president.[96] In 1969, Muḥammad bin Ibrāhīm got sick, fell into a coma, and died after long suffering.[97] Until today, no subsequent Islamic jurist has reached a comparable level of influence in the Saudi judiciary.

3.3.4 The Development of the Appeal Court System

In the subsequent decades, the appeal court system was gradually extended. In 1975, the Code of the Judiciary (Niẓām al-Qaḍāʾ), which addressed the structure of the Saudi court system, installed an appeal court (at the time called Maḥkama Tamyīz) that had jurisdiction over the whole kingdom. There is no evidence that scholars from the Najd refused the new court's authority. One of the reasons for the jurists' support was certainly Muḥammad bin Ibrāhīm's efforts to legitimize judicial reforms among leading ʿulamāʾ.

The prime task of the appeal court was not to revoke judgements but to enter into a dialogue with the first-instance judges. The review was limited to questions of the application of the law; questions of fact were left to the first-instance judges. The appeal court should suggest a different view or, in

92 Al-Qāsim, Fatāwā wa-rasāʾil, 12:380. See also Āl al-Shaykh, *Taṭawwur idārat al-qaḍāʾ*, 96.
93 Al-Qāsim, Fatāwā wa-rasāʾil, 1:20.
94 Ibid., 12:60–61.
95 Āl Khunayn, *Al-Kāshif*, 2:192.
96 Āl al-Shaykh, *Taṭawwur idārat al-qaḍāʾ*, 68–70.
97 Al-Qāsim reports that his coma continued until 1978, but this is most likely due to a mix-up of dates. See Al-Qāsim, *Fatāwā wa-rasāʾil*, 1:23.

case of procedural errors, ask the first-instance judges to correct them. The parties themselves, however, did not come into direct contact with the appeal court judges.

In severe criminal cases, the parties could appeal a judgment on a question of fact.[98] This was limited to cases in which the first instance court decided to punish the defendant with death (*qatl*), cutting hands (*qaṭʿ al-yad*), or stoning (*rajm*). Saudi jurists emphasized that, due to the severe consequences for the defendant, not one judge alone could decide such cases, but a group of judges should give their opinion.

In 2000, a new Code of Civil Procedure (Niẓām al-Murāfaʿāt al-Sharʿiyya) was introduced. Although the code mostly dealt with procedural issues, it also stipulated that the appeal court could only revoke a judgement after having debated the issue with the first instance judge.[99] Article 187 of the 2000 Code of Civil Procedure specifies,

> If the appeal court has remarks regarding the decision, it has to work out a statement and send it to the [first instance] judge. If he disagrees with the appeal court's recommendations, he has to answer and state his view after he has noted this in the court records. If, however, he agrees with them, then he has to inform the parties, listen to their response, register this in the court records, and judge accordingly. This judgement can be appealed if it contains alterations to the previous judgement.

The 1975 Code of the Judiciary initially installed only one appeal court for the whole kingdom. In 2008, the appeal court system was substantially extended by a new Code of the Judiciary. Subsequently, appeal courts were installed in the kingdom's major cities.

---

98 Criminal judgements of the appeal courts could be revoked by the Higher Judicial Council. See ʿAlī bin Ramaḍān Barakāt, *Al-Wasīṭ fī sharḥ niẓām al-qaḍāʾ al-saʿūdī al-jadīd* (Riyadh: Maktabat al-Qānūn wa-l-Iqtiṣād, 1433/2012), 73.

99 Before the new Code of Civil Procedure was issued in 2000, court procedure was mainly regulated by the 1936 Procedural Code (Niẓām al-Murāfaʿāt), which was only amended once, in 1953, and therefore did not address the workings of the appeal court. See Āl Khunayn, *Al-Kāshif*, 1:5.

3.3.5 The Judicial Review of Facts

The 2008 code gave appeal courts the power to also address the facts of a case.[100] Today, the appeal courts have the competence to hear witness testimonies and consider new evidence. Article 17 of the 2008 Code of the Judiciary stipulates,

> The appeal courts review decisions of the first instance courts that are open to appeal. They decide after hearing the parties according to the Code of Civil Procedure and the Code of Criminal Procedure [Niẓām al-Ijrāʾāt al-Jizāʾiyya].

In severe criminal cases, a third level of judicial appeal was introduced. The High Court was now allowed to review de novo the appeal court's judgements that involved corporal punishments.[101]

In 2013, the appeal process for civil cases was again significantly changed by a new Code of Civil Procedure. Article 190 of the code specified that the right to appeal depends on the parties' presence at the court sessions.[102] However, according to the published court judgements and interviews with judges, the appeal process still takes place without direct contact with the parties. Upon appeal, the case is forwarded directly to the appeal court, where it is considered by a minimum of three judges. The judges write short comments, which are sent to the first instance judge as a hardcopy or electronically. In difficult cases, the appeal court judges discuss the case with each other.[103] Generally, the appeal court judges still only decide on questions of law, leaving out questions of fact. The new court structure, however, was implemented only gradually. In 2018, courtrooms for the trials were just about to be constructed.

---

100 According to Article 185/2 of the Code of Civil procedure, the Higher Judicial Council can decide that some legal questions are not open for appeal. However, I have not come across any such limitations.

101 Article 11 of the 1428/2007 Code of the Judiciary. In general, the role of the High Court is difficult to grasp. The 1428/2007 Code of the Judiciary extended its competences immensely. Now, at least in theory, all judgements that are potentially in conflict with Islamic law or the anẓima can be appealed a second time. Yet, I have never encountered published judgements in which the High Court was involved.

102 If, however, the appealing party failed to appear at court, a sixty-day period was granted in which the party could demand the resumption of the appellate procedure.

103 Judge al-Khuḍayrī and Judge Jār Allāh, both judges at the Riyadh Court of Appeal, showed me in detail how they work on files that they receive from the first instance courts.

Despite the extension of the appeal courts, judges still respect normative pluralism in their decision-making process and are very cautious about criticizing decisions of the first-instance courts, especially when it comes to questions of law. According to the published appeal court decisions, the judges never commented on questions of fact and hardly on questions of law. In none of the published cases that I have read did the appeal court render a new judgement. The appeal court judges only recommend that a different opinion should be followed. Technically, they can also refer the case back to another first-instance judge, which does not seem to happen regularly.

It remains to be seen whether the lenient attitude of the ʿulamāʾ, who largely support the current appeal system, will remain once the new court structure is implemented and appeal courts are allowed to review decisions de novo. One of the appeal court judges expressed his scepticism towards those changes. Although he held that judicial appeal was allowed in general, the judge was still unsure whether the introduction of an appeal court that dealt with questions of fact was in accordance with Islamic law.

4 Conclusion

The prevailing practice and the extension of the appeal courts both centralized control over the law. Although the individual judges retained their room for individual ijtihād in issues not covered by prevailing practice, their independence decreased. It was the judges at the higher courts who increasingly determined what opinion should be followed in many matters, a result of a long-standing process towards legal unification and centralization that began in the early twentieth century. Typically, literature on Islamic law associates standardization with the introduction of new forms of text, such as legal handbooks (*mukhtaṣar*) or codified law. However, the developments in Saudi Arabia highlight the crucial role that the organization of the judicial system plays in shaping Islamic legal doctrine.

The interplay between the jurists' reinterpretation of the prevalent practice and the expansion of the appellate court system fulfilled some of the functions of codification. It provided some form of legal stability while not requiring judges to adhere to a single school of Islamic jurisprudence or written code. In fact, the prevalent practice could be seen as a form of proto-codification.

The developments in Saudi Arabia also demonstrate the caution that must be exercized when drawing conclusions based solely on theoretical writings on ijtihād. While the ideal of Saudi jurists is unrestricted ijtihād, they recognize that a functional legal system requires at least a certain level of legal certainty.

CHAPTER 5

Ijtihād in Court

1 Introduction

When Saudi judges write and debate questions of Islamic jurisprudence, they almost never refer to case law. This makes it difficult to assess how the jurists' debates are reflected in their practice in court. For a long time, information on Saudi court practice was hard to obtain. However, with the release of thousands of court decisions beginning in the mid-2010s, Saudi court practice became more transparent. The published judgements include the transcript of the court hearings and thereby provide detailed information on the case and the judges' actions.

By taking child custody as a case study, one of the most contentious areas in the Saudi judiciary,[1] this chapter analyses in depth how Saudi judges undertook ijtihād in their daily work prior to the codification of Islamic family law. Based on the published court decisions, this chapter focuses, on the one hand, on the ways Saudi judges approached their cases and, on the other hand, how their decisions and arguments related to the four major schools of Islamic jurisprudence.[2]

Besides the topic in its substance, there are several other reasons why child custody lends itself very well for analysis: Firstly, we have seen in the analysis of the debate on codification that some Saudi scholars consider child custody one of the prime examples in which legal flexibility is necessary. Secondly, child custody is a field of law that is especially affected by changing technology

1 It is relatively easy to identify important questions in which the judges disagreed. In an article, Muḥammad al-Saʿīdī, the head of the Islamic Studies department at the Umm al-Qurā University in Mecca, listed the most prominent disagreements of Saudi judges. See Muḥammad bin Ibrāhīm al-Saʿīdī, "Ishkāliyat al-taqnīn wa-l-tadwīn," in *Al-Niẓām al-ʿadl fī al-Saʿūdiyya*, ed. Muḥammad bin Saʿūd al-Bashr and Manṣūr bin ʿAbd al-Raḥmān al-Ḥaydarī (Riyadh: Markaz al-Fikr al-ʿĀlamī, 1436/2010), 308. A similar article by Manṣūr bin Fāyiz al-Thubaytī, a judge at the court in Tabūk, in which he presented 150 legal questions on which Saudi judges disagree in their judgements, was made available to me by Manṣūr al-Ḥaydarī. Parts of the text are available online, see www.saaid.net/bahoth/200.htm [last access: 18 March 2023]. Moreover, experienced judges and scholars usually knew which questions were disputed among the judges in their field of interest and referred to them openly.

2 It is sometimes argued that Islamic family law differs fundamentally from other areas of the law in the way the law is applied. Yet, I have not found any evidence for such exceptionalism in my study of Saudi court judgements and in my meetings with Saudi judges.

and social norms. This has led to a growing interest in child custody among Western scholars of Islamic law.[3] Thirdly, child custody is one of the key areas in which women's rights and their role in society are negotiated.

The analysis of the judges' ijtihād in court is based primarily on published court judgments from the years 1434/2012–2013 and 1435/2013–2014 and thus reflects the situation prior to the codification. We will discuss the impact that codification had on custody law in Chapter 7.

2 Child Custody in Islamic Jurisprudence

2.1 *Traditional Understandings of Child Custody*

Islamic jurists understand child custody (*ḥaḍāna*[4]) as the fulfilment of the child's basic daily needs, including cooking for the child, providing it with a safe place to sleep, and dressing and washing it.[5] Especially in premodern legal discourse, ḥaḍāna is deeply associated with femininity, although also men can obtain custody for their children. Masculinity, on the other hand, is identified with guardianship (*wilāya*), which, most importantly, comprises the child's religious and worldly education, the administration of its assets, its legal representation, and in the case of girls, also the approval of the marriage. Custody has to be distinguished from visitation (*ziyāra*). If one parent is appointed as custodian, the non-custodial parent has the right to visit the child and regularly spend time with it. Classical fiqh books usually do not discuss visitation rights in detail but leave their determination to local custom.[6]

In general, Islamic jurists understand custody not as an obligation but as a right. Especially contemporary 'ulamā' consider it a joint right of the child and the custodian. According to their understanding, the child has a right to care but cannot demand a specific person as custodian. Thus, the jurists allow the mother to waive her right to custody only when someone else is capable

3 See, for instance, Ahmed Fekry Ibrahim, *Child Custody in Islamic Law: The Best Interests of the Child in Theory and Practice: Egypt 1517–2014* (Cambridge: Cambridge University Press, 2018); and Nadjma Yassari, Lena-Maria Möller, and Imen Gallala-Arndt, eds., *Parental Care and the Best Interests of the Child in Muslim Countries* (The Hague: T.M.C. Asser, 2017).

4 Some scholars only use the term *ḥaḍāna* for the care of children under seven, whereas the word *kafāla* is applied to the custody of older children. See, for example, Wajnāt bin 'Abd al-Raḥīm Maimanī, "Li-man al-ḥaḍāna?" *Majalla Jāmi'at 'Umm al-Qurā* 14, no. 27 (1424/2003): 371.

5 See, for instance, Al-Raṣā', *Sharḥ ḥudūd Ibn 'Arafa* (Beirut: Dār al-Gharab al-Islāmī, 1993): 324.

6 See, for example, Al-Bahūtī, *Kashshāf al-qinā' 'an matn al-iqnā'* (Beirut: 'Ālam al-Kutub, 1403/1983), 5:502.

and ready to take care of the child. The parents are free to agree on custody arrangements, which happened quite regularly throughout Islamic history.[7] However, the jurists usually prohibit trading custody rights in favour of other rights, like alimony or a khulʿ divorce.[8] Questions of child custody arise after divorce but also during the parents' marriage. Although the husband has the right to demand his wife's return to the matrimonial home at any time, women often live separated from their husbands for several months or even years after a dispute before they managed to get a divorce.

Generally, all schools of jurisprudence assign the custody of a child under seven years to its mother, provided that she is fit and capable. According to a famous narration, the Prophet told the mother of a small child: "You have the right [*aḥaqq*] [to custody] but do not marry."[9] In addition to the Prophet's decision, the jurists argue that no one can be as gentle and caring as the child's mother.[10] It is the mother's odour [*rīḥ*] and her kindness [*luṭf*], Caliph Abū Bakr said, according to a widely quoted account, which make her the better custodian.[11]

When the child has reached the age of seven, the schools disagree on who is the best custodian. The Ḥanafīs held that a boy should be given to his father once he is able to eat, drink, and dress himself, a period they generally associate with the boy turning seven.[12] A girl, on the other hand, should remain with her mother until her menstruation starts.[13] According to most Mālikī scholars, this ruling applies to boys, too, whereas girls should remain with their mothers until they are handed over to their future husbands.[14] Both Mālikīs and Ḥanafīs did not consider the opinion of the child when they allocate custody. A child, they argued, does not know what is best for it.

Ḥanbalīs and Shāfiʿīs, in contrast, allowed children to choose their custodian at least to some degree. Most jurists in the Shāfiʿī tradition held that a child over seven could, independent of its gender, decide who should be the

7 See Ahmed Fekry Ibrahim's chapter on private separation deeds. Ibrahim, *Child Custody*, 111–33.

8 See, for example, Ibn ʿĀbidīn, *Radd al-muḥtār*, 5:258. In Chapter 6, we will discuss khulʿ divorce in Saudi Arabia in detail.

9 Abū Dāwūd, *Sunan Abī Dāwūd*, 3:588 (Nr. 2276).

10 See, for instance, Ibn Qudāma, *Al-Mughnī*, 11:414.

11 Ibn Manṣūr, *Kitāb al-Sunan* (Mumbai: al-Dār al-Salafiyya, 1403/1982), 3:139 (Nr. 2272).

12 Ibn ʿĀbidīn, *Radd al-muḥtār*, 5:267.

13 Al-Qudūrī, *Mukhtaṣar al-Qudūrī fī fiqh al-ḥanafī* (Beirut: Dār al-Kutub al-ʿIlmiyya, 1418/1997), 174.

14 Muḥammad bin Bashīr al-Shaqafa, *Al-Fiqh al-mālikī fī thawbihi al-jadīd* (Damascus: Dār al-Qalam, 1432/2011), 4:594.

custodian.[15] The jurists based their reasoning on another ḥadīth. According to this narration, the Prophet told the child of divorced parents, "This is your mother, and this is your father. Take the hand of one of them as you like."[16] The majority of Ḥanbalī scholars only allowed boys to choose. Girls, on the other hand, had to remain with their fathers until their marriage.[17] The Ḥanbalī jurists gave two main reasons for this distinction: firstly, the father was more capable of protecting the girl, and secondly, it was the father who would marry the girl off to her future husband.[18]

While the child's well-being was of prime importance for the jurist, most schools of Islamic jurisprudence expressed their perception of the best interests of the child in categories along gender and age. Only the Shāfiʿī school gave older children of both genders the right to choose their custodian. None of the schools left much discretionary power to the judge to consider the child's best interests on an individual basis.

2.2 *The Best Interests Principle*

2.2.1 Islamic Custody Law in Arab Countries Today

The custody regimes of the first legislation on family law in the Arab legal systems were influenced by Ḥanafī rulings, a result of the Ottoman patronage of the school. Most laws stipulated strict age limits to determine the parents' custody rights. Beginning in the second half of the twentieth century, the inflexibility of these regimes led women's rights groups in several Middle Eastern countries and international organizations to lobby for reforms.[19]

Lawmakers reacted mainly by extending the mother's period of custody instead of rethinking custody rules more generally. In Syria, for example, the age limit for the mother's period of custody was raised in 2003 from nine to thirteen years for boys and from eleven to fifteen years for girls.[20] Similarly, in Egypt, the limit was raised to fifteen years for both genders in 2005.[21]

---

15 Al-Shirbīnī, *Mughnī al-muḥtāj ilā maʿrifat maʿānī alfāẓ al-minhāj* (Beirut: Dār al-Kutub al-ʿIlmiyya, 1421/2000), 5:198.

16 Muḥammad Nāṣir al-Dīn al-Albānī, *Ṣaḥīḥ Sunan al-Nasāʾī* (Maktabat al-Maʿārif li-l-Nashr wa-l-Tawzīʿ, 1419/1998), 2:502.

17 Ibn Qudāma, *Al-Mughnī*, 11:415–18.

18 Ibid., 11:418.

19 In Egypt, one of the laws that extended the custody of mothers was popularly known as "Jihan's law," referring to former president Sadat's wife, who was one of the most influential figures in the Egyptian feminist movement. See Jasmine Moussa, "Egypt," in Yassari, Möller, and Gallala-Arndt, *Parental Care*, 11.

20 Article 146 of the Syrian 1953 Law of Personal Status (Qānūn al-Aḥwāl al-Shakhṣiyya), amended by Law 18 of 2003.

21 Egyptian Law Nr. 4 of 2005 (Qānūn Raqm 4 li-Sanat 2005 bi-Shāʾn Sinn Ḥaḍānat al-Ṣaghīr).

Other countries introduced more flexibility. In Iraq, for instance, the child's father is generally awarded custody once the child reaches the age of ten, but the judge can prolong the custody of the mother when he considers this to be in the best interests of the child.[22] Some legislatures refer exceptionally to the child's best interests in order to expand the judges' discretionary powers and allow them to deviate from the law in exceptional cases.[23] However, in most countries of the region, the best interests of the child still do not serve as the paramount principle for the allocation of custody.

2.2.2 The Focus on the Child in Islamic and Contemporary Western Jurisprudence

In European and North American jurisprudence, the focus on the child and the consideration of its best interests are considered one of the most important achievements in family law in the last fifty years. For long periods in European legal history, the focus in child custody was on the parents. In Germany, for instance, the allocation of child custody was linked to the circumstances of the parents' divorce. In case one parent was believed to have caused the divorce, the child was given to the other parent.[24] Beginning in the 1950s and '60s, the focus of German law shifted. The individual interests of the child, including the relationship with its parents, were increasingly taken into consideration on a case-by-case basis.[25] In the US, a similar development could be witnessed. Until the 1960s, a mother could lose custody of her children if she was deemed to have caused the divorce.[26] Today, US law recognizes the best interests of the child as the universal standard for the allocation of child custody. In international law, the 1989 UN Convention on the Rights of the Child shifted the focus away from the child's mere protection to the consideration of its best interests.

However, the best interests standard remains ambiguous; it is, as one critic noted, a "vague platitude"[27] and not a legal or scientific standard. The absence of any objective criteria opens up a window for gender biases, speculations,

---

22 Article 57, paragraph 4 of the 1959 Iraqi Law of Personal Status (Qānūn al-Aḥwāl al-Shakhṣiyya).

23 Nadjma Yassari, Lena-Maria Möller, and Imen Gallala-Arndt, "Synopsis," in id., *Parental Care*, 330.

24 Wapler, Friedericke 2015. Kinderrechte und Kindeswohl. Tübingen: Mohr Siebeck, p. 38. However, some exceptions to the law already existed at the time that allowed the judges to consider the child's best interests, see Schwoerer, Julius 1953, Die Rechtsprechung des BGH zu § 74 EheG. JuristenZeitung 8 (1/2), pp. 15–19, 16.

25 Friedericke Wapler, *Kinderrechte und Kindeswohl* (Tübingen: Mohr Siebeck, 2015), 253.

26 Linda Elrod, and Milfred Dale, "Paradigm Shifts and Pendulum Swings in Child Custody: The Interests of Children in the Balance," *Family Law Quarterly* 42, no. 3 (2008): 391.

27 Andrea Charlow, "Awarding Custody: The Best Interests of the Child and Other Fictions," *Yale Law & Policy Review* 5 (1986): 290.

and subjective value judgements.[28] As another author highlighted, the best interests standard can, among other things, disadvantage people with disabilities in custody disputes since they are often categorically considered unsuitable for childcare.[29]

In contrast to Europe and the US, the focus of Islamic jurists was always on the child and not on the parents. The Ḥanbalī jurist Ibn Qudāma, for example, wrote that the primary goal of child custody was the realization of the child's well-being.[30] Instead of granting the judge the power to determine what is best for each child individually, the jurists developed the general custody regime discussed earlier. In most jurisprudential writings, the judges are not called to depart from established rulings if these conflict with the child's best interests.

Some twentieth-century Saudi scholars also first looked at the established rulings before turning to the individual child. For instance, in a fatwa on the custody of two older girls, Muḥammad bin Ibrāhīm (d. 1969) referred to the classic Ḥanbalī opinion without further debate and granted the father custody. Like in all of his other published letters and fatwas on child custody, he did not inquire about the children in question. However, he put his ruling under the condition that no harm is inflicted upon them by the father or his living circumstances.[31]

2.2.3 The Saudi Approach to the Best Interests of the Child

The vast majority of contemporary Saudi ʿulamāʾ have become sceptical of the major schools' rigid custody rules and used the writings of Ibn Taymiyya and his student Ibn al-Qayyim to develop a focus on the child's best interests on an individual basis. On the question as to whether a seven-year-old boy should be allowed to choose his custodian, Ibn Taymiyya replied,

> No general judgement can be made about a father or a mother. It cannot be said that every father is better for the boy. And not every mother is better for him than the father, some fathers are better, and some mothers are better. In one situation, the father might be better, and in [another] situation, the mother might be better. None of them can be determined.[32]

---

28 Richard Warshak, "Parenting by the Clock: The Best-Interest-of-the-Child Standard, Judicial Discretion, and the American Law Institute's 'Approximation Rule,'" *University of Baltimore Law Review* 41, no. 1 (2011): 105.

29 Michael Lanci, "The Child's Best Interests? Rethinking Consideration of Physical Disability in Child Custody Disputes," *Columbia Law Review* 118, no. 3 (2018): 914.

30 Ibn Qudāma, *Al-Mughnī*, 11:418.

31 Al-Qāsim, *Fatāwā wa-rasāʾil*, 11:219.

32 Ibn Taymiyya, *Majmūʿat al-fatāwā*, 34:121–22.

Ibn Taymiyya argued that the reason why custody rules should be understood flexibly lies in the Islamic revelation:

> It must be noted that God does not provide a general provision [*naṣṣ ʿāmm*] that categorically favors one parent. And the scholars agree that none of them can categorically be assigned [custody].[33]

Later, Ibn al-Qayyim elevated the best interests of the child as one of the guiding principles in his reasoning on child custody. When asserting the effects of one parent's change of domicile, he wrote,

> As you can see, there is no textual evidence [*dalīl*] for these views that can be relied on. The proper way is to look and pay attention to the child and consider what is best for it and suits it regarding a change of domicile. What is better and safer for the child prevails. This applies as long as the leaving parent does not intend to hurt the other by taking the child away.[34]

ʿAbd al-Raḥmān bin Nāṣir al-Saʿdī (d. 1957) was especially known among his contemporaries for his excellent knowledge of Ibn Taymiyya and Ibn al-Qayyim, whose books are said to have been the most consulted ones in his library.[35] Thus, it is little surprising that their influence can be seen in Ibn Saʿdī's reasoning on child custody. One of his fatwas illustrates his focus on the best interests of the child:

> Q 5: Who has custody of a girl when she is over seven?
> A: The predominant [*mashhūr*] [opinion] in the school [is]: it is her father. And the second account [in the school is]: it is her mother, provided both [parents] fulfil the required [conditions]. If one of them lacks the requirements for custody of the child or does not fulfil the child's best interests [*yaṣlaḥuhu*], custody is taken away and is given to the other [parent]. What is considered when given preponderance [*tarjīḥ*] over [one of the] two opinions: it is looked at the best interests [*maṣlaḥa*]

---

33 Ibid., 34:132.

34 Ibn al-Qayyim, *Zād al-maʿād fī hadī khayr al-ʿibād* (Cairo: Dār al-Āfāq al-ʿArabiyya, 1428/2007), 4:1433.

35 Abdul Hakim al-Matroudi, *The Ḥanbalī School of Law and Ibn Taymiyyah* (London: Routledge, 2006), 164.

> [of the child]. The child stays with whom its best interests are [fulfilled], because, in this matter, it is [only] looked at the best interests of the child [*maṣlaḥat al-maḥḍūn*].[36]

Ibn Saʿdī gained significant influence in Saudi Arabia, most notably through his pupils, who later occupied key positions in the religious establishment. When Ibn Bāz was asked about the custody of a five-year-old girl, his teacher's influence can be noticed. Ibn Bāz refrained from giving an abstract answer, even though all four schools agreed that the mother has custody of a girl under seven years. Instead, he replied,

> This is a matter of disagreement between the scholars. It depends on the spouses' disagreement. Perhaps this [one] is qualified, and this [one] is not. In any case, the court will look [into this matter].[37]

Prior to codification, Saudi judges explicitly stated in their verdicts that the best interests of the child were the guiding principle for their decisions.[38] A judge in Hāʾil, for instance, referred to Ibn Taymiyya's argument that no general statements about mothers or fathers could be made.[39] Other judges quote Ibn al-Qayyim in order to legitimize their use of the best interests standard. For some judges, the best interests standard seemed so well established that they refer to it without further explanation. A judge in Qilwa, for example, wrote in his verdict,

> Custody is for the protection of the child and the realization of what is in its best interests. The best interests of the child have to be respected, and these differ with the different situations and people.[40]

36 ʿAbd al-Raḥmān bin Nāṣir al-Saʿdī, *Al-Fatāwā al-saʿdiyya* (Riyadh: Maktabat al-Maʿārif, 1402/1982), 553–54.

37 Recording of Ibn Bāz. Available on www.binbaz.org.sa/noor/3016 [last access: 23 February 2023].

38 Appeal court judge Ḥamd al-Khuḍayrī, however, argued that the judges generally "follow the views of the school [*ʿamal bi-l-madhhab*]." If a judge concludes that another legal opinion realizes the child's best interests, al-Khuḍayrī wrote in a 2010 article on judicial procedure in family matters, he could depart from the established teachings. See Ḥamd bin ʿAbd al-ʿAzīz al-Khuḍayrī, "Al-Ijrāʾāt al-qaḍāʾiyya fī l-mushkilāt al-zawjiyya," *Majallat al-ʿAdl* 45 (1431/2010): 137.

39 Jeddah General Court, decision Nr. 34253916 (27.6.1434/08.5.2013).

40 Qilwa General Court, decision Nr. 3475176 (8.4.1434/19.2.2013).

In 2012, the Saudi High Court issued a decision according to which "the assignment of custody follows the best interests of the child."[41] One year later, the Higher Judicial Council directed a statement to the judges highlighting the importance of the child's best interests in custody matters:

> The honourable judges in the courts have to consider the situation of the child and its best interests when giving custody to one of the parents. They have to verify and take seriously what one parent accuses the other of concerning his or her suitability for custody. This aspect has to be given preference, concern, and attention when dealing with cases like that.[42]

Like in Western jurisdictions, the way the best interests of the child are understood largely depended on the judges' assessment of the situation.

3 Ijtihād in Practice

3.1 *Individual Ijtihād within and outside School Boundaries*

3.1.1 The Scope for Individual Ijtihād in Custody Cases

In their reasoning, Saudi judges referred to the best interests standard on two levels: Firstly, in some legal questions, it opened up a space for individual ijtihād that allowed the judges to choose between different views freely. Secondly, in other questions, it allowed the judges to legitimize a prevailing practice that deviated from established teachings or even challenged a widely recognized premodern consensus (*ijmāʿ*).

Let us first look at how references to the best interests of the child allowed for individual ijtihād. Child custody was one of the areas of the law without a comprehensive prevailing practice. Nevertheless, even if the judges were not bound to a particular school or prevailing practice, there were clear boundaries that limited their ijtihād. In the last chapter, we saw that an ijtihād is only valid when it does not contradict the jurists' consensus. However, it is important to keep in mind that the consensus itself is sometimes disputed among

41 Decision of the High Court, Nr. 33/3/3 (1.5.1433/24.3.2012), printed in Markaz al-Buḥūth, *Al-Mabādiʾ wa al-qarārāt*, 197.

42 Decision of the Higher Judicial Council Nr. 279/2/34 (5.6.1434/16.4.2013), printed in the circular letter to the courts by the minister of justice Nr. 376/T (15.7.1434/25.5.2013); A copy of the circular letter is in possession of the author. A Judge in Jeddah also quoted the Council's decision, see Jeddah General Court, decision Nr. 34383118 (confirmed by the Mecca Court of Appeal on 7.7.1435/7.5.2014).

premodern ʿulamāʾ and regularly challenged by contemporary Saudi jurists: "There is not ijmāʿ about ijmāʿ,"[43] as Benjamin Jokisch put it.

In custody cases, the scope for individual ijtihād largely depended on the child's age. Regarding children under the age of seven, premodern ʿulamāʾ agreed that the mother should be their custodian, provided she fulfils the necessary requirements. In these cases, Saudi judges held that the mother's custody is in the best interests of the child und usually referred directly to the consensus in Islamic jurisprudence on this question. A typical reference was made to Ibn Qudāma, who wrote that he did not know of any disagreement.[44] Other judges quoted the Prophetic account according to which a mother gets custody as long as she does not marry without referring to any fiqh books.

3.1.2 Free Ijtihād in Custody Cases Involving Children over Seven

There was generally more room for individual ijtihād when children reached the age of seven. The judges rather deliberately chose a solution among the different existing opinions. Although all schools have developed a predominant (*mashhūr*) opinion, there is still a significant plurality of opinions even inside every school. This heterogeneity allowed Saudi judges to follow their personal understanding within or beyond the rulings of any given school.

Interestingly, the Ḥanbalī scholars are particularly divided on the issue of custody for older children. Ibn al-Qayyim stated that besides the mainstream opinion that a boy over seven could choose his custodian, two other opinions (*riwāyāt*) exist: the first opinion grants custody to the father; the second to the mother.[45] Moreover, disagreement exists also on the question of the custody of a girl over seven. In addition to the mainstream opinion, according to which a girl over seven is given to her father, Ḥanbalī jurists also argued that a girl could stay with her mother until puberty or could choose her custodian.[46] Thus, the Ḥanbalī school alone offers the judges a broad range of options. Considering that the other schools of law present a similar multitude of options, a judge has almost unlimited possibilities to allocate custody while staying within the discursive boundaries of the Islamic legal tradition.

---

43 Benjamin Jokisch, "Ijtihād in Ibn Taymiyya's Fatāwā," in Robert Gleave, Eugenia Kermeli, eds., *Islamic Law: Theory and Practice* (London: I.B. Tauris, 1997), 126.

44 See, for example, the decision of an unknown court in ʿAṣīr Province, decision Nr. 34258488 (3.7.1434/13.5.2013); Ibn Qudāma, *Al-Mughnī*, 11:413.

45 Ibn al-Qayyim, *Zād al-maʿād*, 4:1436.

46 Ibid.

However, the plurality of Islamic jurisprudence was not reflected in the Saudi judges' decisions on the custody of boys over seven. In such cases, the judges simply applied the mainstream Ḥanbalī opinion. Provided that both parents are equally suitable for custody, they let boys choose their custodian, assuming that a boy over seven would know which parent is best for him.

The judges considered this an expression of the best interests standard. Typically, they made no further references to fiqh books but briefly mentioned the Prophetic account. For instance, a judge from Riyadh wrote,

> Given what has been presented as claim and response, the boy's choice to stay with his father and the ḥadīth of Abū Hurayra, according to which a woman came to the Prophet and … the Prophet said, (This is your father, and this is your mother. Take the hand of one of them as you like. He took his mother's hand, and she left with him), narrated by Abū Dāwūd and al-Nasāʾī, I dismissed the plaintiff's claim.[47]

When it comes to the custody of girls over seven, the judges exercized their freedom of ijtihād more extensively. In none of the available court decisions did the judge simply follow the Ḥanbalī mainstream opinion. Some judges even openly dismissed the Ḥanbalī school.

In other cases, the deviation from the Ḥanbalī school's mainstream opinion was more subtle. For instance, a judge in Medina referred to a lesser-known account of Aḥmad bin Ḥanbal, according to which a girl should stay with her mother until she marries.[48] In his verdict, the judge wrote,

> [Regarding] a girl over seven, Imām Abū Ḥanīfa and Mālik, and Aḥmad [bin Ḥanbal] according to an account, stated that the mother gets custody until [the girl] marries or her menstruation starts because she cannot choose, and she cannot be separated [from her mother]. The mother gets custody in the same way as [if the girl were] under seven.[49]

Another judge in Medina explicitly deviated from the majority view in the Ḥanbalī school. In his verdict on the custody of a ten-year-old girl, he argued,

---

47 Riyadh General Court, decision Nr. 34209331 (8.5.1434/20.3.2013).

48 In Chapter 2, we saw that Aḥmad bin Ḥanbal often presented several opinions on an issue without stating his personal preference.

49 Medina General Court, decision Nr. 34205797 (5.5.1434/17.3.2013).

> According to the [Ḥanbalī] school, a girl is with her father when she is over seven. It seems to me that there is no specific provision like this for a girl. [An older girl] is not excluded from the general account of the Prophet (You have the right to custody but do not marry). A girl at this age needs her mother more than ever before.[50]

Other judges elaborated more extensively on the different opinions in Islamic jurisprudence and mixed them with their personal views on femininity and motherhood. For instance, a judge in al-Aḥsāʾ carefully listed the mainstream opinions of the four schools before deciding that the Mālikī opinion was preferable in the given case. In the verdict, it says,

> The two girls are over seven years old. The scholars are in disagreement about which parent gets custody of a girl that age. The Ḥanafīs and the Mālikīs hold the opinion that the mother gets custody of a girl over seven. However, they disagree on the time: according to the Ḥanafīs, until her puberty, according to the Mālikīs, until she is given to her husband. This view preponderates [*yatarajjaḥu*] in my opinion because the mother is closer to her [daughter] than her father. The mother is the one who teaches her useful female matters [*umūr al-nisāʾ*]. She is the one who is with her until her puberty and teaches her the rules and manners that are connected to that, provided that the mother does not marry, because of the account of the Prophet (You have the right to custody but do not marry). This generally [applies] to boys and girls. In contrary, the Shāfiʿī school allows [the girl] to choose like the boy, and the Ḥanbalīs [give] custody to the father at the mentioned age. Based on all that has been presented, I decided to give the custody of the mentioned two girls to her mother until they marry.[51]

Notions of femininity and motherhood were frequently used to justify that a girl should stay with her mother. Women were thereby granted more rights than in premodern Ḥanbalī law. The reason for this is the Saudi jurists' understanding of puberty. For Saudi judges, puberty necessarily demands knowledge of a new set of rules and social codes. The judges held that it was the mother who could best understand the transformation of a girl's body. Whereas premodern Ḥanbalī scholars worried more about the girl's physical safety and

50 Medina General Court, decision Nr. 34249215 (24.6.1434/5.5.2013).

51 Al-Aḥsāʾ General Court, decision Nr. 34339018 (confirmed by the Court of Appeal of the Eastern Region on 7.6.1435/8.4.2014).

thus gave custody to the father in order to protect the child from possible physical dangers, Saudi judges were more concerned with the child's psychological well-being.

The notion of the nuclear family increasingly played a role in the judges' reasoning. Some judges considered the relationship between the child and its siblings in their decision making, an aspect that is largely absent in premodern fiqh literature. A judge in Medina, for instance, argued that it would be best for the girl to stay with her older siblings, who lived with their mother. In order to stay within the boundaries of the Ḥanbalī school, he quoted a commentary on al-Bahūtī's (d. 1641) *Al-Rawḍ al-murbiʿ* by the Najdī scholar ʿAbd al-Raḥmān bin Qāsim (d. 1972). In his verdict, the judge wrote,

> It is best for the girl to stay with her sister [name] and her brother [name], and it says in [Ibn Qāsim's] *Ḥāshiyyat al-rawḍ al-murbiʿ* (7/162): The majority of scholars give preference to the mother [in case of an older girl], and this is the school of Abū Ḥanīfa, and what Mālik says. Ibn al-Qayyim states: This is the most popular opinion of Aḥmad [bin Ḥanbal] and the right [opinion], considering the textual evidence. Because of this, I decided: Firstly, to dismiss the [father's] claim for custody of [name of the older sibling] and [name of the older sibling] because they are grown up. Secondly, I decided to grant the mother custody of [name of the girl].[52]

The disagreement among Ḥanbalī scholars thus allowed the judges to refer to the siblings' relationship without explicitly declaring it a criterion for the allocation of custody.

3.1.3 The Suitability of the Potential Custodian

The judges only undertook individual ijtihād if they considered both parents equally suitable for custody. Even if a child was allowed to choose its custodian, it could not select a parent that was not considered suitable. Only then, the judges regarded the child's choice to be in its best interests. In an important decision, the High Court stated, "The minor (*al-qāṣir*) cannot choose the hand of the one who does not protect and suit him."[53]

---

52 Medina General Court, decision Nr. 34193383 (21.4.1434/4.3.2013). Interestingly, earlier in his commentary, Ibn Qāsim wrote that Ibn al-Qayyim's view was not the authoritative Ḥanbalī opinion. See ʿAbd al-Raḥmān bin Muḥammad al-Qāsim, *Ḥāshiyat al-rawḍ al-murbiʿ sharḥ zād al-mustaqniʿ* (N.p, 1397/1977): 7:162.

53 Decision of the High Court Nr. 6.3.2 (28.2.1432/3.2.2011), printed in Markaz al-Buḥūth, *Al-Mabādiʾ wa al-qarārāt*, 197.

Over the centuries, the ʿulamāʾ established several requirements (*shurūṭ*) for custodians, some of which are disputed between the schools. While some of the requirements should ensure the child's physical safety, others are an expression of the jurists' understanding of a proper Islamic upbringing. The Saudi judges' approach to these requirements reflected their broad understanding of the best interests of the child. Whereas most fiqh books carefully distinguish between the different requirements, the judges simply spoke of the custodian's suitability (*ṣalāḥiyya*).

A potential custodian's suitability only became relevant when the other party questioned it. According to the published decisions, the parties' allegations were manifold and included physical violence, bad treatment, or neglect of the children. In case there was doubt about the suitability of a custodian, the judges inquired whether the living circumstances were generally suitable for children. If the judge was not satisfied with the answer, he could order the court administration to visit the home of a potential custodian.[54] For the judges, a good living environment was not only determined by the available space but, in the case of girls, also by the availability of a *maḥram*[55] to ensure the girl's freedom to move. As the judges expect girls to only leave the house in the company of a maḥram, they believe living in an all-female household may be disadvantageous for them.

Other allegations regarded the children's moral well-being. For example, in one court case from Riyadh, a father complained that the mother of his three children had installed satellite TV and thereby made "immoral" programs, including songs and movies, accessible to them. Furthermore, he invoked her immoral lifestyle, accusing her of going out late at night and sleeping throughout the day. As a result, the mother would disregard her religious duties, not pray, and thus could not supervise the children's religious duties.[56]

The judges also considered behavior that was technically legal in Saudi Arabia but generally disapproved by Islamic jurists. For example, some judges considered smoking, although allowed by Saudi law, a reason why a person should not be granted custody. Even if it could not be proven that the parent

54 For example, this happened in a case in Jeddah, see Jeddah General Court, decision Nr. 34253916 (27.6.1434/8.5.2013).

55 A *maḥram* is every male person with whom the girl is not legally allowed to conclude a marriage, most importantly, the male members of the nuclear family. Many Saudi families still require women to be accompanied by a maḥram whenever they leave the house.

56 The father, however, could not prove his allegations. Since it is not obligatory to do the prayers in a mosque, it was very difficult for the judge to assess whether the mother neglected praying when she was at home. Riyadh General Court, decision Nr. 34172423 (25.3.1434/6.2.2013).

smoked in front of the children, smoking nevertheless was seen as a health risk for children.[57] Likewise, a judge from Yanbuʿ regarded a father's opposition to vaccination as a reason to withhold custody. The father admitted in court that he had not vaccinated the children because he believed that it would harm them.[58]

The published court judgments show that the judges mostly respected female employment. Working mothers, however, pose a challenge to the judges' child-centered approach. Even though the judges held that female employment generally did not violate the child's best interests, they feared that a working mother had no time to care for the child appropriately. During the trial, the judges usually inquired about the parent's exact working hours. The mother's employment was less problematic when the parents cooperated to ensure the child's care. For example, according to a published case from Jeddah, the mother drove her two boys to school in the morning before she went to work. Her ex-husband later picked them up, and the boys usually spent the afternoon with their father. On her way back home from work, the mother stopped by her ex-husband's house and took the boys back to her home. The arrangement was accepted as suitable by the court.[59]

In other cases, the children stayed with their grandparents during their mother's working hours. Women often moved back to their parents when they divorced, since living alone as a woman is uncommon. This made it easier for women to work, since the child could stay at home with its grandparents.

The judges' acceptance of female employment might also have been influenced by the government's efforts to include more women in the workforce. "Vision 2030" ranks women's contribution to the labor market as one of the most important steps towards a non-oil-dependent economy. By 2030, 30% percent of the labor force was supposed to be female. However, in 2015, only 20.2% of working-age women participated in the labor force, compared to 77.8% of all men.[60]

---

57 Nāyif bin Aḥmad al-Ḥamd, "Working paper for the conference 'Intiqāl Ḥaqq al-Ḥaḍāna fī Ḍaw' Mutaghayyirāt al-ʿAṣr' [Transferring the Right to Custody in the Light of the Changes of the Century] at the Imām Muḥammad bin Saʿūd Islamic University in Riyadh on the 23.10.1433/10.9.2012," (1433/2012), 15.

58 Yanbuʿ General Court, decision Nr. 33656540 (confirmed by the Medina Court of Appeal on 26.4.1435/27.2.2014).

59 See Jeddah General Court, decision Nr. 34272410 (confirmed by the Mecca Court of Appeal on 28.1.1435/2.12.2013).

60 See Sana Naseem, and Kamini Dhruva, "Issues and Challenges of Saudi Female Labor Force and the Role of Vision 2030: A Working Paper," *International Journal of Economics and Financial Issues* 7, no. 4 (2017).

3.1.4 Restrictions by the Rules of Evidence

The judges' interference in the parents' personal life was limited by the strict rules of evidence in Islamic jurisprudence. In many cases, the judges were not allowed to consider the parents' lifestyle in their legal reasoning because the raised allegations could not be proven.

According to Islamic jurisprudence, the burden of proof lies on the plaintiff. If the plaintiff cannot provide evidence for the wrongdoing, the judge is generally not allowed to consider the allegations. Because the majority of allegations in custody cases refer to actions that took place inside the private sphere, they are especially difficult to prove. Moreover, close relatives and spouses are believed to potentially follow their personal interest (*tahmiyya*) in their testimony and are considered less credible. For instance, the testimony of one of the parties' father is usually not accepted as evidence.[61]

Even if witnesses are admitted, the judge could demand that their integrity (*ʿadāla*) be verified.[62] The plaintiff then has to call two more witnesses, who testify on the integrity of the primary witnesses. This process is known as *tazkiyya*.[63] For instance, in one case from Hāʾil, a mother demanded custody of her six-month-old daughter, who stayed with the child's father. The judge asked the mother to provide proof for her suitability. She presented two witnesses that testified; however, the judge demanded that the witnesses be checked for their credibility. Subsequently, the mother named two more witnesses that testified on the credibility of the primary witnesses. Likewise, during a court trial in Ṭāʾif, a father questioned the integrity of two witnesses who had testified in favor of the mother. The mother then presented another two witnesses to confirm the integrity of the primary witnesses.[64]

61 Wahba al-Zuḥaylī, *Al-Fiqh al-islāmī wa-adillatuhu* (Damascus: Dār al-Fikr, 1418/1997), 8:6041. Ibn al-Qayyim, however, challenged this view and accepted the testimony of the father in favor of his son.

62 Decision of the Higher Judicial council Nr. 102/3 (7.2.1425/29.3.2004), printed in Markaz al-Buḥūth, *Al-Mabādiʾ wa al-qarārāt*, 549.

63 Agrama described *tazkiyya* as "one of many well-developed techniques of moral inquiry and criticism that were characteristic of the Shariʿa and that were meant to secure and maintain various virtues found in multiple aspects of life, and that were, in fact, central to the Shariʿa's very foundation." He argued that the disappearance of such techniques of moral inquiry was one of the key developments in Egyptian legal history during the twentieth century. See Hussein Ali Agrama, *Questioning Secularism* (Chicago: University of Chicago Press, 2012), 54–59. One lawyer told me that the witnesses' moral integrity and the oral testimony still play a crucial role his practice at Saudi courts.

64 Ṭāʾif General Court, decision Nr. 3560949 (confirmed by the Mecca Court of Appeal on 7.6.1435/8.4.2014).

The judges seemed less concerned with the custodian's integrity than with the integrity of the presented witnesses, provided there was no immediate harm to the child. In their judgements, the judges refrained from explicitly discussing the custodian's moral and religious integrity. For the majority of ʿulamāʾ, integrity is one of the essential requirements for custody. However, Ibn al-Qayyim argued that the custodian's bad integrity could not lead to a loss of custody, as this would reduce the number of possible custodians and put hardship on the Islamic community as a whole. Moreover, he referred to the Prophet and his companions, who apparently did not withdraw custody because of the custodian's immoral behaviour.[65]

Due to the absence of published case law, the situation is even less clear when it comes to the custodian's religious affiliation. Non-Muslims are generally not considered moral (*ʿādil*) in premodern Islamic jurisprudence.[66] The ʿulamāʾ agreed that a non-Muslim mother could not have custody of her Muslim children once they become conscious (*ʿaqala*) of their religion. Some Ḥanbalī scholars went even one step further and did not grant custody to non-Muslim mothers at all.[67]

3.2 *The Institutionalized Use of Minority Opinions*

3.2.1 The Mother's Remarriage

In their decisions, the judges not only departed from the majority opinion in the Ḥanbalī school in their individual ijtihād but often also established a prevailing practice that deviated from the consensus between all four schools. One example of this is the question of the mother's remarriage during her period of custody.

According to the mainstream opinion in all four major schools, a divorced mother forfeits custody of her children if she marries again. Already in the tenth century, the Shāfiʿī jurist Ibn al-Mundhir (d. 930) wrote that the ʿulamāʾ had agreed on this position.[68] The jurists' agreement is not surprising, given that a prophetic ḥadīth explicitly excluded married mothers from custody. In addition to the Prophet's decision, the ʿulamāʾ also referred to the mother's marital obligations towards her new husband. The jurists understood marriage as a synallagmatic contract: in return for alimony, the wife has to devote her full attention to the husband. If the mother remarried, the scholars argued, she would lack the time to properly care for her children due to her obligations

65 Ibn al-Qayyim, *Zād al-maʿād*, 4:1432.

66 Ibid.

67 Al-Bahūtī, *Kashshāf al-qināʿ*, 5:498.

68 Ibn al-Mundhir, *Al-Ijmāʿ* (Ajmān: Maktabat al-Furqān, 1420/1999), 112.

towards her new husband. The Ḥanbalī jurist Ibn Qudāma even compared the remarried mother to a slave.[69]

Moreover, the scholars feared that the stepfather could potentially harm the children. Many ʿulamāʾ thus differentiated whether the mother marries a maḥram of the child or a "stranger" (*ajnabī*).[70] A relative is per se considered gentle and caring to the child and is thus not seen as a danger to it. Until today, most family laws in Arab countries follow the Islamic jurists' consensus. Hence, a mother usually loses custody of her children when she marries a man who is not a close relative of the child.[71]

However, the consensus among early Islamic scholars was not as clear-cut as Ibn al-Mundhir described it. According to Ibn Qudāma, Aḥmad bin Ḥanbal made a significant exception to the general rule: he held that a girl could remain with her mother until she turns seven, regardless of the mother's marital status.[72] However, Aḥmad bin Ḥanbal's opinion was not accepted by subsequent scholars in his tradition. The Ḥanbalī jurist al-Mardāwī (d. 1480) stated in his influential *Al-Inṣāf*, which lists the different opinions in the Ḥanbalī school, that the school's jurists almost unanimously refused custody to a remarried mother.[73]

Ibn al-Qayyim disagreed with the mainstream opinion in his school. Whereas his teacher Ibn Taymiyya followed the classic Ḥanbalī opinion and maintained that a remarried mother would lose custody of her children,[74] Ibn al-Qayyim referred to the children's best interests. He cited an account according to which the Prophet granted a woman custody of her nephew even though she was married to a non-relative of the child. Ibn al-Qayyim came to the conclusion that the new husband would have the right to choose whether his wife could keep custody of her children from her previous marriage. He wrote,

> If the [new] husband wants [his wife to have] custody [of her children] and wants the child to stay with him in his household, [she does] not lose custody. This is the correct [opinion], and it is based on legal theory

---

69 Ibn Qudāma, *Al-Mughnī*, 11:421.

70 See, among many others, the great Ḥanafī scholar al-Nasafī. Al-Nasafī, *Kanz al-daqāʾiq* (Beirut: Dār al-Bashāʾir, 1432/2011): 311.

71 Yassari, Möller, and Gallala-Arndt, "Synopsis," 340. There are, however, exceptions. The Iraqi legislator, for example, allowed judges to assign custody to the remarried mother if they are convinced that this was in the best interests of the child. See Aḥmad al-Kubaysī, *Al-Wajīz fī sharḥ qānūn al-aḥwāl al-shakhṣiyya wa-taʿdīlātuhu* (Baghdad: Maktabat al-Sanhūrī, 2015), 315–16.

72 Ibn Qudāma, *Al-Mughnī*, 11:421.

73 Al-Mardāwī, *Al-Inṣāf fī maʿrifat al-rājiḥ fī al-khilāf* (N.p., 1375/1956), 9:424.

74 Ibn Taymiyya, *Majmūʿat al-fatāwā*, 34:107.

> [*al-aṣl*]. The loss of custody because of remarriage is a consideration of the husband's right since the woman's care of someone else's child spoils his enjoyment of her and makes life with the woman harder for him. It could lead to conflicts of affection and compassion between them. Because of that, it is the husband's right to forbid her to [do] that and concentrate on his rights. Thereby, the child's best interests are neglected. If, [however], the husband persists [that the child stays with him] and demands this and takes care of it, then the cause [*mafsada*] that led to the loss of custody is eliminated. This is legal and has effects. It shows that the loss of custody because of remarriage is not God's right [*ḥaqq Allāh*] but the right of the husband, the child, and its relatives. If the owner of the right agrees, it is permissible.[75]

However, Ibn al-Qayyim's argumentation also did not resonate among subsequent Ḥanbalī scholars. The late medieval jurist al-Bahūtī (d. 1641), for instance, emphasized that there could be "no custody for a [woman] who married a stranger [*ajnabī*] because of the Prophetic hadith, even if the [new] husband agrees."[76]

3.2.2 The Saudi Jurists' Approach to Remarriage

In twentieth-century Saudi Arabia, Ibn al-Qayyim's view became popular. Again, it was Ibn Saʿdī who promoted the departure from mainstream Islamic jurisprudence. Although Ibn Saʿdī acknowledged that the wife could be "occupied" with her new husband and referred to the notion of the "bad stepfather," he eventually left the decision in the hands of the new husband. In one of his fatwas, Ibn Saʿdī stated,

> Q 4: If she marries someone who is not related to the child [*ajnabī*], does she get custody?
> A: [According to] the school: No. Correct is that, when the [new husband] agrees, it remains her right because she loses her [custody] rights in order to fulfil his [marital] rights. If he wants her [custody] rights to remain, they remain. This is the analogy [*qiyās*] of the school regarding all rights.[77]

75 Ibn al-Qayyim, *Zād al-maʿād*, 4:1446–47.
76 Al-Bahūtī, *Al-Rawḍ al-murbiʿ*, 391.
77 Al-Saʿdī, *Al-Fatāwā al-saʿdiyya*, 553.

Prior to the codification, the prevailing practice in Saudi courts followed Ibn al-Qayyim and Ibn Saʿdī. The judges typically granted remarried mothers custody of their children provided that the new husband agreed.

In their decisions, most judges explicitly referred to Ibn al-Qayyim, and sometimes also to Ibn Saʿdī. In addition, the judges regularly pointed to the best interests of the child. For instance, a judge from Jeddah wrote in his verdict,

> In custody disputes, one has to look only at the best interests of the child, and the best interests of the children are [realized] when they stay together with their mother, who protects and looks after them. The [new] husband appeared [before the court] and agreed that the children could remain in his wife's custody in his house. The claimant, the children's grandmother, is old and cannot look after them. Ibn al-Qayyim wrote after he mentions some rulings that are derived from the narration of al-Barāʾ bin ʿAzib about the story of Ḥamza's daughters: Thirdly: "If the [new] husband wants [his wife to have] custody [of her children] and wants the child to stay with him in his household, [she does] not lose custody. This is the right [opinion]." Therefore, I dismissed the case.[78]

Ibn al-Qayyim's focus on the husband's rights allowed women to stipulate their husband's approval in their marriage contract and remarry without risking the immediate loss of custody of their children. According to Islamic jurisprudence, the spouses can grant each other additional rights in the marriage contract and thereby adapt their marriage to their personal needs and wishes.[79] The judges generally accepted a stipulation in the marriage contract as proof of the husband's approval, even if the husband later changes his mind.

However, the consent of the husband was not always sufficient. Despite the judges' open attitude towards the remarriage of the mother, the fear that the stepfather might constitute a danger to the child remained. For instance, in a case from Medina, the plaintiff, the girl's aunt, feared that the mother's new husband would spend time alone with the girl, which would put her in danger.

78 Jeddah General Court, decision Nr. 3441277 (18.7.1434/28.5.2013).

79 For example, Saudi women regularly stipulate in their marriage contracts that their husbands have to provide them with a separate apartment instead of accommodating them with or near the husband's parents. Husbands, on the other hand, occasionally stipulate that their wife stay with their families for some time after marriage. See for example Aḥsāʾ General Court, case Nr. 34282474 (confirmed by the Court of Appeal of the Eastern Region on 1.7.1435/1.5.2014).

The judge shared the aunt's concern, even though the aunt's accusation could not be proven in that specific case.[80]

From the judges' perspective, the new husband and the child should ideally meet only occasionally. In a case from Ṭā'if, for instance, the mother had married a man from al-Kharj, a city almost 1,000 kilometers away. The child's parents had agreed that the new husband would only visit the mother during the holidays when the four-year-old daughter stayed with her father. Whereas in other Arab jurisdictions, a woman would, in this case, lose custody of the child, the judge in Ṭā'if decided that the mother's remarriage would not affect the child at all. In his verdict, he wrote,

> Custody is, in any case, the right of the child. To stay with her mother is the best [for the child] at this age. This form of marriage does not affect the purpose [*maqṣūd*] of the mother's custody. The loss of custody because of the mother's remarriage is not the marriage as such, but it is because the husband lives with his wife and the mother is not there for her children. This is not the case here.[81]

The protocols of the court hearings show that the potential custodian's marital status nevertheless played an important role in court. Typically, the judges asked the parties whether they are married or not. Mothers often emphasized in their complaints that they were married and thus had enough time to take care of the child.

Interestingly, the parties often assumed that a remarried mother would, in any case, lose custody. For example, in one case from Mecca, the maternal grandmother argued that she had the right to custody because the mother had remarried.[82] At the court in Riyadh, even a Saudi lawyer assumed the mother had lost custody rights because of her remarriage.[83]

Although the prevailing practice to grant remarried mothers custody of their children was well established, not all first instance judges seemed to support it. A judge at the court in ʿUnayza, a traditionally conservative city in the Najd, granted the father custody of his daughter on the grounds that the mother had remarried. When the mother took the case to the regional appeal

80 Medina General Court, decision Nr. 34205797 (5.5.1434/17.3.2013).

81 Ṭā'if General Court, case Nr. 3560949 (confirmed by the Mecca Court of Appeal on 7.6.1435/8.4.2014).

82 Medina General Court, decision Nr. 3554245 (confirmed by the Medina Court of Appeal on 11.5.1435/13.3.2014).

83 Riyadh General Court, decision Nr. 33430026 (17.10.1433/4.9.2012).

court, the appeal court judges asked their colleague in ʿUnayza to inquire whether the mother's new husband had agreed that the daughter stayed with his wife. Furthermore, the appeal court judges demanded that the first instance judge investigated whether it would be in the child's best interests to remain with her mother, especially since the girl was less than two years old. In their letter to the first instance judge, they pointed to Ibn al-Qayyim's legal reasoning and stressed that Ibn Saʿdī also shared this view. Although the appeal court judges did not explicitly request that the judge in ʿUnayza followed their opinion, the first instance judge nevertheless changed his judgement and granted the remarried mother custody.[84]

3.2.3 The Father's Remarriage

The judges were not only concerned with the mother's remarriage but were also sceptical of the father's new wife.

Premodern ʿulamāʾ did not fear the stepmother to the same extent as the stepfather. On the contrary, some jurists, especially from the Mālikī tradition, allowed the stepmother to take care of the child. For instance, the Mālikī jurist al-Dardīr (d. 1787) wrote,

> Moreover, regarding male custodians, like the father or others: there has to be a woman with him that takes care of the child, like the [grand]mother or the [father's new] wife, or the aunt.[85]

Ibn Taymiyya, however, considered the stepmother almost as threatening to the well-being of the child as the stepfather. In one of his fatwas, he argued,

> If it is assumed that the father has married a second wife [*ḍarra*] and [the girl] is left with the second wife, [this] is not in her best interests but harms or limits her well-being. [Staying with] her mother is in her best interests and does not harm her. Therefore, her mother is given custody in this [case].[86]

Ibn Taymiyya's legal reasoning once again influenced Saudi court practice. For example, at the court in Qilwa, a father claimed custody of his eight-year-old

---

84 ʿUnayza General Court, decision Nr. 3523017 (confirmed by the Qasīm Court of Appeal on 27.7.1435/27.5.2014).

85 Al-Dardīr, *Al-Sharḥ al-ṣaghīr ʿalā aqrab al-masālik ilā madhhab al-Imām Mālik* (Cairo: Dār al-Maʿārif, 1392/1972), 2:759.

86 Ibn Taymiyya, *Majmūʿat al-fatāwā*, 34:133.

daughter. The mother's lawyer argued that giving the girl to her father would not be in her best interest, since he was married to four wives.[87] In his verdict, the judge quoted Ibn Taymiyya's reasoning on the stepmother and granted the mother custody.[88] Whereas Ibn Taymiyya was afraid that in the context of a polygynous marriage, the competition of the mother with a second wife could harm the child, the judge in Qilwa understood the argument more broadly. For him, the father's polygynous marriage as such threatened the child's best interests.

Other judges did not further explain the stepmother's negative impact on the child. Without referring to scholarly authorities, a judge from ʿUnayza, for instance, listed the father's remarriage as one of the reasons why he did not grant him custody.[89] In Qaṭīf, a judge simply wrote that the mother would better guard the child's best interests because she would be more compassionate than the father's wife.[90] Again, the judges pointed to the supposedly affective relationship between girls and their mothers. In another case from Qilwa, the father worked as a border guard and was often away for half the month. During this time, the girl stayed with his new wife and sometimes with the paternal grandmother. The judge decided,

> [T]here is no doubt that the mother is gentler and sincerer with her daughter than the father's [new] wife. It is in the daughter's best interests to stay with her mother, especially since the mother is a teacher.[91]

Women, on the other hand, could stipulate that their new husbands do not bring children from their first marriage into the new home without their approval.[92] Saudi judges, as we will see now, also referred to the best interests principle when they assessed the influence of new technologies on child custody. Again, this led them away from established teachings in Islamic jurisprudence.

---

87 Another interesting aspect of the case is that the father proposed reconciliation during the trial. The mother should waive her right to alimony in return for the custody of the daughter. Apparently displeased with the father's proposal, the judge noted in the court records that the father's true wish was to avoid alimony payments.

88 Qilwa General Court, decision Nr. 3427056 (confirmed by the Mecca Court of Appeal on 2.11.1434/7.9.2013).

89 ʿUnayza General Court, decision Nr. 32379563 (23.9.1433/11.8.2012).

90 Qaṭīf General Court, decision Nr. 34307034 (confirmed by the Court of Appeal of the Eastern Region on 18.8.1435/17.6.2014).

91 Qilwa General Court, decision Nr. 3475176 (8.4.1434/19.2.2013).

92 See Ṭāʾif General Court, case Nr. 34299245 (confirmed by the Mecca Court of Appeal on 8.7.1435/8.5.2014).

3.3 *The Adaptation of the Law to Modern Life*

3.3.1 Mobility

Mobility is one of the areas of human life which have been fundamentally changed by modern technology. This is especially true for Saudi Arabia. For centuries, moving between the different cities of the Najd was not only dangerous, because of political instability, but also physically challenging. Today, big highways connect the major cities, and good roads between smaller cities have been built.

Premodern Islamic jurists were very familiar with the dangers and hardships of travelling at their time, as many moved between the intellectual centers. This is reflected in their reasoning on child custody. Generally, the ʿulamāʾ wanted to avoid any harm to the child due to travelling or one of the parent's relocation. Since the primary sources remained completely silent on the issue, they based their reasoning on general considerations of safety.

While the jurists agreed that the custodian was not allowed to move to a dangerous place, their views differed if an area was generally considered safe.[93] Most Ḥanbalī, Mālikī, and Shāfiʿī jurists held that the father would get custody if he resided in a town far away from the child, no matter whether he was the one who had moved away or not. In medieval times, comprehensive birth registers did not exist. Hence, in cases where the mother moved to a new town, the child's legitimate descent (*nasab*) could be questioned. If, on the other hand, the child stayed with the father, the medieval Shāfiʿī al-Nawawī (d. 1277) argued, its nasab would be protected and its alimony (*nafaqa*) and education secured.[94]

The jurists made an exception when the parents lived reasonably close to each other. The Mālikīs allowed the mother to move six *burad*[95] (approximately 140 km) away from the child's guardian (*walī*).[96] According to the Ḥanafīs, the mother could move to her hometown, irrespective of the distance, provided the father had married her there. In this case, the Ḥanafīs argued, the child's legitimate descent would be protected since the mother's marriage with the child's father would be known in the local community.[97]

---

93 See, for example, Ibn Qudāma, *Al-Mughnī*, 11:419.

94 Al-Nawawī, *Rawḍat al-ṭālibīn*, 9:106; see also Al-Shirbīnī, *Mughnī al-muḥtāj*, 5:201.

95 *Burad* is the plural form of *barīd*, which is a historical Arabic unit of length. In his *Al-Sharḥ al-kabīr*, the Mālikī jurist al-Dardīr (d. 1786) explained that one barīd equals four *farāsikh* (sing. *farsikh*) and one farsikh equals three Arabic miles. See al-Dusūqī, *Ḥāshiyyat al-Dusūqī ʿalā al-sharḥ al-kabīr* (Beirut: Dār al-Fikr, 1437/2016), 1:561.

96 Al-Dardīr, *Al-Sharḥ al-ṣaghīr*, 2:762.

97 Ibn ʿĀbidīn, *Radd al-muḥtār*, 5:273; see also al-Nasafī, *Kanz al-daqāʾiq*, 312.

Ibn al-Qayyim again challenged the mainstream view in Islamic jurisprudence. He argued that since no clear textual evidence in the revelation (*dalīl*) supports the jurists' reasoning, no general rule could be formulated. Instead, the child's best interests should be considered on a case-to-case basis.[98]

Prior to the codification, Saudi judges generally followed Ibn al-Qayyim's approach in order to adapt their ijtihād to mobility in the twenty-first century. For example, a judge in Khāmīs Mushayṭ wrote in his verdict,

> The correct opinion is that a change of domicile does not affect [custody]. There is no textual evidence [*dalīl*] for the opinion that changing domicile between long distances should affect custody, as Ibn al-Qayyim writes in [his book] *Zād al-maʿād*, especially considering the safety of the country and the streets today, thank God.[99]

Ibn al-Qayyim's critique that there was no basis in the revelation for a generalized ruling opened up a way for Saudi judges to question whether the premises (*taʿlīlāt*) on which premodern jurists based their positions still apply. Without feeling bound by the revelation, the judges freely dismissed their predecessors' opinions as outdated and not suitable in the context of the modern nation-state. In 2012, Nāyif bin Aḥmad al-Ḥamd, at the time president of the General Court in Riyadh, argued,

> There is no doubt that [one must] point to the importance of working with the justifications [*taʿlīlāt*] [that are used] by the jurists. … The justification for the father's custody is that this protects the legitimate descent [*nasab*] of the child. In our times, legitimate descent is protected by official papers, and there are birth registers. And there is the justification that the father teaches the son craftsmanship. Today, teaching takes place in schools, and so on.[100]

In one particularly interesting case, the child's parents had lived together in Riyadh. After the divorce, the mother took the two children with her to Jeddah, where she had lived before. In the court hearing, the father's lawyer argued

98 Ibn al-Qayyim's argumentation is translated above. Ibn al-Qayyim, *Zād al-maʿād*, 4:1433.

99 Khāmīs Mushayṭ General Court, decision Nr. 34205683 (confirmed by the ʿAṣīr Court of Appeal on 22.1.1435/26.11.2013).

100 Nāyif bin Aḥmad al-Ḥamd, "Working Paper for the Conference 'Intiqāl Ḥaqq al-Ḥaḍāna fī Ḍaw' Mutaghayyirāt al-ʿAṣr (Transferring the Right to Custody in the Light of the Changes of the Century)' at the Imām Muḥammad bin Saʿūd Islamic University in Riyadh on the 23.10.1433/10.9.2012" (1433/2012), 14.

that the large distance of more than 1,000 kilometers would make it hard for the father to oversee his children's upbringing. He quoted al-Bahūtī's *Kashshāf al-qināʿ* and Ibn ʿUthaymīn's *Sharḥ al-mumtiʿ* and also referred to Ibn Taymiyya, all of which granted the father custody if the parents' place of residence differed. The judge dismissed the lawyers' argumentation in a remarkable way:

> The agreement of the jurists that the father gets custody if one parent moves away more than the minimum distance for shortening and/or combining prayer (*masāfa qaṣr*) is based on their times, in which there was no public transport and no modern communication available.[101]

Whereas premodern jurists focused on the physical dangers of travelling, Saudi jurists are more concerned about the child's moral well-being and education, especially if one or both parents move to Europe or the US. In the last decades, the Saudi government has set up generous scholarship programs to enable Saudi students to study abroad, most notably in Europe and the US. The judges worried whether the child could receive an Islamic upbringing abroad.

For instance, judge al-Ḥamd referred to a report by the Saudi newspaper Al-Waṭan, according to which five percent of the children of exchange students are put into Christian kindergartens. He demanded that children should be put into Muslim kindergartens or stay with a Muslim nanny, even if Christian kindergartens are cheaper or even free. Otherwise, the parents could lose custody of their child.[102]

3.3.2 Modern Tourism

Another issue in which changing notions of mobility affected the judges' reasoning is modern tourism. Premodern jurists were unaware of the concept of tourism and therefore did not discuss its implications for child custody.

Some premodern ʿulamāʾ, however, debated whether "necessary travel" (*safr al-ḥāja*), for example, in order to visit relatives or to undertake business, could affect child custody. Generally, the jurists expected the custodian to stay near the other parent.[103] The Ḥanbalī jurists argued that if the mother or another female custodian travels even for a short distance, she loses custody.[104] Until

101 It is especially surprising that the judge explicitly rejected the opinion of some of the most respected jurists in Saudi Arabia without referring to the Quran and the Sunna. Riyadh General Court, decision Nr. 33453402 (3.11.1433/19.9.2012), 257.

102 Al-Ḥamd, "Working Paper," 16.

103 Wahba al-Zuḥaylī, *Al-Fiqh al-islāmī wa-adillatuhu* (Damascus: Dār al-Fikr, 1418/1997), 10:7317.

104 Al-Mardāwī, *Al-Inṣāf*, 428.

she returns from her travels, the jurists asserted that the child has to stay with its father. Likewise, the Shāfiʿīs pointed to the dangers of traveling for the child.[105] Only the Mālikī jurists argued that short travels should not affect custody at all.[106] The Ḥanafī position remains unclear since the authoritative works do not discuss the question.[107]

In the twenty-first century, tourism is flourishing in Saudi Arabia. Like many other Saudis, judges spend their summer holidays in Europe, the US, or neighbouring countries.[108] Moreover, increasingly good roads have made travelling inside the kingdom relatively safe and popular. In their reasoning on tourism, the judges again referred to the child's best interests. In 2012, for example, a mother in Mecca sued her ex-husband, who had refused to hand over the passport of their one-and-a-half-year-old girl. The father argued that he did not want the child to accompany her mother on the summer vacations with her family to the Emirates. In his verdict, the judge listed the different opinions and concluded,

> It seems to me that – and God knows it better – what the Ḥanafīs and especially the Mālikīs hold [is preferable]. A normal holiday trip that is not very long does not affect today, in these times, the child's best interests.[109]

If one of the parents is not a Saudi citizen, the judges are much stricter on traveling with the child, albeit for other reasons than the premodern ʿulamāʾ.[110] Since the classic corpus of Islamic jurisprudence predates the modern nation-state, premodern scholars did not discuss how they affect child custody. Saudi judges, however, decided that a parent's foreign citizenship can affect the other parent's custody and visitation rights. In order to prevent a

---

105 Al-Mawārdī, *Al-Hāwī al-kabīr fī fiqh madhhab al-Imām al-Shāfiʿī* (Beirut: Dār al-Kutub al-ʿIlmiyya, 1414/1994), 11:504.

106 Al-Dardīr, *Al-Sharḥ al-ṣaghīr*, 2:762.

107 Ibn ʿĀbidīn, for example, wrote that the mother should not be at all allowed to leave the father's place of residence, except to go to her hometown, provided the child's father had married her there. However, Ibn ʿĀbidīn did not discuss traveling specifically. Ibn ʿĀbidīn, *Radd al-muḥtār*, 5:273.

108 Most judges and scholars I spoke to had visited Europe with their families.

109 Mecca General Court, decision Nr. 33480028 (27.12.1433/12.11.2012).

110 Marriages between non-Saudis and Saudis are still rare. In the hijrī year 1436 (2014/2015), only 4.2 percent of all marriages were concluded between a Saudi and a foreigner. See the Annual Statistic Report of the Ministry of Justice for the year 1436. Available online on the Ministry's website, portaleservices.moj.gov.sa/law/Downloades/Annual_Report_1436_Marriage_Divorce.pdf [last access: 30 March 2018].

non-Saudi father from returning to his home country with the children, the Saudi government instructed the courts to ask for the Saudi mother's permission whenever the foreign father wants to leave the country with the children. Judge al-Ḥamd argued that the Saudi king had to interfere in this case through siyāsa sharʿiyya in order to protect the Saudi mothers' rights. The government feared, he explained, that foreign fathers might file for child custody in their home country, which due to lengthy court procedures and other restrictions, would make it difficult for Saudi mothers to get their children back. Al-Ḥamd emphasized that some Ḥanafī scholars apparently developed a ruling similar to that of the government and that Aḥmad bin Ḥanbal also shared this opinion.[111]

4 Conclusion

As envisioned by leading Salafi scholars, the four major schools lost much of their authority in the judges' reasoning on child custody. Even though Ḥanbalī opinions still played a key role, the schools mostly served as a way to structure legal arguments. However, ijtihād, in its ideal form as an individual journey to discover the correct ruling, was limited to a few legal questions. In most issues, the judges followed a prevailing practice that used opinions from all schools of law and sometimes even completely deviated from established school teachings.

In practice, unrestricted ijtihād in the Saudi judiciary largely remained a myth, despite its prominent place in debates on the Saudi judiciary. The individual judges were left with little discretionary power, whereas influential ʿulamāʾ decided which opinions the judges in the first instance courts had to follow. Hence, Saudi Arabia de facto already had binding – yet very intransparent – custody laws prior to codification, laws which had little in common with mainstream Ḥanbalī teachings.

111 Al-Ḥamd, "Working Paper," 15.

CHAPTER 6

Legal Reform beyond the State

1 Introduction

When we think of legal reform, we usually associate it with the state. However, in Saudi Arabia, the doctrine of siyāsa sharʿiyya puts the interpretation of Islamic law in the hands of the ʿulamāʾ; the king is left with limited influence on the law.

Saudi jurists admit that most rulings in Islamic jurisprudence are tied to human actions. Since traditions and social norms are ever-changing, rulings have to be adjusted accordingly.[1] Only the very basics of Islam and Islamic law, like the distinction between men and women in law or the ban on usury and fraud, are considered unchangeable.[2] Changes in uncodified law are much more difficult to identify than state-led reforms in codified law, as the ʿulamāʾ usually do not mention if a ruling has changed or is currently changing.

By using two case studies, this chapter analyses how legal reform takes place in Saudi Arabia without state interference. It explores the genealogy of new rulings and shows how the ʿulamāʾ's discourse is translated into court practice. The first case study examines how the Quranic punishment of ḥirāba, usually associated with brigandage, was expanded and now also includes drug smuggling. This, as we will see, is the result of the jurists' understanding of drug smuggling as a form of "spreading corruption on earth," an expression that is also used in the Quran.

The second case study deals with the reform of khulʿ divorce.[3] It illustrates how Saudi ʿulamāʾ have reinterpreted Islamic divorce law in order to give

---

1 For instance, to illustrate that rulings were already adjusted in early Islam, Ibn ʿUthaymīn gave the following example in one of his fatwas: "Likewise, this happened with the penalty for drinking wine (*khamr*). The penalty at the time of the Prophet and Abū Bakr did not exceed forty lashes. Then the number of people that drank wine increased, ʿUmar reported this to the companions (*ṣaḥāba*), and they advised that the penalty should be eighty lashes." The fatwā is printed in Khālid bin ʿAbd al-Raḥmān al-Jarīsī, *Al-Fatāwā al-sharʿiyya fī al-masāʾil al-ʿaṣriyya min fatāwā ʿulamāʾ al-balad al-ḥarām* (Riyadh: Muʾassasat al-Jarīsī, 1420/1999), 789.

2 See, for instance, ʿAbd Allāh bin Muḥammad Āl Khunayn, "Ḥaqīqat taghayyur al-fatwā wa-asbābuhu," *Majallat al-Buḥūth al-Islāmiyya* 117 (1440/2019): 31.

3 The second case study is based on an article that was published in German in the journal *Die Welt des Islams*. See Dominik Krell, "Die Reform der Loskaufscheidung (*ḫulʿ*): Lehren aus Saudi-Arabien," *Die Welt des Islams* 60, no. 4 (2020).

 | DOI:10.1163/9789004726314_008

women the possibility to end their marriage against the will of their husbands. While this departure from mainstream Islamic jurisprudence remained almost unnoticed outside the Saudi legal discourse, a similar reform by the Egyptian government stirred great controversy both in the Arab world and in Western scholarship.

Each case study begins with the respective ruling in premodern Islamic jurisprudence and then chronologically traces the development in Saudi Arabia and ends with an analysis of contemporary Saudi court practice.

2 The First Example: the Reinterpretation of Ḥirāba

2.1 *Islamic Jurists on Psychoactive Drugs*

2.1.1 The Rulings on Cannabis and Other Organic Drugs

In 2018, 184 people were executed in Saudi Arabia, which puts the kingdom at number three on the list of countries with the highest number of executions. The majority of them, eighty-four people in total, had been convicted of drug-related offences.[4] Only half (fifty-two percent) of the executed had Saudi citizenship. The harsh punishments thus disproportionally affect the already disadvantaged immigrant population.[5]

Islamic jurisprudence is known for its strict stance on intoxicating substances. The consumption of alcohol is mentioned in the Quran, and the Prophet addressed it on several occasions. While earlier verses[6] accepted alcohol consumption, Q 5:90 forbid any form of drinking:

> "You who believe, intoxicants (*khamr*) and gambling, idolatrous practices, and [divining with] arrows are repugnant acts – Satan's doing – shun them so that you may prosper."[7]

While some jurists, mostly from the Ḥanafī school, argued that only wine made from grape juice could be considered khamr, the vast majority of jurists held that the revelation forbids all forms of alcohol.[8]

---

4 Amnesty International. *Amnesty International Global Report: Death Sentences and Executions 2019* (*London: Amnesty International*, 2020), 13.

5 Ibid., 39.

6 See Q 2:219, Q 4:43, and Q 16:67.

7 All translations of the Quran are taken from Muhammad Abdel Haleem, *The Qur'an* (Oxford: Oxford University Press, 2008).

8 See Mustapha Sheikh and Tajul Islam, "Islam, Alcohol, and Identity: Towards a Critical Muslim Studies Approach," *ReOrient* 3, no. 2 (2018).

The most important non-alcoholic intoxicant in the premodern Islamic world was cannabis[9] (*ḥashīsh*), followed by henbane (*banj*) and opium (*afyūn*).[10] According to Ibn Taymiyya, the consumption of cannabis started in the late twelfth century (sixth century hijrī) with the arrival of the Mongols.[11] Ibn Taymiyya's association of cannabis with the Mongols might be a result of his anti-Mongol views. Yet, the term *ḥashīsh* to describe cannabis[12] first appeared in Islamic legal writings around that time.[13]

There are fundamental differences between the jurists' debate on alcohol and nonalcoholic intoxicants. While the ʿulamāʾ agreed that alcohol was forbidden, they differed on their definition of nonalcoholic intoxicants. The starting point for the jurists' reasoning was a narration according to which the Prophet said, "Every *muskir* (intoxicant) is khamr, and every muskir is forbidden."[14] The jurists disagreed about the meaning of muskir. The key debate was on how a substance has to influence the mind in order to be classified as a forbidden drug. Some jurists, especially from the Ḥanbalī school, held that every substance which affects the mind is muskir. The rest of the Ḥanbalīs, the Shāfiʿīs, and the Ḥanafīs only considered hallucinogens muskir, while others, especially Mālikīs, required that a hallucinogen also causes ecstasy. Some ʿulamāʾ further differentiated between liquids and solids. The Mālikī jurist al-Dardīr (d. 1787), for instance, wrote,

> The ḥadd punishment [for muskir] is limited to liquids. However, for solids that affect the mind, there is nothing but chastisement. Likewise, it is not forbidden except in quantities that affect the mind, not in less.[15]

9 Throughout the text, I use the term cannabis to describe the psychoactive parts of the cannabis plant. It is important to keep in mind that cannabis plants served as an important source for fiber and ropes in the premodern Muslim world and were widely cultivated.

10 Al-Dardīr also mentions datura, a poisonous flower known as devil's trumpet. See Al-Dardīr, *Al-Sharḥ al-ṣaghīr*, 3:183.

11 Ibn Taymiyya, *Majmūʿat al-fatāwā*, 34:205.

12 However, as Franz Rosenthal pointed out, the jurists were often unaware or not interested in the differences between substances and potentially applied the term ḥashīsh to mixtures, tinctures, or pastes in which cannabis was only one of many ingredients. See Franz Rosenthal, *The Herb: Hashish versus Medieval Muslim Society* (Leiden: Brill, 1971), 19.

13 Ibid., 43.

14 Ibn Ḥajāj, *Ṣaḥīḥ Muslim* (Riyadh: Dār Ṭayba li-l-Nashr wa-l-Tawzīʿ, 1427/2006), 2:965.

15 Al-Dardīr, *Al-Sharḥ al-ṣaghīr*, 4:499.

While some jurists held that a potentially mind-affecting substance could not be consumed at all, others like al-Dardīr argued that the ban only applied to amounts that affect the mind.[16]

The idea that not all mind-affecting substances must necessarily be considered muskir left some earlier jurists to assume that Islamic law allowed the consumption of cannabis. For instance, the twelfth-century grammarian and jurist al-ʿUkbārī (d. 1219) wrote,

> Know that the pure sharīʿa has not indicated that the use of drugs that cause joy such as saffron, bugloss, and others whose action is similar to that of this drug [ḥashīsh] is forbidden. No indication has come down from the Prophet to the effect that it is forbidden as such and that a ḥadd punishment has been established for eating it. Because there has been no tradition on this matter, people have permitted it and have used it.[17]

This relaxed stance towards cannabis forwarded by early thirteenth-century scholars like al-ʿUkbārī might result from the established principle in Islamic jurisprudence that everything should be allowed as long as it is not explicitly forbidden. However, this open stance towards cannabis did not last long.

Later in the thirteenth century, the Mālikī jurist al-Qarāfī (d. 1285) wrote that the ʿulamāʾ of his time had agreed on the ban on cannabis.[18] Ibn Taymiyya became one of the strictest enemies of mind-affecting substances and discussed cannabis consumption at length in his treatise on siyāsa sharʿiyya and in his fatwas.[19] He advocated punishing everyone who even consumes small amounts of intoxicants, whether as solids or liquids.[20] Those who declared that cannabis did not affect the mind like henbane, he stated, were mistaken. The dangers of cannabis were even greater than that of alcohol (*khamr*) since cannabis affected the mind more and was more addictive. The claim that cannabis was harmless, he continued, was a "call to consume it."[21]

---

16 Today, this plays an important role for the ruling on drinks that only include minor quantities of alcohol, like nonalcoholic beer or champagne. See, for instance, a fatwa by Ibn ʿUthaymīn on nonalcoholic beer, which is available on his official website, binothaimeen.net/content/3222 [last access: 13 January 2021].

17 Translated in Rosenthal, *The Herb*, 101.

18 Al-Qarāfī, *Al-Furūq: Anwār al-burūq fī anwāʾ al-furūq* (Beirut: Dār al-Kutub al-ʿIlmiyya, 1418/1998), 1:372.

19 Ibn Taymiyya, *Al-Siyāsa al-sharʿiyya fī iṣlāḥ al-rāʿī wa-l-raʿiyya* (Riyadh: Wizārat al-Shuʾūn al-Islāmiyya, 1419/1998), 87–88.

20 Ibn Taymiyya, *Majmūʿat al-fatāwā*, 34:205.

21 Ibid., 206.

2.1.2 The Punishment for Cannabis Consumption

Even if most later jurists agreed that the consumption of cannabis violates Islamic law, they differed on the punishment. Broadly speaking, Islamic criminal law recognizes three different categories of crimes:

The first are the *ḥudūd* crimes, which are those mentioned in the Quran or the Sunna. To commit a ḥadd crime is considered a violation of God's right (*ḥaqq Allāh*). Since the punishment is prescribed by the revelation, neither the victim of the crime nor the judge can decide differently. Once a ḥadd crime can be proven, the often very harsh punishments have to be applied. However, even a minor doubt can prevent the application of the ḥudūd, which limits their practical relevance considerably. Moreover, the requirements of evidence for ḥudūd crimes are especially strict, as we will see later in this chapter. The number of recognized ḥudūd crimes and the terms to describe them differ from school to school but usually include theft (*sariqa*), unlawful sexual intercourse (*zinā*), false accusation of *zinā* (*qadhf*), the consumption of intoxicants (*shurb khamr*), brigandage (*ḥirāba*), and apostasy (*ridda*).[22]

The second category are the *qiṣāṣ* crimes, which prescribe retaliation for acts of wounding and killing. In contrast to the ḥudūd, wounding and killing others is considered a matter between individuals or smaller groups, not God or the community. The jurists have developed rulings on how death or injuries should be compensated or, if not possible, retaliated. Since the focus in the qiṣāṣ is on the relationship between individuals, the ruler again has only limited power to interfere in the process or the punishment.

The third category, the *taʿzīr* crimes, encompass all violations of Islamic legal doctrine that do not fall under the ḥudūd. Contrary to the qiṣāṣ, the execution of the taʿzīr penalties is a part of the ruler's task of enforcing Islamic law. While the ḥudūd address the relationship between the individual and God, taʿzīr penalties sanction the rights of other individuals and the community granted by Islamic law. Taʿzīr crimes comprise, on the one hand, offences that could potentially be punished as ḥadd but did not fulfil their strict requirements, and, on the other hand, actions that violate Islamic teachings that are not sanctioned as ḥudūd. It is a matter of siyāsa sharʿiyya to determine exactly which actions should be punished with taʿzīr, and therefore the jurists acknowledged that what is punished as a taʿzīr crime varies with the social, technological, and economic circumstances.

Thus, the question of whether the consumption of intoxicating substances constituted a ḥadd crime or should be punished by taʿzīr had implications for

22 Rudolph Peters, *Crime and Punishment in Islamic Law: Theory and Practice from the Sixteenth to the Twenty-first Century* (Cambridge: Cambridge University Press, 2005), 53.

the standard of evidence used in a trial and the severity of the punishment. Usually, the jurists considered the consumption of alcohol a ḥadd punishment.[23] When it came to cannabis, those jurists who regarded it as mind-affecting also recommended a ḥadd punishment but differed on the number of lashes (forty or eighty). Others, who excluded the consumption of cannabis and other nonalcoholic substances from the ḥadd punishment, like the Mālikī al-Dardīr, regarded it as a matter of taʿzīr.[24]

Today, there is still disagreement about whether the ḥadd penalty should be applied to the consumption of nonalcoholic intoxicating substances. The influential Syrian jurist Wahba al-Zuḥaylī (d. 2015), for instance, argued that the punishment for cannabis consumption was based on the general principle in Islamic law that harming oneself is forbidden, not on the substance's intoxicating effect. In contrast to alcohol, cannabis consumption did not lead to joy (*ṭarab*) and pleasure (*ladhdha*) and did not cause addiction.[25]

Similarly, Ibn ʿUthaymīn distinguished between alcohol and other mind-affecting substances. Even though nonalcoholic substances did affect the mind like alcohol, he wrote without further explanation, there could only be a ḥadd punishment for alcohol consumption. Ibn Uthaymīn leaves the taʿzīr punishment for the use of cannabis and other drugs to the ruler's discretion (*ijtihād al-imām*).[26]

2.2 *The Development of a Broader Understanding of Ḥirāba*

2.2.1 The Ḥirāba Punishment

For most Islamic jurists, ḥirāba is synonymous with brigandage (*qiṭāʿ al-ṭarīq*). Some ʿulamāʾ even refrain from using the word ḥirāba and call the ḥadd punishment qiṭāʿ al-ṭarīq.[27] The basis for the jurists' conception of ḥirāba lies in Q 5:33, which states,

> Those who wage war against God and His Messenger and strive to spread corruption in the land should be punished by death, crucifixion, the amputation of an alternate hand and foot, or banishment from the land:

---

23 There is, however, a small group of jurists who considered the consumption of alcohol a taʿzīr crime, since the punishment itself is not mentioned in the Quran. See, for instance, Maḥmūd Shaltūt, *Al-Islām: ʿAqīda wa-sharīʿa* (Cairo: Dār al-Shurūf, 2001), 287.

24 Al-Dardīr, *Al-Sharḥ al-ṣaghīr*, 3:183.

25 Wahba al-Zuḥaylī, *Al-Fiqh al-islāmī wa-adillatuhu* (Damascus: Dār al-Fikr, 1418/1997), 7:5505.

26 Muḥammad bin Ṣāliḥ bin ʿUthaymīn, *Al-Sharḥ al-mumtiʿ ʿalā zād al-mustaqniʿ* (Dammam: Dār Ibn al-Jawzī, 1428/2007), 14:303.

27 See, for instance, ibid., 14:368.

> a disgrace for them in this world, and then a terrible punishment in the hereafter, unless they repent before you overpower them – in that case, bear in mind that God is forgiving and merciful.

However, there are limitations to the crime of ḥirāba, which prevent the application of harsh punishment in many robbery cases. For some ʿulamāʾ, only brigandage taking place outside of dwellings can be classified as ḥirāba. Others, especially the Mālikīs, apply the ḥirāba punishment for every robbery, even inside cities.[28] There is also disagreement on the subject of the robbery. For some, like Ibn Qudāma, ḥirāba necessarily involves the unlawful taking of property while carrying arms,[29] while for others, "frightening" or killing without taking property is enough to be classified as a brigand (*muḥārib*).[30]

However, all jurists required that a muḥārib take advantage of people's helplessness and spread fear among them.[31] In other words, the offender has to severely breach public safety by attacking the community. Sherman Jackson argued that the rulings on ḥirāba in premodern Islamic law correspond to a large extent to the understanding of domestic terrorism in US law today.[32] Especially earlier jurists also understood violent rebellion as a form of ḥirāba and treated rebels as brigands.[33] Later scholars, however, developed a separate law of rebellion (*aḥkām al-bughāt*), which excluded organized rebel groups with a political agenda from the harsh punishment of ḥirāba.[34]

There is also substantial disagreement between the ʿulamāʾ on the penalty, especially on the question of whether the ruler is allowed to choose between the penalties mentioned in Q 5:33. The Mālikīs argued that the death penalty should not be applied to all brigands but only to those who had killed. In other cases, the ruler had the power to choose between killing, crucifixion, and amputation.[35] Other premodern ʿulamāʾ allowed the ruler to also apply

---

28 Ibn Rushd, *Bidāyat al-mujtahid wa-nihāyat al-muqtaṣid* (Cairo: Maktabat Ibn Taymiyya, 1415/1994), 4:417.

29 Ibn Qudāma, *Al-Mughnī* (Riyadh: ʿĀlam al-Kutub, 1417/1997), 12:474.

30 Some jurists discussed ḥirāba together with theft, which shows the strong association of the concept with the protection of property. See, for instance, al-Qudūrī, *Mukhtaṣar al-Qudūrī fī fiqh al-ḥanafī* (Beirut: Dār al-Kutub al-ʿIlmiyya, 1418/1997), 201.

31 Sherman Jackson, "Domestic Terrorism in the Islamic Legal Tradition," *The Muslim World* 91 (2001): 296.

32 Ibid., 293.

33 Khaled Abou El Fadl, *Rebellion and Violence in Islamic Law* (Cambridge: Cambridge University Press, 2001), 131.

34 See for a discussion of the differences between the law of ḥirāba and the law of rebellion Jackson, "Domestic Terrorism," 301–3.

35 Ibn Rushd, *Bidāyat al-mujtahid*, 4:419.

the death penalty for offenders who had not killed. However, the majority held that the punishment had to follow the gravity of the act of ḥirāba. Hence, if someone had killed without taking property, he should be executed. If he also took property, he should first be executed and then crucified. If he only took money without killing, his left foot and right hand should be amputated. Those who neither killed nor took money but spread fear should be exiled.[36]

In later centuries, the scope of ḥirāba was extended step by step. Rashīd Riḍā, for instance, considered every attempt to prevent the application of Islamic law ḥirāba, while for Sayyid Quṭb, the organized opposition against the legitimate Muslim ruler should be subject to the ḥirāba punishment.[37]

2.2.2 Ḥirāba and Drug Trafficking in Contemporary Saudi Arabia

Contemporary Saudi jurists have adopted a broad understanding of ḥirāba. However, they often refrain from using the technical terms ḥirāba or *muḥāraba* but speak more generally about spreading corruption (*fasād*) on earth, a term that is also mentioned in Q 5:33. For the jurists, every violation of public order can potentially constitute spreading corruption (*fasād*). While ḥirāba is a ḥadd crime, it is not always clear whether the jurists classify spreading corruption as a ḥadd or a taʿzīr crime. The distinction between the two concepts often remains blurred.

The idea of spreading corruption as a distinct form of criminal offence seems to have first appeared in the Ottoman empire, where it was used to punish spying, rebellion, disrespecting political sovereigns, and counterfeiting coins.[38] Habitual offenders were also considered spreaders of corruption and could thereby be sentenced to death without the strict requirements of the ḥudūd.[39]

The extension of the scope of ḥirāba in Saudi Arabia took place as a gradual process. The first significant change happened in 1981 when the Council of Senior Scholars addressed the issue for the first time.[40] King Khālid had asked the Council for their advice on two problems that he saw himself confronted with: the number of severe cases of robbery and kidnapping inside the cities rose, and drug consumption increased.[41] In the first part of their decision,

---

36 Jackson, "Domestic Terrorism," 300.

37 See for more information on Riḍā's and Quṭb's understanding of ḥirāba Ibid., 303–5.

38 See also Khālida Ribḥī al-Nāṭūr and Muḥammad Aḥmad al-Quḍāh, "Jarīmat al-mutājara bi-l-mukhadirāt min ṣuwar jarīmat al-ifsād fī al-arḍ," *Al-ʿUlūm al-Sharīʿa wa-l-Qānūn* 41, no. 1 (2014): 269.

39 Peters, *Crime and Punishment*, 90.

40 The 1981 fatwa is also briefly discussed by Peters. See ibid., 151–52.

41 Ibid., 151.

which was issued on 9 September 1981, the Council's jurists advocated for the Mālikī view, according to which actions inside towns could also be classified as ḥirāba and therefore judges could decide on the death penalty.[42] Moreover, the Council decided that abduction for sexual motives also falls under ḥirāba.[43]

The second part of the decision addressed drug consumption and dealing. Generally, Saudi jurists distinguish between the trade and the consumption of drugs. The Council asserted that drug consumption fell under the general ruling on the consumption of muskir; the punishment, however, was taʿzīr, not ḥadd. Drug dealing, on the other hand, should first be punished with prison, fines, or lashing. If someone repeatedly committed a drug-related offence, the Council decided that they had spread corruption on earth and, therefore, could be killed.

According to Islamic jurisprudence, the death penalty can only be imposed in cases of ḥadd crimes, although some jurists permit exceptions, such as for instances where a Muslim has committed treason against other Muslims.[44] To justify the death sentence for drug trafficking, the Council relied on the writings of Ibn Taymiyya, who maintained that if the only way to stop a criminal was by killing them, the death penalty could be imposed as taʿzīr. Although King Khālid explicitly asked the Council for a verdict on drug smugglers and not only on dealers or consumers, the Council's jurists remained silent on the question.[45]

In 1987, Khālid's successor, King Fahad, turned to the Council of Senior Scholars and asked them for a more extensive ruling on drug trafficking. Drugs, the king wrote to the Council, had lately poured into the kingdom, and threatened the well-being of Saudi citizens. It was necessary, King Fahad argued, to impose sanctions to stop the trafficking.[46] In their decision of 20 February 1987, the Council's members distinguished between the trafficking of drugs into the kingdom and their distribution inside. The jurists wrote without further

42 Ibid.

43 According to the published court decisions, Saudi courts today use the concept of ḥirāba most importantly in abduction cases that involve sexual violence.

44 Wizārat al-Awqāf wa-l-Shuʾūn al-Islāmiyya al-Kuwaitiyya, *Al-Mawsūʿa al-fiqhiyya al-kuwaitiyya* (Kuwait City: Wizārat al-Awqāf wa-l-Shuʾūn al-Islāmiyya al-Kuwaitiyya, 1404/1983), 12:263.

45 The Council's decision was published in the Council's journal *Majallat al-buḥūth al-islāmiyya*. The text is available on the Council's homepage. www.alifta.gov.sa/Ar/Magazine/Pages/issues.aspx?cultStr=ar&View=Page&PageID=1673&PageNo=1&BookID=2 [last access: 8 January 2023].

46 The Council's decision is printed in Muḥammad bin ʿAbd al-ʿAzīz al-Musnad, ed., *Fatāwā islāmiyya* (Riyadh: Dār al-Waṭan), 379.

explanation that drug trafficking should be punished with death since it corrupted not only the drug trafficker but also damaged society as a whole. In the decision, it says,

> Firstly: Concerning the drug smuggler [*muharrib*], his punishment is death, since what he causes, the smuggling of drugs and them entering into the country, constitutes great corruption [*fasād*] not limited to the smuggler himself, immense damage, and enormous dangers for the umma as a whole. The [term] smuggler applies to a person who imports or receives drugs from abroad and provides them to the drug dealers [*murawwijūn*].[47]

Drug dealing, on the other hand, should only be punished with death in cases where a person repeatedly deals with drugs. The Council argued that by repeatedly distributing drugs, a drug dealer had spread corruption on earth. The decision justified the taʿzīr death penalty for habitual offenders in length and cited both Ibn Taymiyya and a prophetic account according to which a person who does not stop an illegal act should be killed.[48]

Although the Council's jurists clearly applied the concept of ḥirāba to drug smuggling, they refrained from using the term, since, for them, the term ḥirāba is still associated with brigandage. The difference between ḥirāba and spreading corruption on earth, however, remains blurry. For instance, when asked about the nature of ḥirāba and drug trafficking, Ibn Bāz replied,

> Ḥirāba is one of the greatest wrongdoings. It is brigandage [*qaṭʿ al-ṭarīq*] and attacking people with a weapon in order to take their possessions. This is called ḥirāba. They are called brigands; they are called spreaders of corruption on earth [*mufsidūn fī al-arḍ*].[49]

However, in another fatwa, Ibn Bāz draw similarities between ḥirāba and drug smuggling and applied Q 5:33 to drug smugglers:

> The Council of Senior Scholars has studied the rulings on drugs and the resulting great evil for Muslims, the huge corruption and the loss of many young men and others because of their drug use, their insistence and

47 Ibid., 380.

48 Ibid., 380.

49 A transcript of the audio recording of the fatwa can be found on binbaz.org.sa, bit.ly/3mteHKg [last access: 19 December 2022].

> persistence on it. [The Council] has looked into the scholars' opinions and decided based on that: he who smuggles drugs from here to there must be killed because of his corruption of the world [*fasādihi fī al-arḍ*]. Because it is a part [*bāb*] of the corruption of the world, and also because it is worse than brigandage [*muḥāraba*]. If the brigand [*muḥārib*], who takes the peoples' possessions on the road, is killed, then the one who corrupts peoples' minds should be killed even more.
>
> However, he who distributes drugs through buying and selling them is disciplined and punished according to the opinion of the ruler [*walī al-amr*] with prison or [other forms of] disciplinary [measures]. He who relapses has to be killed because killing him protects the minds of the Muslims and their lives. It is part of God's grace to the humans that He allowed the death penalty [*taʿzīr bi-l-qatl*] if someone does not refrain because of flogging, prison, and other [measures].
>
> This is the reason for the issued ruling. Because it is corruption of the earth, because it is worse than brigandage, where people's possessions are taken illegally on the roads, and similarly in town, with force. If the one who takes people's possessions or frightens them on the way is killed or crucified or his hand and leg are amputated, then the one who corrupts people's minds and smuggles what damages their minds and corrupts them in their religious and worldly [life] should be killed even more with this penalty.[50]

The jurists' decisions guided the judges' ijtihād until King ʿAbd Allah issued the Code against Drugs and Mind-affecting Substances (Niẓām Mukāfaḥat al-Mukhadirāt wa-l-Muʾathirāt al-ʿAqliyya) in 2005. The code transformed many of the jurists' ideas on drug-related offences into statutory law and extended it, for instance, by providing a detailed list of the drugs considered mind-affecting. Moreover, it provided a clear framework for the medical use of mind-affecting substances. In Article 37, the code addresses the issue of drug smuggling:

> First: With consideration of Section 2 of this article, anyone who is proven to have committed one of the following actions is punished with death [*qatl taʿzīrān*]:
>
> 1. Smuggling [*tahrīb*] of drugs or mind-affecting substances.
> 2. Accepting drugs or mind-affecting substances from a smuggler.

---

50 A transcript of the audio recording of the fatwa can be found on binbaz.org.sa, bit.ly/2LMpZwG [last access: 18 January 2021].

3. The transportation, importing, exporting, creation, production, transformation, extraction, growing, and receiving of drugs or mind-affecting substances with the aim to distribute them without being authorized according to this code.
4. Voluntary complicity in the undertaking of one of the actions mentioned in the numbers before.
5. Distributing drugs or mind-affecting substances for the second time through buying, offering, circulating, delivering, receiving, or transporting them, under the condition that a verdict was issued before proving the conviction of drug distribution for the first time.
6. Distributing [drugs or mind-affecting substances] for the first time if a guilty verdict of undertaking one of the actions mentioned in numbers 1, 2, and 3 of this article had previously been issued.

Secondly: The court is allowed – for reasons that it decides – to change the death penalty to a prison sentence of not less than fifteen years, flogging [*jald*] of not more than fifty floggings at one time, and a fine of not less than 100,000 riyal.

Thirdly: If the following circumstances apply to a criminal [*jānī*] who is not punished with death according to Section 1 of this article, he is punished with a prison sentence of not less than twenty-five years and flogging [*jald*] of not more than fifty floggings at one time, and a fine of not less than 150,000 riyal. These circumstances are the following:
1. If the criminal repeats to commit one of the crimes after he was sentenced because of committing one of them and the punishment was based on the text [*naṣṣ*] of this article.
2. If the criminal was a public servant or employee or someone in charge of enforcing the rulings of this code or delegated to fight drugs and mind-affecting substances or supervise their distribution and possession.
3. If the criminal was a member of an organized enterprise and the smuggling of drugs or mind-affecting substances or selling them or the provision to consume them was among the enterprise's objectives. Or if his crime is connected with an international crime [*jarīma dawliyya*], like arms smuggling, counterfeiting, or terrorism.
4. If the criminal was armed and used his arms while undertaking the crime.

While the Council of Senior Scholars decided that the drug smuggler's punishment was death in any case, the 2005 code explicitly allowed judges to decide against the death penalty. Death, however, still remains the prime form of punishment for drug smuggling in the code.

The 2005 code translated the jurists' discourse into the structure of a modern law while upholding the main elements of the Council of Senior Scholars' decisions. However, the references to the idea of spreading corruption and Ibn Taymiyya's argument that habitual offenders could be punished with death are missing. At least at first glance, this makes it difficult to notice that the code's origins lie in Islamic jurisprudence.

2.3 *Saudi Court Decisions on Drug Smuggling*

2.3.1 Judgements Not Involving the Death Penalty

Due to the severity of the crime, Saudi courts deal with comparably few cases that involve drug trafficking. As a result, only a small number of court decisions on the issue have been published. Some of the published cases involve drug trafficking for personal use, for which the punishment is much lighter, namely flogging and prison for up to two years.[51] For instance, in one case from Qaṭīf, a man was caught by Saudi customs at the border with Bahrain carrying cannabis and three and a half amphetamine pills. The judges noted that since the amount was small, it was likely that the man smuggled the amphetamine for personal use only and sentenced him to sixty days of prison and sixty lashes.[52]

Even if larger amounts of drugs are smuggled, the judges do not always decide to punish the accused with death. In one case from Najrān, three Yemeni men were caught by Saudi border control with more than twenty-five kilograms of cannabis when they tried to illegally cross the border with Yemen by foot. The public persecutor suggested the death penalty; the judges, however, noted in their verdict that the death penalty was only a possibility but not mandatory. The men's repentance (*tawba*), the judges wrote, seemed honest. Since the men also confessed, the judges sentenced the three men to twelve years in prison, 1,200 lashes (fifty lashes every thirty days) and a fine of 100,000 Saudi riyals.[53] In a similar case, judges in Jāzān decided against the death penalty due to the accused's young age.[54]

Many published cases deal with qat, which is popular and socially accepted in Yemen but considered a forbidden drug according to the Saudi Code

---

51 Article 41 of the 1426/2005 Code against Drugs and Mind-affecting Substances.

52 Qaṭīf General Court, decision Nr. 3416899 (19.1.1434/3.12.2012).

53 Najrān General Court, decision Nr. 3452825 (2.3.1434/14.1.2013).

54 Since all personal data is erased from the published court cases, the exact age of the accused remains unknown. Jāzān General Court, decision Nr. 33331714 (7.7.1434/17.5.2013).

against Drugs and Mind-affecting Substances. Qat smugglers, however, receive relatively mild sentences, especially if they smuggle for personal consumption only.

2.3.2 Cases Involving the Death Penalty

There are only two published cases in which the judges decided on the death penalty for drug smuggling. In the first one, a case from Jeddah, a Pakistani man had arrived at the airport carrying 852 grams of heroin in his stomach. He claimed that four people in Pakistan had forced him to transport the drug by threatening to kill him. However, the man could not provide evidence for his claim. The judges discussed whether the sheer possibility that someone was forced to transport drugs could raise enough doubt of the man's guilt that it prevents the death penalty.[55] However, they concluded that the man could have contacted the police both in Pakistan and in Saudi Arabia before entering the country.[56]

In this first case, the judges barely explained the legal basis for their judgement and simply referred to Article 37 of the Code against Drugs and Mind-affecting Substances. The judges in the second published case, by contrast, elaborated on their legal reasoning in length. In the second case, a middle-aged man was accused in Tabūk of smuggling 209,110 pills of Captagon from Jordan into Saudi Arabia. Saudi authorities had found the Captagon pills, an amphetamine popular in many Arab countries, hidden in the fuel tank of his car. During his interrogations with the police, the man had initially confessed that he had modified the fuel tank in Jordan with the help of a local taxi driver. However, during the trial, he denied the accusations and declared that he did not know that he was carrying the pills. Before crossing the border, the man told the judges, he had given the car to another man who needed it to bring his brother to the hospital and who then hid the Captagon pills in the fuel tank.[57]

In their verdict, the judges first discussed the legal effects of the man's withdrawal of his confession. As we have seen earlier, Islamic jurisprudence places great attention on doubt, especially in ḥudūd crimes. According to a well-known principle (*qāʿida*) of Islamic law, the ḥadd punishments should

55 Interestingly, the judges at the Appeal Court later also argued that it was possible that the man's claims were true and called for the careful handling of the death penalty. However, they eventually accepted the first instance judges' decision.

56 Jeddah General Court, decision Nr. 34157062 (confirmed by the Mecca Court of Appeal on 15.7.1435/15.5.2014).

57 Tabūk General Court, decision Nr. 34279643 (25.7.1434/4.6.2013).

be averted in case of doubt (*al-ḥudūd tudraʾ bi-l-shubhāt*). The great majority of Islamic jurists argued that the withdrawal of a confession could create enough doubt to prevent the ḥadd punishment, even if there are good reasons to believe that the confession was accurate.[58] In practice, the withdrawal of a confession is one of the prime reasons why Saudi judges rarely impose ḥadd punishments.

As we have seen, the Council of Senior Scholars and other Saudi jurists emphasized that although drug smuggling is related to ḥirāba, it never constitutes a ḥadd crime. The judges in Tabūk likewise considered drug smuggling to be not a ḥadd but a taʿzīr crime and discussed whether the principle that doubt averts the punishment could be applied in this case. They concluded that the withdrawal of a confession in a taʿzīr case was not possible and quoted Ibn Qudāma, who stated that the jurists had agreed that a withdrawal of a confession only has legal effects in ḥadd cases.[59]

The judges then turned to their justification for the death penalty. They first cited Q 5:33 and then quoted two paragraphs from al-Bahūtī's (d. 1641) *Kashshāf al-qināʿ*, according to which it was generally possible to impose the death penalty in a taʿzīr case. The first paragraph from al-Bahūtī's book states,

> Taʿzīr is done by hitting, slapping, reproach, isolation, and withdrawal of [the offender's] legal competence [*ʿazl ʿan al-wilāya*]. In *Al-Ikhtiyarāt* [by Ibn Taymiyya], it is said that if the purpose is to fight corruption [*fasād*] and it can only be stopped by killing, then he is killed. If someone repeats [committing] a form of corruption and it cannot be prevented by the recognized ḥudūd, but he continues with the corruption, he is like the assailant [*ṣāʾil*], who cannot be defeated unless he is killed, and he is killed.[60]

Hence, according to the judges, drug smuggling can only be stopped by killing the smuggler. Even though the alleged smuggler in the case in question did not have any prior record of drug smuggling, they nevertheless applied Ibn Taymiyya's and al-Bahūtī's rulings on a habitual offender to him. This can also be seen in the second paragraph of the *Kashshāf al-qināʿ*, which they quoted in the verdict:

---

58 Wizārat al-Awqāf wa-l-Shuʾūn al-Islāmiyya al-Kuwaitiyya, *Al-Mawsūʿa al-fiqhiyya al-kuwaitiyya*, 6:72.

59 See Ibn Qudāma, *Al-Mughnī*, 7:278.

60 Al-Bahūtī, *Kashshāf al-qināʿ*, 6:124.

> The shaykh [Ibn Taymiyya] said that an offender is punished in the way that stops him, because the reason [for the punishment] is prevention, and he said that an offender is punished with death, if this is needed.[61]

After establishing the possibility of applying the death penalty in a taʿzīr case like this, the judges quoted the Council of Senior Scholars' decision. The judges used the Council's argument to justify that the death penalty can be imposed not only generally in taʿzīr crimes but specifically in the crime of drug smuggling. Only in the very last step of their legal reasoning did the judges briefly refer to Article 37 of the Code against Drugs and Mind-affecting Substances and quoted the beginning of the article without discussing it further.

The legal reasoning of the judges in Tabūk thus reflects the genealogy of the ruling on drug smuggling in Saudi Arabia. Even though an explicit regulation on drug smuggling can be found in the Code against Drugs and Mind-affecting Substances, the judges nevertheless considered drug smuggling first and foremost as a matter of fiqh.

Surprisingly, the association of drug smuggling with ḥirāba can also be seen in how Saudi authorities communicate the execution of drug smugglers. In another case from Tabūk, two men were executed for drug smuggling in 2019. The Ministry of Interior's announcement of the execution started by quoting the full text of Q 5:33 before the names of the convicts and their crime were listed.[62] Media reports also frame death sentences for drug smuggling as ḥirāba punishments. For instance, in 2014, the Saudi newspaper Al-Waṭan reported that the court in Najrān applied the ḥirāba punishment (*ḥadd al-ḥirāba*) on two alleged drug smugglers and sentenced them to death.[63]

3 The Second Example: the Reform of Khulʿ Divorce

3.1 *The Concept of Khulʿ Divorce*

3.1.1 The Wife's Ability to File for Divorce in Islamic Law

From a women's rights perspective, divorce is among the most contested areas in Islamic law. One of the key questions is whether a woman has the right to dissolve her marriage against her husband's will. Technically, Islamic law only grants the husband and the judge the right to dissolve a marriage. Usually, it

61 Ibid., 6:126.

62 The announcement was printed in a local newspaper. I want to thank Ingo Schendel from the German Embassy in Riyadh for providing me with a copy of the article.

63 The article can be found on the newspaper's homepage, see bit.ly/2KqELIV.

is the husband who ends the marriage through repudiation (*ṭalāq*). The husband does not have to present grounds for the repudiation, but some ʿulamāʾ even argued that the husband does not even have to inform his wife about the divorce.[64]

The wife, on the other hand, only has two ways to end the marriage: first, she can file for dissolution (*faskh*) of the marriage in court, and second, she can try to obtain a khulʿ divorce. In order to get the marriage dissolved, the wife has to present specific grounds to the judge. The general idea in all schools of Islamic jurisprudence is that if the wife suffers any physical or psychological damage (*ḍarar*) from the marriage, she should be free to dissolve the marriage without further costs. The schools, however, disagree on what constitutes damage. The jurists mostly accept that physical violence by the husband, his absence for a longer period of time, his refusal to pay alimony, and his impotence or inability to father children can damage the wife's well-being.

In case the wife cannot prove any damage, the only option left for her is to obtain a khulʿ divorce. In a khulʿ divorce, the wife offers to return claims or payments that she has received from her husband during the marriage, usually her dowry (*mahr*), in exchange for the divorce. According to Islamic jurisprudence, every woman is entitled to a dowry when she marries, which is usually negotiated before the marriage and laid down in the marriage contract.[65]

The limited access to divorce for women in Islamic law is regularly criticized by women's rights activists as well as human rights NGOs and others. In Egypt, the critique led in 2000 to the issuing of a controversial law on khulʿ, which enabled a wife to file for khulʿ divorce without her husband's consent. The law stipulated that the wife has to renounce all claims she has against her husband and return her dowry entirely. Furthermore, she has to declare in court that she detests living with her husband and is afraid to transgress the boundaries (*ḥudūd*) set by God.[66]

The Egyptian law served as a role model for similar reforms in various Arab countries.[67] For instance, the 2001 reform of divorce law in Jordan explicitly

---

64 Mathias Rohe, *Das islamische Recht: Geschichte und Gegenwart* (Munich: Beck, 2009), 92.

65 Nadjma Yassari, *Die Brautgabe im Familienvermögensrecht: Innerislamischer Rechtsvergleich und Integration in das deutsche Recht* (Tübingen: Mohr Siebeck, 2014), 34.

66 Article 20 of the Egyptian Law Nr. 1 of 2000 regulating certain situations and judicial procedures in personal status matters (Qānūn Raqm 1 li-Sanat 2000 bi-Iṣḍār Qānūn Tanẓīm Baʿḍ Awḍāʿ wa-Ijrāʾāt al-Taqāḍī fī Masāʾil al-Aḥwāl al-Shakhṣiyya).

67 Lynn Welchman, *Women and Muslim Family Laws in Arab States: A Comparative Overview of Textual Development and Advocacy* (Amsterdam: Amsterdam University Press, 2007), 119–22.

referred to the Egyptian law.[68] The Egyptian law also received much attention in Western literature.[69] It was seen as a turning point in the history of Islamic law and the beginning of a new era. In a much-cited article, Oussama Arabi claimed that the Egyptian khulʿ law was an example that Islamic law could be substantially reformed by modern state legislation. Although Arabi acknowledged that the Egyptian government based the reform on accounts of the Prophet and consulted al-Azhar, he argued,

> [T]he historically established corpuses [sic] of over a millennium of Muslim legal thought – the immense intellectual effort of past generations of school jurists sedimented in the treatises of jurisprudence and in community legal practices – are, to a large measure, constitutionally neutralised.[70]

Arabi's analysis has become the standard narrative on the development of khulʿ divorce and deeply influenced subsequent research on Egyptian family law.[71] Yet, despite the lack of state legislation in family law, a similar development of judicial khulʿ can be observed in Saudi Arabia.

---

68 Ibid., 116. In the United Arab Emirates, a similar regulation was included in the 2005 family law codification. However, the Emirati legislators explicitly distanced themselves from the Egyptian and Jordanian reforms. See Lena-Maria Möller, *Die Golfstaaten auf dem Weg zu einem modernen Recht für die Familie* (Tübingen: Mohr Siebeck, 2015), 171.

69 See among others Nadia Sonneveld, *Khulʿ Divorce in Egypt: Public Debates, Judicial Practices, and Everyday Life* (Cairo: American University in Cairo Press, 2012); Essam Fawzy, "Muslim Personal Status Law in Egypt: The Current Situation and Possibilities of Reform through Internal Initiatives," in *Women's Rights and Islamic Family Law: Perspectives on Reform*, ed. Lynn Welchman (London: Zed Books, 2004); Dawoud El-Alami, "Remedy or Device? The System of Khul' and the Effects of Its Incorporation into Egyptian Personal Status Law," *Yearbook of Islamic and Middle Eastern Law* 6 (1999); Nathalie Bernard-Maugiron, "The Judicial Construction of the Facts and the Law: The Egyptian Supreme Constitutional Court and the Constitutionality of the Law on the Khulʿ," in *Narratives of Truth in Islamic Law*, ed. Baudouin Dupret, Barbara Drieskens, and Annelies Moors (London: I.B. Tauris, 2008); Hendrik Denker, "Die Wiedereinführung des ḫulʿ und die Stärkung der Frauenrechte," in *Leipziger Beiträge zum Islamischen Recht IV*, ed. Silvia Tellenbach and Thoralf Hanstein (Frankfurt am Main: Lang, 2004).

70 Oussama Arabi, "The Dawning of the Third Millennium on Sharīʿa: Egypt's Law No. 1 of 2000, or Women May Divorce at Will," *Arab Law Quarterly* 16, no. 1 (2001), 21.

71 See, for instance, Sonneveld, *Khulʿ Divorce in Egypt*, 41; Javaid Rehman, "The Sharia, Islamic Family Laws and International Human Rights Law: Examining the Theory and Practice of Polygamy and Talaq," *International Journal of Law, Policy and the Family* 21, no. 1 (2007): 120; Maurits Berger and Nadia Sonneveld, "Sharia and National Law in Egypt," in *Sharia Incorporated: A Comparative Overview of the Legal Systems of Twelve Muslim Countries in Past and Present*, ed. Jan Michiel Otto (Leiden: Leiden University Press, 2010), 76; Clark

3.1.2 The Concept of Khulʿ Divorce in Islamic Jurisprudence

The premodern jurists' rulings on khulʿ divorce are based on several Quranic verses and one important account of the Prophet Muḥammad. In Q 2:229, it says,

> Divorce can happen twice, and [each time] wives can either be kept on in an acceptable manner or released in a good way. It is not lawful for you to take back anything that you have given [your wives], except where both fear that they cannot maintain [the marriage] within the bounds set by God: if you [arbiters] suspect that the couple may not be able to do this, then there will be no blame on either of them if the woman opts to give something for her release. These are the bounds set by God: do not overstep them. It is those who overstep God's bounds who are doing wrong.

Moreover, Q 4:4 states,

> Give women their bridal gift upon marriage, though if they are happy to give up some of it for you, you may enjoy it with a clear conscience.

Based on the Quranic text, the ʿulamāʾ agreed that a wife could generally return her dowry in exchange for divorce. However, more important than the Quranic verses was a narration of the Prophet Muḥammad which set a precedent for khulʿ divorce. In al-Bukhārī's ḥadīth collection, it says,

> The wife of Thābit bin Qays came to the Prophet and told him: Messenger of God, I do not blame Thābit bin Qays for his character or his religion, but I hate [to commit] disbelief [*akrahu al-kufr fī al-islām*]. The Messenger of God replied: "Give his garden back to him [that he gave you as dowry]." She said: "Yes." [Then] the Messenger of God said [to Thābit]: "Accept the garden and divorce her once" [*iqbal al-ḥadīqa wa-ṭalliqhā taṭlīqatan*].[72]

Several different versions of the ḥadīth exist, and the last sentence of the account became especially contested. In another version of the story, the

---

Lombardi, "The Constitution as Agreement to Agree: The Social and Political Foundations (and Effects) of the 1971 Egyptian Constitution," in *Social and Political Foundations of Constitutions*, ed. Denis Galligan and Mila Versteeg (Cambridge: Cambridge University Press, 2013), 421, n. 22; Jasmine Moussa, *Competing Fundamentalisms and Egyptian Women's Family Rights: International Law and the Reform of Sharīʿa-Derived Legislation* (Leiden: Brill, 2011), 196.

72 Al-Bukhārī, *Ṣaḥīḥ al-Bukhārī*, 1344 (Nr. 5273).

Prophet said to Thābit: "Take what she got from you [*khūdh alladhī lahā ʿalayka*] and let her go her way."[73] In yet another version, he simply stated: "Take it [the garden]."[74]

However, the different versions have only minor implications for the jurists' understanding of khulʿ divorce. The ʿulamāʾ agree that khulʿ divorce is a contract between the spouses, in which both agree that the wife gives back assets provided to her by the husband in return for divorce.

The requirements of khulʿ divorce resemble those of other contracts: first of all, there has to be an offer from the wife's side to which the husband has to agree.[75] Since khulʿ divorce is an exercize of the spouses' private autonomy, the involvement of a judge or any other official is not required.[76] Most importantly, the wife does not have to present any reasons for the divorce. It is sufficient that she no longer wants to live with her husband.[77]

The details of khulʿ divorce are, however, disputed between the different schools. One of the key questions is the amount of the compensation. Some jurists considered the return of at least a part of the mahr a requirement for khulʿ divorce. For some Ḥanbalīs, this was not mandatory: they argued that the wife could initiate a khulʿ divorce even without returning any assets.[78] The jurists also intensively debated if the wife could offer to return more than she has received from her husband.[79] Equally disputed was the legal nature of khulʿ divorce: is it a repudiation (*ṭalāq*) or a dissolution (*faskh*) of the marriage?[80] Since spouses are generally only allowed to remarry if the husband has not uttered the ṭalāq three times, the question is of great practical importance.[81] A faskh divorce, on the other hand, does not have any further legal consequences for a potential remarriage of the spouses.[82]

73 Al-Nasāʾī, *Sunan al-Nasāʾī*, 543 (Nr. 3497).

74 Abū Dāwūd, *Sunan Abī Dāwūd*, 3:544 (Nr. 2227).

75 The Islamic jurists did not develop a general law of contracts but instead addressed fundamental problems of contract law in the law of sales. The sales contract (*ʿaqd bayʿ*) became a model contract, to which the jurist referred when discussing other forms of contracts. See Oberauer, *Islamisches Wirtschafts- und Vertragsrecht*, 15.

76 See al-Zuḥaylī, *Al-Fiqh al-islāmī wa-adillatuhu*, 9:7012; Al-Sarakhsī, *Al-Mabsūṭ* (Beirut: Dār al-Maʿrifa, 1409/1989), 6:173; Ibn Qudāma, *Al-Mughnī* (Riyadh: ʿĀlam al-Kutub), 10:268.

77 See, for example, al-Shīrāzī, *Al-Muhadhdhab fī fiqh al-Imām al-Shāfiʿī* (Damascus: Dār al-Qalam, 1413/1996), 4:254.

78 Ibn Qudāma, *Al-Mughnī*, 10:287.

79 See, for instance, Ibn Rushd, *Bidāyat al-mujtahid*, 3:132.

80 Ibn Qudāma, *Al-Mughnī*, 10:274.

81 See See Munir, "Triple Ṭalāq.".

82 Al-Mawārdī, *Al-Ḥāwī al-kabīr fī fiqh al-Imām al-Shāfiʿī* (Beirut: Dār al-Kutub al-ʿIlmiyya, 1414/1994), 10.

3.1.3 Can the Husband Be Forced to Agree to a Khulʿ Divorce?

In a case where her husband does not want the divorce, the primary question for the wife is whether she can nevertheless end the marriage. The premodern ʿulamāʾ pointed to the contractual nature of khulʿ divorce and argued that the husband's agreement is always needed in order for the divorce to take place. Islamic jurisprudence usually places great emphasis on contractual freedom, and the ʿulamāʾ generally refuse the idea of an obligation to contract. In the case of khulʿ divorce, the jurists agreed that, like in all other contracts, both parties' agreement is needed for the contract to be valid.

However, can the husband be forced to give his agreement, or can a court subsidize it? Premodern ʿulamāʾ discussed whether the prophet's decision to give back the garden could be understood as a binding rule. The four major schools agreed that the Prophet's order to take back the garden in return for the divorce should be seen as advice, which is not binding, but only recommended (*mustaḥabb*) to follow. This made it impossible for a judge to force a husband to agree to his wife's offer to khulʿ divorce.[83] Due to the consensus among the early ʿulamāʾ on the issue, most postclassical fiqh works refrained from extensively discussing the question.

This is not to say that all premodern scholars followed the mainstream opinion of the schools. The Mālikī jurist al-Bājī (d. 1101), for instance, held that the Prophet's decision to take back the garden did not even result in a moral obligation to agree to the divorce,[84] while, about six-hundred years later, the Yemenī scholar Muhammad bin Ismāʿīl al-Ṣanʿānī (d. 1768) argued that, at its core, the Prophet's command should be understood as binding. Al-Ṣanʿānī ruled that the husband is bound to agree to the wife's offer to khulʿ divorce; however, he did not discuss whether the husband has to agree to the wife's offer right away or if the wife has to go to court and force the husband to consent.[85] Al-Ṣanʿānī was not alone: in the Mālikī tradition, a few scholars in their school opposed the school's doctrine and considered the Prophet's command binding.[86] However, their opinion fell into obscurity.[87]

---

83 Ahmed Fekry Ibrahim, *Pragmatism in Islamic Law: A Social and Intellectual History* (Syracuse: Syracuse University Press, 2015), 211.

84 ʿAbd Allāh bin Muḥammad Āl Khunayn, *Al-Khulʿ bi-ṭalab al-zawja* (Riyadh: Dār Ibn Farḥūn, 1421/2001), 65.

85 Muhammad bin Ismāʿīl al-Ṣanʿānī, *Subul al-salām sharḥ bulūgh al-marām* (Riyadh: Maktabat al-Maʿārif, 1427/2006), 3:454.

86 Ibrahim, *Pragmatism in Islamic Law*, 211.

87 A comprehensive contemporary work on the Mālikī school, for instance, clearly states that the husband in any case has to agree to the khulʿ divorce. See Muḥammad bin Bashīr al-Shaqafa, *Al-Fiqh al-mālikī fī thawbihi al-jadīd* (Damascus: Dār al-Qalam, 1432/2011), 4:272.

3.1.4 Saudi Views on Forced Khulʿ Divorce

Contemporary Saudi scholars also see khulʿ divorce as a private contract between the spouses. For instance, Ibn Khunayn wrote in his 2010 book on khulʿ divorce,

> There is no doubt that [khulʿ divorce] is an agreement between the spouses and [constitutes] the wife's obligation to return [what she has been given] to the husband or a third person. The husband is not forced to [agree], nor is the wife forced to return [her assets].[88]

Starting from the middle of the twentieth century, Saudi scholars increasingly discussed whether a judge could dissolve a marriage despite the husband's refusal to khulʿ divorce. The key question was whether exceptions to khulʿ divorce's contractual nature could be made. Like jurists from the other schools, Ḥanbalī ʿulamāʾ traditionally held that the husband's agreement was only desired and that the judge could only intervene if the husband violated his marital duties.

Muḥammad bin Ibrāhīm (d. 1969) was the first prominent Saudi scholar to diverge from the mainstream opinion in the schools. He referred to the famous Ḥanbalī book *Al-Inṣāf* by ʿAlāʾ al-Dīn al-Mardāwī (d. 1480), which lists the various opinions held by Ḥanbalī scholars in the fifteenth century. Al-Mardāwī wrote that, except for Ibn Taymiyya, the Ḥanbalī scholars agreed that the husband's consent to a khulʿ divorce could not be forced. However, al-Mardāwī also briefly stated that some judges in the Levant at his time did force the husband to agree.[89] Muḥammad bin Ibrāhīm quoted al-Mardāwī's brief reference to the Levantine judges and presented their practice as a legitimate minority opinion in the school.[90] However, he remained silent on the proceedings that the judges should undertake in a forced khulʿ divorce and explicitly left this to the judges' ijtihād.[91] Despite Muḥammad bin Ibrāhīm's great influence on the judiciary, he did not manage to establish his view on khulʿ divorce as the prevailing practice in the kingdom. Some judges followed Muḥammad bin Ibrāhīm's opinion, whereas others preferred the mainstream view.[92]

Muḥammad bin Ibrāhīm was not the only major twentieth-century Saudi scholar to grant forced khulʿ divorce. Ibn ʿUthaymīn (d. 2001) also allowed

88 Āl Khunayn, *Al-Khulʿ bi-ṭalab al-zawja*, 20.

89 Al-Mardāwī, *Al-Inṣāf*, 8:382.

90 Muḥammad bin ʿAbd al-Raḥmān al-Qāsim, (Ed.). Fatāwā wa-rasāʾil samāḥat al-shaykh Muḥammad bin Ibrāhīm Āl al-Shaykh. Mecca: Maṭbaʿat al-Ḥukūma, vol. 10, p. 288.

91 Al-Qāsim, *Fatāwā wa-rasāʾil*, 10:298.

92 This was told to me by several senior judges that I interviewed in Riyadh.

judges to force a husband to consent to a khulʿ divorce. Although Ibn ʿUthaymīn briefly referred to Ibn Taymiyya, he forwarded a very pragmatic argument: it was the judge's obligation to solve the dispute between the spouses. However, if the wife does not want to remain with her husband and the husband insists on his refusal of the divorce, the only way left for the judge to solve the conflict was to dissolve the marriage.[93]

Saudi court practice substantially changed in 1974, when King Fayṣal asked the Council of Senior Scholars for a fatwa on forced khulʿ divorce. For the Council, the question of forced khulʿ divorce is connected to the wife's "disobedience" (*nushūz*). According to Islamic jurisprudence, the wife owes the husband obedience (*ṭāʿa*) in return for the provision of alimony. If the wife refuses to obey, for example, if she moves out of the marital home without the husband's consent, she is considered disobedient (*nāshiza*).[94] As a result, she loses her right to alimony until she returns to her husband.[95] Since Saudi women usually move out of the marital home once a serious marital dispute arises, the Council's members assumed that the wife is disobedient whenever the question of forced khulʿ arises. For them, the wife's disobedience contradicts the goal of the marriage, namely the peaceful cohabitation of man and woman. If it was possible for the spouses to settle their dispute, the Council demanded that a judge should dissolve the marriage.[96]

In addition to the aforementioned Quranic verses and the account of Thābit and his wife, Saudi ʿulamāʾ pointed to a famous prophetic ḥadīth that also serves as a basic principle (*qāʿida*) in Islamic jurisprudence: No harm shall be inflicted or reciprocated (*lā ḍarar wa-lā ḍirār*).[97] The principle is used in different ways. Ibn Khunayn, for instance, argued that the unhappy marriage itself constituted harm to the wife. Since it was the imperative of Islamic law to reduce harm, an unhappy marriage should be ended in any case, if necessary, through a forced khulʿ divorce.[98]

Today, Saudi jurists discuss the question of forced khulʿ divorce in much greater detail than earlier scholars like Muḥammad bin Ibrāhīm. For example, Ibn Khunayn not only refers to Ḥanbalī works but also carefully analyzes the opinions in the other schools. Moreover, he is much more concerned with the procedural aspects of forced khulʿ divorce. For Ibn Khunayn, the prevailing

93 Al-ʿUthaymīn, *Al-Sharḥ al-mumtiʿ*, 12:480.
94 Wizārat al-Awqāf wa-l-Shuʾūn al-Islāmiyya al-Kuwaitiyya, *Al-Mawsūʿa al-fiqhiyya al-kuwaitiyya*, 40:287.
95 Al-Zuḥaylī, *Al-Fiqh al-islāmī wa-adillatuhu*, 10:7364–66.
96 Al-Amāna al-ʿĀmma li-Hayʾat Kibār al-ʿUlamāʾ, *Abḥāth hayʾat kibār al-ʿulamāʾ*, 1:658.
97 For more information on the principle see Zakariyah, *Legal Maxims*, 158–72.
98 Āl Khunayn, *Al-Khulʿ bi-ṭalab al-zawja*, 72.

opinion in Saudi Arabia today resembles the Egyptian khulʿ law issued in 2000. He emphasized that Saudi jurists had come up with their ruling decades before the Egyptians, and, therefore, he could not understand the debates surrounding the Egyptian law. For him, forced khulʿ divorce should be a given today.[99]

3.2 *Forced Khulʿ in Saudi Legal Practice*

3.2.1 The Prevailing Practice in Saudi Courts before Codification

Prior to the codification of family law, the prevailing practice in Saudi courts followed the majority opinion among Saudi scholars. According to the published court decisions, the judges forced husbands to consent to a khulʿ divorce whenever reconciliation failed, and the wife insisted on the divorce. Moreover, according to several judges I spoke to, the appeal courts usually revoked judgements if the first instance judge refused to grant a forced khulʿ divorce. Muḥammad Jār Allāh, for instance, a senior judge at the Riyadh Court of Appeal, explained that he referred all decisions in which women were denied a khulʿ divorce back to the first instance court.[100] According to Ibn Khunayn, the courts were de facto bound to the Council of Senior Scholars' decision, and a group of young lawyers from Riyadh confirmed that forced khulʿ divorce had become a routine procedure at Saudi courts. It was hard for them to imagine that a woman could be denied a khulʿ divorce as it was argued by the authoritative jurists of the four major schools.[101]

In order to obtain a forced khulʿ divorce, the wife had to file a lawsuit at court, which is free of charge.[102] Often, a forced khulʿ divorce took place in the context of a lawsuit concerning the wife's disobedience. If the wife moved out of the marital home, the husband could file a lawsuit to force her to return to the marital home. However, according to the published court decisions, such a case was difficult to win. Instead of forcing the wife to return to the husband, the judges often started the procedure for a khulʿ divorce.[103] Even if a judge decided that the wife should return to the husband, she could not be forced to

99 Interview with Ibn Khunayn in his house in Riyadh, 1 August 2018.

100 Interview with Muḥammad Jār Allāh in his office at the Riyadh Court of Appeal, 31 July 2018.

101 Interview with five lawyers of Manṣūr al-Dhufayrī law firm at the law firm's offices in Riyadh, 13 May 2018.

102 Court actions are generally free of charge in Saudi Arabia. See Shaʿīshaʿ, *Al-Tanẓīm al-qaḍāʾī al-jadīd*, 459.

103 In some of the published court cases, however, the wife agreed to return to the marital home after financial incentives from the husband See, for instance, the decision of the Badāʾiʿ General Court, decision Nr. 34121653 (confirmed by the Qaṣīm Court of Appeal on 10.4.1435/11.2.2014).

do so, since according to the Code of Enforcement (Niẓām at-Tanfīdh), such a decision could not be enforced.[104] However, the judgement could deprive the wife of her alimony since she would be officially declared disobedient.

3.2.2 The Role of the Arbitrators

The khulʿ procedure at court usually started with the appointment of the two arbitrators (*ḥakamān*). The institution of the arbitrators has its roots in the Quran. In Q 4:35, it says,

> If you fear that a couple may break up, appoint one arbiter from his family and one from hers. Then, if the couple wants to put things right, God will bring about a reconciliation between them: He is all knowing, all aware.

The arbitrators' task is to reconcile the couple. However, they can also negotiate the divorce. Most premodern jurists deduced from the clear wording of the Quranic verse that the arbitrators have to be members of the spouses' families. Prior to the codification, Saudi judges asked the parties who they want to nominate as arbitrators. Some couples chose to contact professional marriage counsellors. For instance, in one case from Tabūk, the couple unanimously nominated a nonprofit family counselling center as arbitrator.[105] In other cases, the mediation center (*qism al-ṣulḥ*) at the court, an institution that assists the judges often in family disputes, was nominated as an arbitrator for both parties.[106] However, according to the head of the mediation center at the family court in Riyadh, many spouses still preferred to nominate arbitrators from their families.[107]

The arbitrators' decision was not binding for the spouses. For instance, in the aforementioned case from Tabūk, the family counselling center concluded that it was best to end the marriage, due to the hostility between the spouses. The counselling center suggested that the wife should only return a bit more than half of her dowry, but the husband refused the center's decision and demanded that the wife give back all of her dowry.[108]

104 Article 75 of the 1433/2012 Code of Enforcement.

105 Tabūk General Court, case Nr. 34116147 (confirmed by the Tabūk Court of Appeal on 1.3.1435/3.1.2014).

106 See, for instance, ʿUnayza General Court, decision Nr. 3486983 (confirmed by the Qasīm Court of Appeal on 8.2.1435/12.12.2013).

107 Visit of the Riyadh Family Court, 9 August 2018.

108 Tabūk General Court, case Nr. 34116147 (confirmed by the Tabūk Court of Appeal on 1.3.1435/3.1.2014).

Even if one or both spouses refused the arbitrators' decision, the judges nevertheless often followed it, especially when the mediation center at court served as arbitrator. When all efforts to reconcile the couple failed, the mediation center at court almost always proposed that the marriage should be ended and suggested the amount of the dowry that the wife had to pay back. If the couple had been married for a long time and the wife's responsibility for the divorce was unclear, the center often decided that the wife did not have to return her dowry at all.

Sometimes one of the spouses rejected the arbitration procedure entirely. In another case from Tabūk, for instance, the wife refused to appoint an arbitrator because she was determined to separate from her husband. The judge then appointed the mediation center as arbitrator and listed the wife's refusal as one more sign of the failure of the marriage.[109]

3.2.3 The Judges' Legal Reasoning

In their decisions, the judges did not always directly refer to the Saudi scholars we discussed earlier, even though the judges followed them in their legal reasoning. Instead, they usually started their verdicts by quoting the prophetic account of the story of Thābit bin Qays and his wife. In addition, the majority of decisions referred to premodern fiqh writings. For instance, one judge quoted Ibn al-ʿArabī (d. 1149), who wrote,

> Long term contracts [*ʿuqūd al-abdān*] are only concluded through agreement, harmony [*taʾāluf*] and good relations [*ḥusn al-taʿāshur*] [between the parties]. If this is missing, [only] the outer appearance of the contract remains. It is [thus] beneficial to dissolve [the contract] by appropriate means.[110]

Other judges, however, also quoted the decision of the Council of Senior Scholars or referred to the fatwas of Muḥammad bin Ibrāhīm.[111] In addition, the judges often used more general principles of Islamic jurisprudence, especially when they referred to the wife's disobedience. The published court

109 Tabūk General Court, case Nr. 34134206 (confirmed by the Tabūk Court of Appeal on 29.7.1435/29.5.2014).

110 Ibn al-ʿArabī, *Aḥkām al-Qurʾān* (Beirut: Dār al-Kutub al-ʿIlmiyya, n.d.), 1:541. See also Tabūk General Court, case Nr. 34134206 (confirmed by the Tabūk Court of Appeal on 29.7.1435/29.5.2014).

111 See, for example, Dammam General Court, case Nr. 33450534 (confirmed by the Court of Appeal of the Eastern Provinces on 26.2.1434/9.1.2013).

decisions show that the women usually had left the marital home a couple of months, in some cases even some years, before the court trial.

The wife's disobedience, the judges often argued, contradicted the goal of the marriage.[112] Some judges went one step further and, like Ibn Khunayn, maintained that an unhappy marriage constitutes a form of harm (*ḍarar*) for the wife.[113] Since Islamic jurisprudence demands that all harm should be avoided, the judges considered it imperative to dissolve the marriage. A judge from Riyadh even wrote that an unhappy marriage violated the wife's dignity (*karāma*).[114] In a couple of cases, the judges simply copied arguments from the Council of Senior Scholars' decision without indicating it. Sometimes the judges also presented less technical arguments: a judge from Dammam, for instance, stated in his verdict that marriage was a matter of the heart, which could not be forced.[115]

Once a judge had decided that the marriage should be ended, the question of compensation arose. Whereas earlier Saudi scholars had left the determination of the compensation largely in the hands of the individual judge, Ibn Khunayn developed criteria for the judges to decide the wife's compensation, which some judges quoted.[116] For Ibn Khunayn, the amount of the compensation depended on the spouses' fault in the divorce. If none of the spouses could be determined to be responsible for the divorce, the wife only had to pay back half of what she had received from the husband. If the judge concluded that the husband had caused the divorce, the wife normally did not have to return any assets.[117]

Women regularly accused their husbands of serious wrongdoing, mostly physical or psychological mistreatment. If there was evidence for the allegations, the wife was granted a divorce without having to pay compensation; however, in most cases, the allegations could not be proven.

112 See, for instance, Riyadh General Court, decision Nr. 3438447 (confirmed by the Riyadh Court of Appeal on 7.5.1434/19.3.2013).

113 See, for instance, 'Unayza General Court, decision Nr. 3486983 (confirmed by the Qasīm Court of Appeal on 8.2.1435/12.12.2013).

114 Riyadh General Court, decision Nr. 3460936 (confirmed by the Riyadh Court of Appeal on 18.7.1434/28.5.2013).

115 Dammam General Court, case Nr. 33450534 (confirmed by the Court of Appeal of the Eastern Provinces on 26.2.1434/9.1.2013).

116 See, for instance, 'Unayza General Court, decision Nr. 3486983 (confirmed by the Court of Appeal of the Qasīm Region on 8.2.1435/12.12.2013).

117 Āl Khunayn, *Al-Khulʿ bi-ṭalab al-zawja*, 166.

3.2.4 The Widespread Scepticism of Khulʿ Divorce

Even though forced khulʿ divorce was a standard procedure at Saudi courts, many ʿulamāʾ still regarded it with scepticism. The jurists often quoted a narration according to which the Prophet said, "Any woman who asks her husband for divorce without reason will not be allowed to smell paradise." The ʿulamāʾ demanded that a wife should have patience (*ṣabr*) with her husband before demanding a divorce.[118] According to the court transcripts, judges regularly quoted the prophetic account in court hearings. For instance, in one case from Dammam, the judge instructed a woman that it was ḥarām to ask for a divorce when no harm is caused.[119] In another case, a judge in Medina reminded the wife that patience in marriage was among the best virtues.[120]

It is crucial to note that the possibility of forced khulʿ divorce was not only significant in cases in which the husband was forced to consent to the divorce, but its prime importance lay in the power it gave to women in their marriages. Men could not anymore prevent the dissolution of the marriage, which put the women in a better bargaining position.[121]

---

118 This view does not originate only from Saudi customs but can also be found in premodern jurisprudence. See Al-Bahūtī, *Al-Rawḍ al-murbiʿ sharḥ zād al-mustaqniʿ* (Cairo: Dār al-Ḥadīth, 1425/2004), 344.

119 Dammam General Court, case Nr. 33450534 (confirmed by the Court of Appeal of the Eastern Provinces on 26.2.1434/9.1.2013).

120 Medina General Court, case Nr. 3426340 (confirmed by the Mecca Court of Appeal on 22.5.1434/3.4.2013).

121 This is illustrated by one of my experiences at the family court in Riyadh, where I had the chance to attend a mediation (*ṣulḥ*) session. In many family law cases, mediation is either required before a lawsuit is filed or judges send the two parties to the mediation center (*qism al-ṣulḥ*) at the court in order to find a mutual agreement. The setting of the mediation session resembled a court hearing. The shaykh was sitting in the middle of the room behind a huge desk. Before him, the wife, dressed in niqāb, and the husband, who was wearing the traditional Saudi dress sat on chairs. The wife wanted the divorce, her husband, however, claimed to still be in love with her. He wanted her to stay with him and refused to pronounce the divorce. The wife seemed to be familiar with the basics of Islamic family law. She accused her husband of drinking and stated that he neglected the prayers. Both accusations theoretically are enough reason for the dissolution of the marriage. Several high ranking Saudi ʿulamāʾ even hold that someone who does not pray can be considered an infidel (*kāfir*). In the course of the ṣulḥ session, the shaykh tried to convince both parties separately that they should find a solution for their problems. The woman should give her husband another chance, the husband, on the other hand, should try to behave better or pronounce ṭalāq. Both declined, and the women made clear that she did not want, under any circumstances, to continue the marriage. By the end of the session, the shaykh had told the husband that there were two options for him: his wife was determined to get a divorce, and he could do nothing to prevent that. So, he might as well divorce her now. Additionally, the shaykh quoted from the Qur'an. This left an impression, and the husband promised to later pronounce the ṭalāq in front of the court.

The scepticism towards khulʿ divorces was reflected in the numbers: although khulʿ divorces had become more popular over the last decades, the numbers still remained much lower than that of ṭalāq divorces.[122] According to Al-Arabiya, eighty-one ṭalāq divorces were registered every day in the kingdom in the year 1432/2010–11, but only four khulʿ divorces per day.[123]

4 Conclusion

The two case studies illustrate that legal change can occur silently over decades, entirely through the jurists' discourse and without significant public debate. In many cases, Saudi jurists developed the law in ways that conflict with the consensus (*ijmāʿ*) as it is recognized by the four major schools of Islamic jurisprudence. Usually, the jurists relate and continue premodern debates, often inside the Ḥanbalī school.

The development of the death penalty for drug smuggling shows that not only can the law change without the government's interference, but sometimes the discourse of the jurists can also serve as the basis for state law reform. Similar developments can be seen in Islamic family law, which will be discussed in the next chapter. The case study on drug smuggling also illustrates that for many judges, Islamic jurisprudence is still the main point of reference, even in legal questions addressed by codified law.

Legal change in Saudi Arabia does not follow one single direction. On the one hand, it can strengthen the position of women, as seen in the case of khulʿ divorce, and to some extent, in child custody. On the other hand, it can undermine fundamental human rights and lead to harsh criminal punishments, as illustrated by the case study on drug smuggling.[124]

---

122 Observers argue that Saudi women today know more about their possibilities for divorce, which has led to a rise in khulʿ divorces in the last years See www.arabnews.com/saudi-arabia/news/814866 [last access: 20 November 2022].

123 However, this includes not only forced but also consensual khulʿ divorces. The article can be accessed under bit.ly/2s1mB6q [last access: 30 September 2022].

124 A similar development can be witnessed in the question of unlawful intercourse (*zinā*). While premodern ʿulamāʾ did not accept the pregnancy of an unmarried women as evidence for zinā, Saudi scholars argued that the pregnancy fulfilled the requirements for the ḥadd punishment. See Krell, "Saudi Arabia," 311.

CHAPTER 7

What Happens When Islamic Law Is Codified

1 Introduction

On March 8, 2022, International Women's Day, Saudi Crown Prince Muhammad bin Salman announced that a codification of Islamic family law had been approved by the Council of Ministers and would be enacted in ninety days. The new personal status law (Niẓām al-Aḥwāl al-Shakhṣiyya, PSL), the prince stated, represented a "quantum leap" (*naqla nawʿiyya kubrā*) for the Saudi judiciary.[1]

Saudi government officials praised the codification as a significant reform of Islamic family law, highlighting that it ensures the "protection" (*ḥifāẓ*) of the rights of Saudi women, children, and the family more generally. Moreover, the new law, they said, safeguards human rights (*ḥuqūq al-insān*). Yet, at the same time, government officials emphasized that the codification does not deviate from Islamic law. Instead, the government chose those opinions (*aqwāl*, sing. *qawl*) from the Islamic legal tradition that were believed to best fit the current social and economic situation in the kingdom. The Minister of Justice at the time, Walīd al-Samaʿānī, emphasized that the new law was based on the principles of jurisprudence (*maqāṣid al-sharīʿa*) and incorporated the best modern judicial practices and teachings while acknowledging the changes and challenges of modernity.[2]

Although Saudi government officials and many commentators outside Saudi Arabia regarded the new code as the start of a new era of law in Saudi Arabia, it generated little visible interest within the Saudi legal community. The scholarly establishment largely remained silent, and commentators on Twitter only vaguely criticized some aspects of the new law. The lack of criticism was not surprising, given the current state of freedom of speech in the kingdom. Nevertheless, it was noteworthy that scholarly institutions, such as the Council of Senior Scholars, which seldom miss an opportunity to formally praise the Saudi leadership, refrained from commenting on the law. Those jurists who commented on the law remained very brief. For instance, Saʿūd bin ʿAbd Allāh al-Muʿjab, the general prosecutor of Saudi Arabia and a member of the Council

1 This was reported by several Saudi newspapers. See, for instance, the article in the Mecca Newspaper, https://bit.ly/3W2gjfz [last access: 24 January 2023].

2 https://www.okaz.com.sa/news/local/2099481 [last access: 16 January 2023].

of Senior Scholars, released a short statement praising the Saudi leadership and merely superficially pointing to the alleged benefits of the new law.[3]

This chapter explores whether the codification constitutes a departure from the way Islamic family law was conceptualized and applied in the kingdom before the new law was issued. To do this, it analyzes (1) how the codification of family law came into being and (2) how it relates to the writings of Saudi jurists and court practice before the codification.

2 How the New Code Came into Being

The new code law put an end to the almost 100-year-long debate in the kingdom on the codification of Islamic law, during which several attempts had been made to codify the law. In the early twentieth century, King ʿAbd al-ʿAzīz planned to establish a committee of religious scholars, which should choose rulings from all four schools of Islamic jurisprudence and publish them in the form of a modern law code. Since the nineteenth century, Islamic scholars outside Saudi Arabia had been publishing compilations of Islamic law, which were mostly called *majallāt* (sing. *majalla*). The most important compilation was the Ottoman majalla (*Majallat al-aḥkām al-ʿadliyya*), which was published and enforced in most parts of the Ottoman empire between 1870 and 1877.[4] It was a remarkable effort to transform late Ḥanafī doctrine into a systematic and comprehensive law code.[5]

The idea of a systematic codification was not new to Ottoman jurists, since European-style codes had already been introduced in some areas of the law. The majalla, however, was the first effort to codify the core of Islamic private law. Family law was left out, but soon other compilations were created to fill that void. Most importantly, it was the work of the Egyptian jurist Qadrī Bāshā,

3 See an article in the Saudi newspaper Sabq, available on the newspaper's homepage https://bit.ly/3WfC2Rm [last access: 16 January 2023].

4 Asad, *Formations of the Secular*, 211.

5 To what extent the majalla still represents Islamic law is disputed among historians of Islamic law. While Schacht argued that the majalla was a secular, not an Islamic code, other scholars see it more as a digest of Islamic law than a code in the European sense. For an overview over the literature on the Ottoman majalla see Guy Burak, "Codification, Legal Borrowing and the Localization of 'Islamic law,'" in *Routledge Handbook of Islamic Law*, ed. Khaled Abou El Fadl, Ahmad Atif Ahmad, and Said Fares Hassan (London: Routledge, 2019), 394.

who compiled Ḥanafī family law. Qadrī Bāshā's work never had any binding effect but served as the primary source for the 1917 Ottoman family code.[6]

In Saudi Arabia, King ʿAbd al-ʿAzīz's plan to create a compilation of Islamic law failed, apparently due to the complexity of the project.[7] After the king's efforts proved unsuccessful, Saudi judge Aḥmad al-Qārī decided to continue the king's project and started to work on a compilation of Islamic law in 1925. Instead of incorporating other schools of Islamic jurisprudence, as imagined by King ʿAbd al-ʿAzīz, al-Qārī decided to limit the compilation to those Ḥanbalī books that were mentioned in the 1928 decree of the Higher Judicial Authority.[8] Al-Qārī died before he could finish the compilation, but his work was later finished by two other scholars, ʿAbd al-Wahhāb Abū Sulaymān and Aḥmad Ibrāhīm ʿAlī.[9] They published al-Qārī's extensive compilation of the rulings of the Ḥanbalī School in 1927. Although al-Qārī's compilation never had any binding effect, it is still popular among Saudi judges and lawyers as an introduction to Ḥanbalī law due to its easy accessibility.

Inspired by the spread of comprehensive codifications in the region, more and more Saudis demanded a binding law code in the subsequent decades. The debate reached its peak when the Council of Senior Scholars discussed and finally refused any form of binding law in 2000.[10] King Fahd had turned to the Council in order to legitimize his plan to codify Islamic law. However, the decision of the Council was by no means unanimous. In several statements, six of the Council's twenty-one scholars supported the king's plan. Among them were such influential figures as Rāshid bin Khunayn, a relative of ʿAbd Allāh bin Khunayn, and Ṣāliḥ bin Ghaṣūn. Interestingly, the vast majority of the dissenters had worked in the judiciary before they became members of the Council.[11] Whereas the Council's final decision did not refer to fiqh literature,

---

6 Hans-Georg Ebert, *Die Qadrî-Pâshâ-Kodifikation* (Frankfurt am Main: Peter Lang, 2010), 19.

7 Aḥmad bin ʿAbd Allāh al-Qārī, *Majallat al-aḥkām al-sharʿiyya* (Jeddah: Tiḥāma, 1401/1981), 29.

8 Ibid., 30. See Chapter 2.

9 Al-Fāyiz, *Taqnīn al-aḥkām al-qaḍāʾiyya*, 48.

10 The decision is published together with the dissenting opinions in al-Amāna al-ʿĀmma li-Hayʾat Kibār al-ʿUlamāʾ, Abḥāth hayʾat kibār al-ʿulamāʾ, 3:115–271. Some newspaper reports mention that the Senior Scholars had already refused codification in 1973. However, the decision does not seem to have been published and there is no information about it.

11 This was pointed out by Nāṣir bin ʿAbd Allāh al-Maymān in a lecture on the codification of Islamic law, available on YouTube: www.youtube.com/watch?v=LR6-EaA3OYI&t=942s, min 1 [last access: 21 April 2023].

many of the dissenters built their case on the writings of various premodern and contemporary jurists.[12]

As a result of the Council's decision, King Fahd refrained from codifying Islamic law.[13] In the early 2010s, the discussion on codification again intensified. Around the year 2012, rumors spread that the Council of Senior Scholars had released a new decision on the possibility of codification.[14] However, according to Ibn Khunayn, who at the time was a member of the Council, the senior scholars did not release a second decision.[15]

Despite the refusal of a binding codification of Islamic law by the Council of Senior Scholars, King ʿAbd Allah formed a committee of Saudi jurists in 2010 which was tasked with developing a compilation (*tadwīn*) of Islamic law. By 2018, a compilation of the major areas of civil and criminal law had been completed and was in the editing process but not announced publicly. The compilation was meant to be binding for the judges.[16] The jurists of the drafting committee had continued from where past efforts to codify and systematize Islamic law in Saudi Arabia had stopped: In commercial matters, they based their code mainly on Aḥmad al-Qārī's compilation of Ḥanbalī law. In family, inheritance, and criminal law, they aimed to codify the prevailing practice.[17]

However, in February 2021, the Crown Prince refused the committee's proposition. The code did not satisfy the needs of the Saudi people, Muhammad bin Salman announced. Instead, he promised that family, private, and criminal law codes would be issued by the end of the same year.[18] The new codes

12 The dissenting opinions can be found in al-Amāna al-ʿĀmma li-Hayʾat Kibār al-ʿUlamāʾ, *Abḥāth hayʾat kibār al-ʿulamāʾ*, 3:240–71.

13 Instead of focusing on codifying the law, the Saudi government increasingly concentrated on other ways to establish legal security, as we saw in Chapter 4.

14 ʿAbd Allāh al-ʿIlmī, "Hadhihi al-fatwā ghayr mulzima," article in the newspaper Al-ʿArab, 17 December 2014. Available on the website of Al-ʿArab: bit.ly/2JLeDa5 [last access: 18 June 2022]; Saʿad al-Utaybī mentions these rumors, see al-ʿUtaybī, *Maqālāt fī al-siyāsa al-sharʿiyya*, 17. Frank Vogel writes that he also heard rumors that the Council issued a favorable decision in 2010. See Vogel, Saudi Business Law, 32.

15 Interview with Ibn Khunayn in his home in Riyadh, 24 April 2018. Manṣūr al-Ḥaydarī was also not aware of another decision by Council. Interview with Manṣūr al-Ḥaydarī in the Ministry of Justice in Riyadh, 8 May 2018.

16 This was confirmed to me in 2018 by Manṣūr al-Ḥaydarī, who was a member of the drafting committee. Interview with Manṣūr al-Ḥaydarī in the Ministry of Justice in Riyadh, 8 May 2018.

17 Interview with Manṣūr al-Ḥaydarī and Bashār al-Mufadda in the Ministry of Justice in Riyadh, 8 May 2018.

18 The crown prince's statement was made public by the Saudi Press Agency, see www.spa.gov.sa/2187777 [last access: 15 February 2021].

should be "modern" codifications, which include "international modern court practices" (*mumārasāt al-qaḍā'iyya al-dawliyya al-ḥadītha*).[19] Of course, the king added, the code could not violate the fundamentals of Islamic law but remained silent on the details. A bit more than a year later, the PSL was issued as the first of the announced codifications of Islamic law in Saudi Arabia.[20]

Very little is known about the law-making process. Before the PSL was issued, a draft law (Mashrūʿ Niẓām al-Aḥwāl al-Shakhṣiyya) was promulgated, but no details on the sources used or people involved were published. As we will see, the enacted PSL largely followed the draft but deviated from it in important aspects.

3 Is There Anything New in the 2022 Family Code?

3.1 *The Ministry of Justice's Claims*

Shortly after the new code was issued, the Ministry of Justice and other government officials highlighted what they saw as its major accomplishments.[21] Among them were several improvements in procedural matters. It is now mandatory to register divorce (*ṭalāq*), reconciliation after a divorce (*rajaʿa*), and other changes in a person's personal status. The new law also allows women to register their divorce, which is of high practical importance.

But the Ministry highlighted that the law also introduced new rulings in a range of legal questions. In the following, I will investigate the most commonly made claims to analyse to what extent they deviate from Saudi court practice before codification.[22] Surprisingly, Saudi officials did not mention inheritance law in their announcements of the new law, which makes up a large part of the PSL. Instead, they focused on marriage, divorce, and child custody.

The most widespread claims were the introduction of (1) a minimum age of marriage, (2) new ways to prove paternity, (3) a new ruling on the triple ṭalāq,

19 https://www.okaz.com.sa/news/local/2099337 [last access: 31 March 2022].

20 As of early 2023, the other codifications of Islamic law have not yet been issued.

21 The list was shared on social media but also in newspapers. See, for example, the news website Mubasher https://bit.ly/3irmqMM.

22 My investigations into the new law are partly based on some of my earlier work on Islamic law in Saudi Arabia. See Dörthe Engelcke, Dominik Krell, and Nadjma Yassari, "Underage Marriage: Legal and Social Practice in Muslim Jurisdictions," *Arab Law Quarterly* (forthcoming); Krell, "Saudi Arabia"; and Dominik Krell, "Was kann man von Saudi-Arabien für die Entwicklung des islamischen Familienrechts in Europa lernen?" in *Migration und Heimatrecht*, ed. Irene Schneider, Hatem Elliesie, and Silvia Tellenbach (Wiesbaden: Harrassowitz, 2022).

(4) improvements of the rights of children in custody law, and (5) women's right to divorce on their own will in some instances. We have already touched on several of these issues in earlier chapters, which is not surprising given that they are among the most contentious issues in Islamic family law today.

3.2 *The Introduction of a Minimum Age of Marriage*

In general, Islamic jurisprudence does not specify a minimum age of marriage. According to the four major schools, a girl and a boy can be married well before puberty. However, this does not imply that sexual intercourse is permitted. The marriage is only consummated once the wife has been handed over to her husband following the marriage ceremony, which typically occurs after she has reached puberty.[23]

Saudi scholars have long permitted minor marriage. When asked about the marriage between a 14-year-old boy and a girl aged 10 to 14, the Permanent Committee responded that such a marriage was valid if the marriage guardians agreed.[24] In another fatwa, the Committee stated that there was no reason why a marriage of a 12-year-old child should be prohibited.[25] Referring to plans to institute a minimum age of marriage in the Emirates, Ibn Bāz condemned any restrictions on marriages of children under the age of 18, emphasizing that there would not be any age limit for marriage in Islamic law. He wrote that "nobody can legislate (*sharaʿ*) contrary to what God and the Prophet have legislated" and reminded the Emirati legislators of their obligation to adhere to Islamic law.[26]

The Saudi government and the Saudi Human Rights Organisation (Hay'at Ḥuqūq al-Insān) have worked for decades towards the prohibition of minor marriages.[27] Plans to introduce a minimum age of marriage were presented by the Ministry of Justice around 2009. The plans faced severe criticism from leading Saudi ʿulamāʾ. ʿAbd al-Raḥmān bin Nāṣir al-Barrāk, a former professor at Riyadh's Imām University, strongly urged the Saudi government to reconsider

23 For more information on minor marriage in Islam and in the legislation of other Arab countries, see Engelcke, Krell, and Yassari, "Underage Marriage"; and Dominik Krell, "The Role of Jurists in Contemporary Islamic Family Law," *Arab Law Quarterly* (forthcoming).

24 Aḥmad bin ʿAbd al-Rāziq al-Dawīsh, *Fatāwā al-Lajna al-Dāʾima li-l-Buḥūth al-ʿIlmiyya wa-l-Iftāʾ* (Riyadh: Riʾāsat Idārat al-Buḥūth al-ʿIlmiyya wa-l-Iftāʾ, n.d.), 9:16.

25 Ibid.

26 Ibn Bāz, *Majmūʿ fatāwā wa-maqālāt mutanawwiʿa*, 4:126–28.

27 See ʿAbd al-Muḥsin bin Ḥamd al-ʿAbād's polemic reaction against the government's plans. The fatwa is printed in ʿAbd al-Raḥmān bin Saʿd al-Shithrī, *Ḥukm taqnīn manʿ tazwīj al-fatayāt aqall min 18 sana wa-taḥdīd sinn al-zawāj* (Al-Fayyūm: Dār al-Falāḥ. 1431/2010), 104.

its plans, since Islamic law did not allow, he said, for such a restriction. Social problems caused by minor marriages, he argued, should be addressed through Islamic law rather than through the introduction of positive law (*qānūn waḍʿī*).[28] ʿAbd al-Muḥsin bin Ḥamd al-ʿAbād, a professor at Medina University, emphasised that not only were minor marriages permitted but there were also no restrictions on the age gap between the spouses.[29] He mentioned Muḥammad bin Ibrāhīm, who allegedly married two minor girls when he was old, although al-ʿAbād did not specify their exact age. Because Islamic law did not set a minimum age of marriage, al-ʿAbād held that no one would be allowed to pass any legislation that forbids minor marriage.[30] Ṣāliḥ bin Fawzān al-Fawzān even accused journalists who advocated for a minimum age of marriage of being either ignorant of the rulings of Islamic law or of opposing them.[31]

Other Saudi scholars are more critical of minor marriage and, more specifically, of the marriage of prepubescent children. Those jurists point to the views of some early scholars, such as Ibn Shubrama (d. 761), who held that minors should not be married at all. According to Ḥātim bin ʿĀrif al-ʿAwnī, a lecturer at Mecca's Umm al-Qurā university, the early jurists' opinions demonstrated that there is no consensus (*ijmāʿ*) in Islamic jurisprudence on minor marriage. In a fatwa, al-ʿAwnī referred to the debate on "triple ṭalāq," which will be discussed later in this chapter, where some scholars falsely assumed a consensus and thereby ignored Ibn Taymiyya's important minority opinion. Al-ʿAwnī argued that even if there was a consensus in Islamic jurisprudence that allowed the marriage of minors, this would not necessarily mean that instituting a minimum age of marriage was in conflict with Islamic law. In other questions, Saudi ʿulamāʾ (he explicitly addressed Ṣāliḥ bin Fawzān al-Fawzān) would have used the concept of "blocking the means" (*sadd al-dharāiʿ*) to declare an otherwise permissible action forbidden in order to prevent unlawful or undesirable actions from taking place.[32] The same, al-ʿAwnī asserted, could be argued in the case of the introduction of a minimum age of marriage.[33]

The most prominent Saudi scholar to advocate for restrictions on minor marriage was Ibn ʿUthaymīn. He argued that although a boy could be married off before puberty by his father, a girl could only be married in extraordinary

---

28 The fatwa is printed in ibid., 94.

29 The fatwa is printed in ibid., 99.

30 Ibid., 100.

31 The fatwa is printed in ibid., 88.

32 The most famous example of this is the ban on female driving.

33 The fatwa can be found on al-ʿAwnī's homepage: https://www.dr-alawni.com/articles.php?show=61 [last access: 21 November 2022].

cases when the marriage was in her best interest. In his *Al-Sharḥ al-mumtiʿ*, Ibn ʿUthaymīn wrote,

> Some ʿulamāʾ, however, state that there is consensus that he can marry her off, relying on the ḥadīth of ʿĀʾisha, and I have stated the difference. Ibn Shubrama, [one] of the renown jurists, said: He can never marry off a girl that has not reached puberty. Because if we say that consent is a requirement [for marriage], then her consent cannot be considered. [If] we say that a pubescent girl cannot be forced, then this is even more so. And this is the correct opinion. The father cannot marry off his daughter until she reaches puberty. If she reaches puberty, he can only marry her off if she agrees.
>
> But if we assume that the father is of the opinion that the groom is equal (*kufʾ*), and he [himself] is old, and fears that if he dies, the girl will find herself under the guardianship of her brothers, who abuse her and marry her off at their convenience, this is not in her best interests. If he sees that it is in the girl's interest that he marries her off to an equal [groom], he can do this without a doubt. However, she can choose when she grows up. If she wishes, she can say: I do not want this and I do not need it.[34]

Other Saudi scholars argue that, while minor marriages were not prohibited, the Saudi government could restrict them. Ṣāliḥ bin ʿAwād al-Maghāmsī, for example, a popular scholar and imam, argued that the introduction of a minimum age of marriage was a question of siyāsa sharʿiyya. As a result, the Saudi king could impose restrictions if he considered this to be in the public benefit, most importantly by prohibiting the registration of such marriages. However, the king could not declare minor marriages to be void.[35]

In December 2019, the Ministry of Justice sent a circular to the courts. It prohibited the registration of a marriage in which one of the spouses was under eighteen. The ministry had issued implementing regulations for the Child Protection Law (Niẓām Ḥimāyat al-Ṭifl), according to which it must be assured that the marriage of a person under eighteen, whether male or female, does not lead to any damages and is in the minor's best interests. Referring to the Child Protection Law, the Ministry wrote to the courts,

---

34 Ibn ʿUthaymīn, *Al-Sharḥ al-mumtiʿ*, 12:58.

35 The shaykh gave a fatwa on the question of minor marriage in his TV show Al-Abwāb al-Mutafarriqa. See https://www.youtube.com/watch?v=2fXIfEYmCe8 [last access: 21 November 2022].

> In response, there have been inquiries regarding the marriages of persons under the age of eighteen. For this, we want to inform the assistants (*ma'dhūnūn*) allocated to the courts to not register any marriages of persons who are under the age of eighteen and to refer those who reject this to the competent court to execute what appears in the abovementioned paragraph and to dismiss those assistants who do not comply with this.[36]

The PSL builds on the Ministry's directive and the Child Protection Law. Article 9 of the PSL stipulates,

> The registration of a marriage contracted by a person under the age of eighteen is prohibited. The court allows such a minor, male or female, to marry if he or she is of age, and it has been determined that the marriage is in his or her best interests. The [implementing] regulations to this law determine the requirements and the necessary procedure.

Hence, the PSL does not completely forbid underage marriage. Children under eighteen can still marry with the permission of the court. Moreover, the new law does not state that underage marriages cannot be contracted, since it only prohibits the registration of such a marriage. In Saudi Arabia, as in most other Arab countries,[37] a marriage can be contracted without the involvement of state institutions. This type of marriage is usually called customary marriage (*zawāj ʿurfī*). In theory, customary marriages entail the same legal effects as officially registered marriages. Because the conclusion of underage marriages as such is not illegal, minors can marry early and register their marriage later.[38]

3.3 *New Technologies to Establish Paternity*

Paternity (*nasab*) plays a key role in Saudi society.[39] As Sebastian Maisel has pointed out, "the large majority of Saudi citizens define their identity first by

36 Circular letter (no. 13/t/7969 of 26.4.1441 (24.12.2019), The circular is available on the Ministry of Justice's homepage, see https://portaleservices.moj.gov.sa/TameemPortal/TameemList.aspx?id=37403 [last access: 26 October 2022].

37 See Engelcke, Krell, and Yassari, "Underage Marriage."

38 However, the failure to prove a marriage can result in harsh penalties. Saudi criminal law prohibits premarital sexual relations (*zinā*), which can include being alone with the opposite gender. In the past, Saudi judges have imposed harsh taʿzīr penalties in cases where opposite sexes simply met. Because the police can check marriage certificates, whether during an ongoing investigation or in public, not having registered the marriage can lead to accusations of premarital sexual relations.

39 For more information on filiation in Saudi Arabia prior to the codification, see Krell, "Saudi Arabia."

bloodlines and then geographically."[40] Despite the government's efforts to foster a national Saudi identity, such as through the celebration of the national day (*yawm al-waṭan*), the importance of tribal affiliation appears to have increased in recent decades. Navid Samin has documented the growing interest among Saudis in their family histories, primarily to confirm their tribal affiliation. Thousands of books and articles have been published to trace a particular family's ancestry.[41]

Paternity refers to the male bloodline, which is evident in the Saudi naming system that includes the father's and grandfather's names. As we will discuss later in this chapter, paternity also plays a crucial role in determining marriage equality (*kafāʾa*), which limits a woman's freedom to choose her spouse. Paternity is first and foremost established through a valid marriage. If a child is born into a valid marriage, the child is automatically attributed to the mother's husband, even if another man is the child's biological father. This is based on an account of the Prophet Muḥammad according to which a child is attributed to the marital bed (*firāsh*).[42] Children who do not have a legally recognized father often face discrimination. As a result, Saudi ʿulamāʾ are traditionally cautious about denying a child paternity.[43]

In the past, one way in which children born out of wedlock were attributed to a legal father was the assumption in premodern Islamic jurisprudence that women could be pregnant for several years. According to the Ḥanafīs, a pregnancy could last up to two years.[44] The Shāfiʿīs[45] and Ḥanbalīs[46] set the maximum length of pregnancy to four years, and Mālik, the founder of the eponymous school, even held that women could be pregnant for up to five years.[47] The Ẓāhirī jurist Ibn Ḥazm, on the other hand, criticized his contemporaries for believing rumors rather than facts and set one year as the maximum length of pregnancy. The jurists' rulings, however, allowed children born from extramarital relationships to claim paternity to either their mother's divorced or deceased husband.

---

40 Sebastian Maisel, "The New Rise of Tribalism in Saudi Arabia," *Nomadic Peoples* 18, no. 2 (2014): 103.

41 Navid Samin, *Of Sand or Soil: Genealogy and Tribal Belonging in Saudi Arabia* (Princeton: Princeton University Press, 2015).

42 Al-Bukhārī, *Ṣaḥīḥ al-Bukhārī*, 1686 (No. 6818).

43 Krell, "Saudi Arabia," 310.

44 Ibn ʿĀbidīn, *Radd al-muḥtār*, 5:230.

45 Al-Ramlī, *Nihāyat al-Muḥtāj* (Beirut: Dār al-Kutub al-ʿIlmiyya, 1424/2003), 7:112.

46 Al-Bahūtī, *Kashshāf al-qināʿ*, 5:414.

47 Ibn Rushd, *Bidāyat al-mujtahid wa-nihāyat al-muqtaṣid*, 3:219.

With the advent of modern medicine, the extensive lengths of pregnancy assumed in premodern Islamic jurisprudence were abolished in the Arab world and one year was widely accepted as the maximum length of pregnancy. Saudi Arabia was long an exception: several of the prominent twentieth-century Saudi jurists held that the maximum length of pregnancy could, in rare cases, far exceed nine months. Ṣāliḥ bin Fawzān al-Fawzān, for example, followed the traditional Ḥanbalī opinion and maintained that women could be pregnant for up to four years.[48] Ibn ʿUthaymīn even claimed that no maximum length of pregnancy could be determined:

> A child born more than four years [after the death of the testator] does categorically not inherit according to the [Ḥanbalī] school as four years is the maximum length of pregnancy. [But] the correct [opinion] is that it inherits if no sexual intercourse has taken place after the death of the testator, because the time of pregnancy can exceed four years, as it happens.[49]

Similarly, Muḥammad bin Ibrāhīm assumed that pregnancies could last longer than the four years maximum established in the Ḥanbalī school. He argued that no time limit could be set because justice must be upheld even in rare cases when women would be pregnant for more than nine months. Muḥammad bin Ibrāhīm cited Ibn al-Qayyim, who observed a case where a pregnancy lasted fourteen years and the child was born with all its teeth.[50]

Saudi courts have in the past assumed pregnancy lengths that contradict modern medicine. In 2009, Saudi jurist ʿAbd al-ʿAzīz al-Ghāmdī reported that there was still uncertainty among Saudi judges about the maximum length of pregnancy.[51] A year earlier, in 2008, a judge in Mecca attributed a boy that was born nearly two and a half years after the mother's husband had died to the deceased. He contended that the time between the death of the mother's husband and the birth of the boy did not exceed the maximum length of pregnancy in Islamic jurisprudence.[52] The PSL diverged from the Saudi jurists' ruling by introducing a maximum pregnancy length of ten months, from which the court may only deviate based on a medical report. Article 68, paragraph 2 states,

---

48 Ṣāliḥ bin Fawzān al-Fawzān, *Mulakhkhaṣ al-fiqhī* (Riyadh: Dār al-ʿĀṣima, 1423/2002), 2:416.

49 Ibn ʿUthaymīn, *Tashīl al-farāʾiḍ* (Riyadh: Dār al-Ṭayba, 1404/1983), 102.

50 Al-Qāsim, *Fatāwā wa-rasāʾil*, 11:151.

51 ʿAbd al-ʿAzīz bin ʿAlī al-Ghāmdī, "Aqall muddat al-ḥaml wa-aktharuha bayna al-fiqh wa-l-ṭibb," *Majallat al-ʿAdl* 43 (1430/2009): 221.

52 Mecca General Court, decision Nr. 11/29/16 (14.3.1429/22.3.2008).

> The maximum length of pregnancy is ten months. The court may decide differently based on a recognized medical report.

While the PSL aligns Islamic law with modern medicine, it deprives some children who would otherwise be considered born out of wedlock from claiming paternity. However, several judges confirmed to me that cases involving the maximum length of paternity were rare. When no financial rights were claimed, Saudi courts usually did not hear paternity disputes.[53]

The introduction of a maximum length of pregnancy is one way in which the orientation towards modern medicine affects children born out of wedlock. Another, and perhaps more important, development is the introduction of DNA testing. Saudi jurists long had a critical stance towards the use of DNA tests in paternity cases. They were concerned that DNA tests would call established family relationships into question, creating conflicts and unrest. As a result, DNA tests were generally not permitted to prove paternity prior to the PSL.

If the mother was married, her marriage was a more significant factor for determining paternity than a DNA test revealing that the mother's husband was not the biological father.[54] In case the mother was unmarried, the four major schools of Islamic jurisprudence agree that the child cannot be attributed to the biological father, even if the biological father acknowledges paternity. Important Saudi scholars, including the Permanent Committee[55] and the former Grand Muftis Muḥammad bin Ibrāhīm[56] and Ibn Bāz[57] shared the opinion that a child born out of wedlock can under no circumstances have a legal father.

Other Saudi scholars refer to Ibn Taymiyya and his disciple Ibn al-Qayyim. Both held that a child born out of wedlock can be attributed to the biological father, despite the prophetic account according to which a child can only be attributed to the marital bed.[58] The two scholars argued that the Prophet's statement only applied if the mother was married. If the parents were

53 Saudi jurists usually discuss the question of the maximum length of pregnancy in the context of succession law. It is therefore likely that disputes regarding the paternity of children arise in practice during the division of a person's estate.

54 See for instance Jeddah General Court, decision Nr. 3432937 (9.2.1434/23.12.2012). However, some Saudi judges have ordered DNA testing before starting the *liʿān* procedure, through which men can deny paternity.

55 Al-Dawīsh, *Fatāwā al-lajna al-dāʾima*, 20:389.

56 Al-Qāsim, *Fatāwā wa-rasāʾil*, 11:146.

57 Ibn Bāz, *Majmūʿ fatāwā*, 12:402.

58 Ibn Taymiyya, *Majmūʿat al-fatāwā*, 16:73; Ibn al-Qayyim, *Zād al-maʿād*, 5:381.

unmarried, no specification could be found in the revelation, and thus, there was no reason to deny the child legitimate descent. Furthermore, they pointed to an account according to which ʿUmar bin al-Khaṭṭāb attributed a child born out of wedlock to its biological father.[59]

In 2001, the appellate court in Riyadh ruled that a child born out of wedlock could not claim paternity from its biological father, referring to the majority opinion in Islamic law.[60] Twelve years later, in 2013, the Saudi High Court decided that, although children resulting from unlawful intercourse could not be attributed to the "fornicator" (*zānī*), children conceived before the parents were married could be attributed to the husband at the judge's discretion. However, the judge would have to consider the specifics of the individual case in order to do so.[61]

Due to the great stigma in Saudi society surrounding extramarital relationships, there are few court cases and even fewer published decisions involving children born out of wedlock. A high-ranking judge at the Riyadh Court of Appeal assured me that judges allowed a child born out of wedlock to claim paternity from its biological father, thereby following Ibn Taymiyya's and Ibn al-Qayyim's opinion. The judge explained that otherwise, the child would face serious difficulties through no fault of its own. The Saudi judiciary, however, did not make this public to maintain public morality.

The PSL now allows for DNA testing in cases involving the paternity of a child born out of wedlock. If a DNA test reveals that the father and child are biologically related, the child can be attributed to the father regardless of whether it was born as a result of unlawful sexual intercourse. Article 60 stipulates,

> In exceptional cases or if the paternity of the child is disputed or on the basis of a request from a competent body, the court decides to have a DNA test carried out. This is done on the basis of principles drawn up for this purpose. The court must rule on the basis of the final results of the DNA test. The court only decides [on the DNA test] if the following is fulfilled:
> 1. the child is of unknown descent
> 2. the age difference is such that paternity of the child is possible.

59 Ibn Taymiyya, *Majmūʿat al-fatāwā*, 16:73.

60 ʿAdnān bin Muḥammad al-Daqaylān, "Nasab walad al-zinā," *Majallat al-ʿAdl* 22 (1425/2004): 138.

61 Decision of the High Court Nr. 12/M (10.5.1435/12.3.2014), printed in Markaz al-Buḥūth, *Al-Mabādiʾ wa-l-qarārāt*, 194.

The PSL thus represents a shift from a social definition of paternity to a biological one, while also continuing the liberal stance towards children born out of wedlock advocated by Ibn Taymiyya and Ibn al-Qayyim.

3.4 *The Debate on "Triple Ṭalāq"*

Another new feature of the law, at least according to Saudi officials, is its ruling on the question of three divorce (*ṭalāq*) utterings in a close temporal context, a legal problem often referred to as "triple ṭalāq." The question of triple ṭalāq is one of the most disputed issues in Islamic legal history.[62] According to Islamic jurisprudence, a man can only pronounce ṭalāq to his wife three times in his lifetime; otherwise, the marriage is permanently divorced, and reconciliation is impossible. Whereas after the first and second ṭalāq, the husband can take the wife back during the waiting period (*ʿidda*) following the ṭalāq or marry her again (after the waiting period has expired), this is prohibited after the pronouncement of the third ṭalāq. The divorce then becomes irrevocable (*baynūna kubrā*). The only way to overcome the marriage prohibition is for the woman to marry another man, consummate the marriage, and then obtain a divorce. Scholars and laymen alike have sought ways to circumvent this strict rule throughout Islamic legal history. In particular, attempts have been made to soften the requirement that the marriage must be consummated with a third party.[63]

According to the unanimous view of the four major schools of jurisprudence, the three ṭalāq utterings do not need to be made separately in time to be effective. The divorce also becomes irrevocable if the ṭalāq utterings occur at one concurrence (*majlis*), that is, in a close temporal connection. It also makes no difference whether the triple ṭalāq is pronounced in a single sentence (*anti ṭāliq thalāthan*; "you are divorced three times") or three times in a row (*anti ṭāliq, anti ṭāliq, anti ṭāliq*; "you are divorced, you are divorced, you are divorced").[64] In practice, this means that a single emotional dispute can be the end of an otherwise happy marriage.

Ibn Taymiyya opposed the strict rule and recognized the triple ṭalāq as a single ṭalāq.[65] Like scholars before him, Ibn Taymiyya believed that the triple ṭalāq constitutes a sin.[66] However, he cited several accounts to show that

62 The following part is based on Krell, "Was kann man von Saudi-Arabien lernen."

63 Yossef Rapoport, *Marriage, Money, and Divorce in Medieval Islamic Society* (Cambridge: Cambridge University Press, 2005), 94.

64 Munir, "Triple Ṭalāq," 32.

65 Ibn Taymiyya, *Majmūʿat al-fatāwā*, 16:73; Ibn al-Qayyim, *Zād al-maʿād*, 33:8–9.

66 Carolyn Baugh, "Ibn Taymiyya's Feminism?: Imprisonment and the Divorce Fatwās," in *Muslima Theology: The Voices of Muslim Women Theologians*, ed. Ednan Aslan, Marcia Hermansen, and Elif Medeni (Berlin: Peter Lang, 2013), 185.

during the time of the Prophet and the first Muslims, the triple ṭalāq was considered merely one divorce uttering.[67] Contemporaries of Ibn Taymiyya were highly critical of his opinion. Reportedly, his stance on the triple ṭalāq even led to his imprisonment in the citadel in Damascus.[68]

Ibn Taymiyya's opinion had a significant influence on Saudi ʿulamāʾ, but there was longstanding disagreement about it among them. In one letter, Muḥammad bin Ibrāhīm wrote that the practice in Saudi courts was to count each utterance as a separate ṭalāq.[69] In a subsequent letter, he criticized a judge at the court in Mecca for stating that three ṭalāq utterances should be counted as a single ṭalāq.[70] Later, the Council of Senior Scholars also issued a ruling in which the Council's jurists followed the majority opinion.[71]

Other Saudi scholars were sceptical of the majority view in Islamic jurisprudence. Ibn Bāz, for example, distinguished based on the man's intention. Did he really want to pronounce the ṭalāq three times, or had he only uttered the divorce several times when in fact he only wanted a single ṭalāq? Ibn Bāz argued that if the husband pronounced the divorce three times in a row, this should be seen as an irrevocable divorce, but the triple ṭalāq in one expression (*anti ṭāliq thalāthan*) should be considered a single ṭalāq. Thereby, Ibn Bāz followed Ibn Taymiyya's minority opinion with qualifications. Frank Vogel reports a court case from 1983 in which a couple, after the husband had pronounced the ṭalāq three times in one sentence, sought to prevent a final divorce. The couple first obtained a fatwa from Ibn Bāz and later went to court. In his decision, the judge followed Ibn Bāz's fatwa. He told Vogel that if the couple had come directly to him, he would have been obliged to follow the majority view.[72]

Ibn ʿUthaymīn, on the other hand, closely adhered to Ibn Taymiyya, leading to a conflict between him and Ibn Bāz. In a letter to Ibn ʿUthaymīn, Ibn Bāz urged him to depart from his opinion.[73] Ibn Bāz, who was already Grand Mufti at this time, had received a court decision from the court in Dammam.[74]

---

67 Munir, "Triple Ṭalāq," 37–40.

68 Baugh, "Ibn Taymiyya's Feminism?," 184.

69 Al-Qāsim, *Fatāwā wa-rasāʾil*, 11:30.

70 Ibid., 11:37.

71 Frank Vogel, "The Complementarity of Iftaʿ and Qaḍa: Three Saudi Fatwas on Divorce," in *Islamic Legal Interpretation: Muftis and Their Fatwas*, ed. Muhammad Khalid Masud, Brinkley Messick, and David Powers (Harvard: Harvard University Press, 1996), 266.

72 Ibid., 268. Vogel notes that if the wife had insisted on divorce, the judge would probably have followed her wish despite Ibn Bāz's fatwa.

73 Ibn Bāz, *Majmūʿ fatāwā*, 21:304–6.

74 Unfortunately, the letter is not dated, but Ibn Bāz served as Grand Mufti of Saudi Arabia from 1993 until his death in 1999.

A man had pronounced his pregnant wife three consecutive ṭalāq (*hiya ṭāliq, hiya ṭāliq, hiya ṭāliq*). In his decision, the judge referred to Ibn ʿUthaymīn and allowed the man to return to his wife. Ibn Bāz sharply criticized this, stating that Ibn Taymiyya's opinion, which Ibn ʿUthaymīn had invoked, was incorrect because it contradicted the sources (*adilla*) of Islamic law. It was, he said, no secret that Ibn Taymiyya, like any other scholar, could be mistaken. Ibn Bāz called on Ibn ʿUthaymīn to correct the judge.[75] This direct criticism of Ibn Taymiyya is noteworthy, given his otherwise strong influence on Saudi scholars.

Before the PSL, large segments of the judiciary still followed the majority opinion.[76] However, the court cases published by the Ministry of Justice contain numerous rulings in which judges applied Ibn Taymiyya's opinion.[77] In 2013, for example, the appellate court in Mecca upheld the decision of a judge from al-Muwayḥ, a small town between Riyadh and Mecca. The judge quoted Ibn Taymiyya extensively in his ruling and decided that a ṭalāq uttered three times in a row should only be counted as one ṭalāq.[78] The PSL also follows Ibn Taymiyya's opinion. Article 83 of the law states,

> A ṭalāq that consists of more than one expression or sign and occurs in a [single] meeting [*majlis*] shall be considered a singular ṭalāq.

Article 83 thus did not introduce a new ruling but rather codified an opinion that was already widely held in the Saudi legal discourse. Moreover, from a comparative perspective, the article is not exceptional: since the beginning of the twentieth century, reforms in the vast majority of Islamic countries have moved away from the majority view on triple ṭalāq.[79] Egypt was the first to introduce Ibn Taymiyya's opinion by law in 1929. The majority opinion was perceived as unjust for women because the man could arbitrarily end the marriage permanently without an opportunity for reconciliation.[80]

---

75 At the end of the letter, Ibn Bāz gets surprisingly direct: "I request you to take up the matter and inform His Eminence [*faḍīlat al-shaykh*] the judge at the high court in Dammam of your renunciation of the fatwa. By doing so, you give precedence to the law and uphold the sources of Islamic law," Ibid., 306. Unfortunately, Ibn ʿUthaymīn's reply is not printed.

76 Ḥamd bin ʿAbd al-ʿAzīz al-Khuḍayrī, *Al-Ijrāʾāt al-qaḍāʾiyya* (n.p., n.d.), 108.

77 Interestingly, no judgments on ṭalāq can be found in the first collection of judgments from 1434.

78 Muwayḥ General Court, decision Nr. 3544607 (26.2.1435/30.12.2013).

79 See Article 37, paragraph 2 of the Iraqi or Article 92, paragraph 1 of the Syrian Personal Status Law. Ibn Taymiyya's opinion is particularly popular among the scholars of the Ahl al-Ḥadīth in India and Pakistan, see Munir, "Triple Ṭalāq," 37.

80 While Ibn Taymiyya's opinion is followed by most Islamic scholars today, it remained controversial in India until it was introduced by law in 2019. The law was controversial

3.5 *A Woman's Right to Separate according to Her Own Will*

In several of its announcements, the Ministry of Justice emphasized that the new law grants women the right to end (*faskh*) their marriages according to their own will in "a number of circumstances" (*al-ʿadīd min al-ḥalāt*).

As we have seen in the previous chapter, a woman can, at least according to the major schools of jurisprudence, only end a marriage against her husband's will if she suffers any kind of damage (*ḍarar*) from the marriage. The PSL specifies four grounds for a woman to end her marriage due to damages caused by the husband. First, if the husband refuses or is unable to pay her maintenance (Article 107). Second, if she can prove that her husband causes her harm, making a normal life with him impossible (Article 108). Third, if her husband declares that they have not had intercourse for more than four months or refuses to have intercourse (Article 113). Fourth, if the husband has been absent for more than four months for reasons unrelated to his work (Article 114), or fifth, if the husband is missing or his whereabouts are unknown (Article 115). These grounds for divorce are largely in line with Mālikī doctrine, which, when compared to the other schools of jurisprudence, has the broadest understanding of damage, and is followed by most other Arab family law codifications.

But what happens if the husband cannot be accused of any wrongdoing and refuses the divorce? In this scenario, the only way for the wife to obtain a divorce is through forced khulʿ, as discussed in the previous chapter. Initially, the draft law adopted the Saudi ʿulamāʾ's opinion and permitted forced khulʿ. Forced khulʿ was addressed within the draft law in the section "Dissolution of Marriage" (*faskh*[81] *ʿaqd al-zawāj*). Article 125, paragraph 1 of the draft law stipulated,

> The court shall dissolve the marriage if the wife so requests, the husband refuses her a divorce [*ṭalāq*] or a [extrajudicial] khulʿ [mukhālaʿa], she detests living together [with the husband], she returns what she has received as a dowry [*mahr*], and reconciliation between the wife and the husband is impossible.

---

because it also criminalized uttering the ṭalāq three times. Men can now be punished with up to three years imprisonment, see https://www.bbc.com/news/world-asia-india-49160818 [last access: 24 March 2022].

81 In terms of legal consequences, a divorce in Islamic law is considered either ṭalāq or faskh, regardless of how it came about. In the case of khulʿ, it is disputed whether it should be regarded as ṭalāq or faskh. While the Ḥanafīs, Mālikīs, and Shāfiʿīs considered khulʿ to be ṭalāq, the majority of Ḥanbalīs saw it as faskh. See al-Zuḥaylī, *Al-Fiqh al-islāmī wa-adillatuhu*, 9:7035.

However, in the final version of the PSL, this provision was limited to marriages that have not yet been consummated. Article 112, paragraph 2 of the PSL states,

> The court shall dissolve the marriage before consummation [*dukhūl*] or the meeting in private [*khilwa*] if the wife so requests, the husband refuses her a divorce [*ṭalāq*] or a [extrajudicial] khulʿ [mukhālaʿa], she returns what she has received as dowry, and reconciliation between them is impossible.

For already consummated marriages, the PSL's provisions on arbitration in the event of a rift (*shiqāq*) apply.[82] As we have discussed in Chapter 6, the spouses each elect arbitrators (*ḥakamān*)[83] during the shiqāq procedure, who are family members or professional family counsellors. The arbitrators are tasked with investigating the reasons for the discord and mediating between the spouses.[84] If they do not succeed, the arbitrators agree to dissolve the marriage and determine whether and to what extent the wife must return assets to the husband.[85]

However, what happens if the arbitrators are unable to reach an agreement on the separation, as it is frequently the case in practice? The PSL provides no clear answer.[86] It is also unclear whether the spouses are bound by the

82 The shiqāq procedure was already included in the draft law. However, the draft law did not specify whether the conciliation procedure is a part of judicial khulʿ. As we have seen in Chapter 6, most Saudi scholars presuppose that the arbitration procedure has to take place during the khulʿ procedure in court.

83 Article 109 PSL: "If no harm can be proven, which makes it impossible to maintain cohabitation in an ordinary way, the rift (*shiqāq*) between the spouses persists, and mediation is impossible, each of the spouses chooses an arbitrator from his or her family within a time limit set by the court. If not, the court, if possible, appoints two arbitrators from the two families. If [no one from their families can be appointed], then someone who can be expected to have the capacity to mediate. The court sets a time limit for the proceedings, which cannot exceed sixty days from the date of the appointment of the arbitrators."

84 Article 110 PSL: "The arbitrators hear the spouses, ascertain the reasons for the rift, and attempt to mediate between them. The refusal of one of the spouses to cooperate with the arbitrators does not affect their work."

85 Article 111 PSL: "If it is impossible for the arbitrators to settle [the dispute] between the spouses, they decide on the separation, either with or without compensation (*ʿiwaḍ*). It can never exceed the dowry paid to the woman. The arbitrators submit a report to the court containing everything they have done to reconcile the spouses and the opinion they reached together with an account of the positions on which it is based."

86 Here lies the crucial difference between the arbitration procedure recognized by all four major schools of law in the event of a rift between the spouses and judicial khulʿ. None of the schools of law allow a woman to divorce if the arbitrators cannot reach an agreement or decide to continue the marriage. The Ḥanbalīs and Ḥanafīs limit the role of the arbitrators solely to mediation between the spouses and do not allow them to decide on the

arbitrator's decision. Therefore, it remains to be seen whether the judges will continue the prevailing practice at the courts and allow women to obtain a divorce against their husband's will, or whether the PSL is in fact a step backwards with regard to women's divorce rights in Saudi Arabia.

3.6 *The Rights of Children and the Best Interests of the Child*

Another key aspect of the new law, Saudi government officials claimed, was the protection of children's rights and the consideration of their best interests in custody cases. As discussed in Chapter 5, the question of how long children should stay with their mothers was one of the few issues in which Saudi judges employed free ijtihād. The PSL ends this practice. It introduces fixed age limits and allows children over the age of fifteen to choose their custodian. Article 135, paragraph 1 and 2 stipulate:

> (1) If the child has turned fifteen years of age, he or she may choose to live with one parent, if the best interests of the child do not require otherwise.
> (2) Child custody ends when the child is eighteen years old.

However, the consideration of the child's best interests is not a new approach. Before the PSL, Saudi 'ulamā' already extensively referred to the principle of the child's best interests to deviate from established opinions in Islamic jurisprudence, as we have seen in Chapter 5.

Remarried mothers' right to child custody was one of the most significant departures from the teachings of the major schools of jurisprudence. If their new husbands agreed, Saudi judges regularly appointed remarried mothers as custodians for their children. The PSL addresses the issue of a mother's remarriage in Article 126, Number 1, which states that a woman can only be appointed as custodian if she is not married to a stranger (*ajnabī*) to the child unless the best interests of the child require otherwise. Compared to the prevailing practice at Saudi courts before the codification, the PSL thus restricts the rights of remarried mothers. Following Ibn al-Qayyim, Saudi judges assumed that a child's best interests were served by staying with their remarried mother unless

divorce. The Mālikīs allow the arbitrators to decide on the separation of the spouses, by which the judge is bound. However, if the arbitrators cannot reach an agreement about the separation, no divorce takes place. According to one opinion within the Shāfiʿī school, the arbitrators can be authorized by the spouses to end the marriage (either as khulʿ or as ṭalāq without restitution). Another opinion within the Shāfiʿī school allows the arbitrators to act as agents against the will of the spouses. In doing so, the arbitrators can also decide to continue the marriage against the wife's will. See Wizārat al-Awqāf wa-l-Shu'ūn al-Islāmiyya al-Kuwaitiyya, *Al-Mawsūʿa al-fiqhiyya al-kuwaitiyya*, 29:53–55.

proven otherwise. By establishing the loss of custody as the general rule in the case of a mother's remarriage, the PSL now makes it more difficult for judges to grant custody to remarried mothers.[87]

The concept of the child's best interests is also mentioned in the order of the custodians (Article 127), where a judge can deviate from the stipulated order if the child's best interests require the appointment of another custodian. A further reference is made with regard to the disobedience (*nushūz*) of the mother (Article 133). According to the PSL, a mother who moves out of the marital home only loses custody of her children if it is in their best interest. All of these regulations correspond to the prevailing practice at Saudi courts before codification.

The PSL's provisions concerning situations where one parent relocates significantly far away from the other or takes the child on trips outside the country are likewise not new. As we have seen in Chapter 5, Saudi jurists have departed from the rule in premodern Islamic jurisprudence that the mother loses custody if the parents do not live in close proximity. The ʿulamāʾ's opinion has been incorporated into Article 128, paragraph 2 of the PSL. According to the article, custody is only lost "if the custodian travels to a place in order to live there, which is not in accordance with the best interests of the child."

In the case of travelling with children, the PSL also largely follows the prevailing practice prior to the codification. The PSL allows a parent to travel outside of Saudi Arabia for ninety days without the permission of the other parent.[88] Article 129 stipulates,

> With consideration of other related provisions, travel with the child outside of the kingdom is subject to the following rules:
> (1) If the custodian is one of the parents, he or she cannot travel with the child outside the kingdom for more than ninety days in one year without the agreement of the other parent or the guardian [*al-walī ʿalā al-nafs*], in case the father has died.
> (2) A custodian other than the parents cannot travel with the child outside the kingdom for more than thirty days in a year without the agreement

87 The PSL addresses the issue also in the context of a woman's obligation to live with her husband and allows that a mother lives with her children from an earlier marriage if the husband agrees. Article 57, paragraph 2 stipulates, "The wife may reside with her children from other than her husband if they do not have another guardian or if they are harmed by her departure, or if the husband agrees explicitly or implicitly and the husband may divorce whenever he incurs harm from that."

88 The PSL contains no provisions for travel within the kingdom.

of the parents or one of them, in case the other parent has died, or the guardian in case both have died.

Contrary to the claims of the Saudi government, the PSL thus did not introduce new rulings in the field of child custody but merely codified the prevailing practice, which built on the ʿulamāʾ's deviations from the rulings of the major schools of Islamic jurisprudence.

4 The Enduring Influence of Tribal Affiliation

When the PSL was issued, the topic that received the most attention from Saudi lawyers and activists on social media was the equality of spouses (*kafāʾa*) in marriage. According to Islamic jurisprudence, a woman can only marry a man who is equal to her. If it turns out after the marriage that the man is not equal to the wife, she and her family have the right to petition the court to dissolve the marriage. Women, on the other hand, are not required to be equal to their husbands.

Aside from the Gulf region, marriage equality is nowadays primarily determined by the husband's socioeconomic status. However, in the Gulf states, the spouses' nasab traditionally plays an important role, as discussed earlier. In the context of marriage equality, nasab encompasses both affiliation to a male line as well as to a specific social group.[89] This also includes what we know as "race" today.

In debates on marriage equality in Saudi Arabia, nasab is mostly associated with affiliation to a particular Arab tribe[90] (*qabīla*). According to Ibn ʿUthaymīn, anyone who "has his roots in the Arab tribes"[91] is of lineage (*nasīban*). Ibn ʿUthaymīn holds that the affiliation to an Arab tribe is based solely on blood and not on language, as one can be Arab without speaking or understanding Arabic.[92] The majority of premodern Islamic jurists including the Ḥanbalīs permitted nasab to be considered in determining marriage equality. The Shāfiʿī jurist al-Khaṭṭābī (d. 998) wrote,

89 ʿAbd Allāh bin Aḥmad al-Muḥammādī, "Al-Kafāʾa bayna al-zawjayn fī al-nasab wa-taṭbiqātuhu al-qaḍāʾiyya," *Majallat al-ʿAdl* 8 (1422/2001): 27–28.

90 In anthropological literature, the concept of tribes is criticized due to its evolutionary connotations. However, as Sebastian Maisel has pointed out, the concept of tribes on the Arab peninsula reflects indigenous perceptions of identity and can therefore be used. See Maisel, "New Rise of Tribalism," 101.

91 Ibn ʿUthaymīn, *Al-Sharḥ al-mumtiʿ*, 12:101.

92 Ibid., 12:104.

> Most jurists define marriage equality according to four aspects: religion [*dīn*], freedom [*ḥuriyya*] [i.e., not being a slave], nasab, and craftsmanship [*ṣanāʿa*]. Some jurists also include mental and physical sanity and solvency.[93]

The most important factor was nasab in the sense of tribal affiliation. The jurists, however, disagreed about which tribes could intermarry. According to most scholars, a woman of the Quraysh, the tribe of the Prophet, could not marry a man from another Arab tribe. Other jurists argued that women of the Hāshimites and the Bānū Muṭṭalib should not intermarry with other Arab tribes, whereas another group of jurists permitted all Arab tribes to intermarry.

But some premodern jurists were also critical of the consideration of nasab in marriage equality. This view was primarily promoted by the Mālikī school, which focused solely on religious piety and the husband's physical condition.[94] However, the opposition to the majority view was not limited to the Mālikīs: Ibn Ḥazm, for example, wrote that, since "Muslims [*ahl al-Islām*] are all brothers, it is not forbidden for the son of the "blacks" [*ibn min al-zanjiyya*] to marry a daughter from the Hāshimites."[95]

Ibn Taymiyya and Ibn al-Qayyim, too, took a strong stance against the inclusion of nasab in marriage equality. Marriage equality, according to Ibn al-Qayyim, could only be measured by religious piety, not by nasab, freedom, craftsmanship, or wealth. Non-Qurayshī men could thus marry Qurayshī women, and non-Hāshimite men could marry Hāshimite women.[96] Ibn Taymiyya wrote that there were some people among the non-Arabs who were far better than most of the Arabs. He maintained that although Islamic law granted certain rights only to Arabs, as, for example, only a man of the Quraysh can become a caliph, no general privilege of the Arabs existed in Islamic law, and thus also not in marriage law.[97]

Saudi ʿulamāʾ have traditionally been critical of the role of tribes in Saudi society. In their view, Muslims should first and foremost identify as members of the community of believers (*umma*), not as members of a tribe.[98]

---

93 Al-Khaṭṭābī, *Maʿālim al-sunan* (Aleppo: Al-Maṭbaʿa al-ʿIlmiyya, 1352/1933), 3:207.

94 Mohammed Fadel, "Reinterpreting the Guardian's Role in the Islamic Contract of Marriage: The Case of the Maliki School," *Journal of Islamic Law* 3, no. 1 (1998): 14.

95 Ibn Ḥazm, *Al-Muḥallā bi-l-Athār* (Beirut: Dār al-Kutub al-ʿIlmiyya, 1425/2003), 9:151 (Nr. 1867).

96 Ibn al-Qayyim, Zād al-maʿād, 5:145.

97 Ibn Taymiyya, Majmūʿat al-fatāwā, 19:30.

98 The same argument is made regarding nationalism. Muḥammad Nāṣir Al-Albānī, for instance, issued a controversial fatwa criticizing Palestinian nationalism. Instead of

Nonetheless, some Saudi scholars have supported the consideration of nasab in marriage equality. Muḥammad bin Ibrāhīm, for instance, argued in one of his fatwas that equality in nasab was a requirement for marriage.[99] In another fatwa, Muḥammad bin Ibrāhīm maintained that members of the Arab tribes were always equal to one other.[100] He criticized the Fatimids (*fāṭimiyyūn*) for refusing to give their daughters to other Arab tribes as they did not want to share the proceeds of their religious endowments (*awqāf*) and therefore preferred to intermarry with non-Arabs.[101] Muḥammad bin Ibrāhīm argued that although piety (*taqwā*) was the correct measure of marriage equality, marrying another Arab was preferable.[102]

Similarly, the current head of the Higher Judicial Institute (Maʿhad al-ʿĀlī li-l-Qaḍāʾ), ʿAbd Allāh bin Aḥmad al-Muḥammādī, supported the view that nasab should be taken into consideration. He argued against focusing on piety (*taqwā*) in marriage equality, since only God and no human could determine someone's piety. Furthermore, many of the verses in the Qurʾan and the Sunna that are employed to reject the consideration of nasab address the equality of believers in the afterlife and could not be applied to this world (*dunyā*) through analogy (*qiyās*). Al-Muḥammādī acknowledged that people were equal in their rights and obligations in this world but emphasized that they were not equal in their status and class.[103] Inequality of status and class were inherent to human nature, and Islamic law could not change this because the division of society along these lines did not violate Islam's basic teachings.[104]

He asserted that the consideration of nasab was not mandatory, unlike the other commonly acknowledged aspects of marriage equality such as piety or freedom. However, Islamic law was obligated to respect local customs, including the social importance of a person's nasab. This ensured a successful marriage and a good and respectful relationship with the wife's relatives.[105] Al-Muḥammādī highlighted that once Arab society stops focusing on tribal

---

fighting for a Palestinian state, al-Albānī argued that Palestinians should concentrate on their religion and follow a religious lifestyle. He claimed that because of the Israeli occupation, a religious lifestyle was not possible, and Muslims should therefore leave Palestine. See Lacroix, "Al-Albani's Revolutionary Approach," 6.

99 Al-Qāsim, *Fatāwā wa-rasāʾil*, 10:121.

100 Ibid., 10:122.

101 Ibid.

102 Ibid., 10:123.

103 Al-Muḥammādī, "Al-Kafāʾa bayna al-zawjayn," 37.

104 Ibid., 38.

105 Ibid., 46.

affiliation, nasab will no longer be a legal requirement in marriage law.[106] Until then, Arab women could not marry non-Arab men. However, according to al-Muḥammādī, there are no distinctions between different Arab tribes or between Arabs of different nationalities.[107]

Other Saudi scholars are more sceptical of the role of nasab in marriage equality. For instance, Ibn ʿUthaymīn held that nasab was not required at all for marriage equality.[108] He complained that, according to some scholars, even distant relatives could end a successful marriage that has lasted for many years. Moreover, Ibn ʿUthaymīn criticized the majority opinion in the Ḥanbalī school, which allows a son who has become his mother's guardian to go to court and demand the dissolution of his mother's marriage.[109] Ibn ʿUthaymīn called this ruling and, more generally, the pride in one's tribe, a pre-Islamic (*jāhiliyya*) custom.[110] Ibn Bāz, too, was critical of the inclusion of nasab in marriage equality. He made an interesting argument: the consensus in Islamic jurisprudence that allows Arab men to marry non-Arab women as long as they are Muslim, Christian, or Jewish demonstrated that only religion should be considered in marriage, not tribal affiliation. Ibn Bāz emphasized that Muslims were equal before God and, as a result, equal to each other in marriage.[111]

Before the codification of family law, the Saudi judiciary did not consider nasab when determining marriage equality. In 2007, the Higher Judicial Council ruled that piety (*dīn*) was the only criterion for marriage equality. Additionally, the council decided that it was wrong to allow the wife's brother or other family members to end the marriage and overrule her explicit will and that of her marriage guardian.[112] Three years later, the High Court argued that since neither the Quran nor the teachings of the Prophet prohibit marriage between people of unequal nasab, such a marriage was valid.[113] In 2016, a spokesperson of the Ministry of Justice emphasized that the reference to nasab could not be used to dissolve a marriage, and Saudi courts would not end marriages due to allegedly unequal nasab. The spokesperson was responding to a controversy

---

106 Ibid., 47.
107 Ibid., 48.
108 Ibn ʿUthaymīn, *Al-Sharḥ al-mumtiʿ*, 12:101.
109 Ibid., 12:104.
110 Ibid., 12:105.
111 Ibn Bāz, *Majmūʿ fatāwā*, 20:401–3.
112 Decision of the Higher Judicial Council Nr. 5/1228 (1.8.1428/15.8.2007), printed in Markaz al-Buḥūth, *Al-Mabādiʾ wa al-qarārāt*, 181.
113 Decision of the Higher Judicial Council Nr. 3/3/8 (10.2.1431/26.1.2010), printed in Markaz al-Buḥūth, *Al-Mabādiʾ wa al-qarārāt*, 181.

sparked by a decision of the court in ʿUyayna, a town north of Riyadh, which dissolved a marriage due to the, in the eyes of the judge, unequal nasab of the couple.[114]

The draft of the PSL followed the prevailing view among Saudi jurists that piety alone should be used to determine marriage equality. Article 14, paragraph 2 of the draft stated,

> Decisive for the marriage equality of a man is his piety [*dīn*]. Nothing else is considered in [marriage] equality.

In the version later adopted by the Council of Ministers, however, a half-sentence was added, stating that local custom, i.e., tribal affiliation, could also be considered. Article 14 (2) of the PSL stipulates,

> Decisive for the marriage equality of a man at the time of the marriage is his piety [*ṣalāḥ dīnihi*] and all that is considered according to local custom [*kull mā qāma al-ʿurf ʿalā iʿtibārihi*].

Because local custom in large parts of Saudi Arabia includes the consideration of nasab, the PSL moved away from the line of thinking developed by Ibn ʿUthaymīn and others. Furthermore, the PSL greatly expanded the scope of the relatives' rights to end a seemingly unequal marriage. Unlike the draft law, which allowed only the wife and her father (if he was her marriage guardian) to end the marriage when they discovered that the husband was not equal, the PSL grants this right to "every relative who has an interest (*maṣlaḥa*) – until the third grade – and is affected by the inequality of the marriage" (Article 14, paragraph 3).

The regulation of marriage equality in the PSL breaks both with the prevailing practice at Saudi courts and with an important tradition among Saudi ʿulamāʾ which provided autonomy in choosing one's marriage partner. It is also a step backwards for the rights of those who are not members of one of the prominent Arab tribes, leading to further discrimination on the basis of tribal affiliation.

114 See an article by the Saudi newspaper Sabq, https://bit.ly/3Vl8Fgt [last access: 23 November 2022].

5 Conclusion

The chapter demonstrated that the PSL introduced only very few changes to family law compared to court practice before the codification, despite the claims by the Saudi government that it was a reformist project. Instead of reforming Islamic family law, the PSL largely rephrased legal opinions that had been developed by Saudi jurists over the last decades, and which the Saudi government then labelled as significant adjustments in Islamic legal doctrine. In some important legal questions, as the chapter has shown, the law can even be considered a step backwards.

At the same time, the PSL illustrates to what extent the Saudi leadership is still tied to Islamic law as defined by the ʿulamāʾ in matters related to the judiciary. Notwithstanding Muḥammad bin Salmān's announcement that international standards should be incorporated into the PSL, the chapter has demonstrated that the code does not include significant aspects of any foreign or non-Islamic law. This shows that the doctrine of siyāsa sharʿiyya has not (yet) lost its authority in the Saudi state. Fundamental changes to Islamic family law, one of the key areas of Islamic jurisprudence, would have been a clear break with the doctrine and, as a consequence, also with the Basic Law of Governance. As long as a codification of Islamic law does not deviate from the ʿulamāʾ's understanding, it does not violate the king's commitment to implementing Islamic law in the legal sector and therefore does not constitute a major shift in the political constitution of the kingdom.

Nevertheless, it remains to be seen how closely judges will follow the PSL and other future codifications of Islamic law. A few indicators point to a growing opposition among judges. This is remarkable in light of the increasingly authoritarian climate in Saudi Arabia. During a meeting with the presidents of the personal status courts in June 2022, minister of justice Walīd al-Samaʿānī saw himself forced to emphasize that the judges are required to apply the PSL.[115]

The PSL does not mark the end of Islamic jurisprudence in family law in Saudi Arabia. Even though the law is very detailed, especially when compared to the family laws of other Arab countries, not all issues are addressed. In cases not covered by the PSL, the law obliges judges to apply the opinion in Islamic jurisprudence most consistent with the codification. In these cases, it is to be expected that judges will continue to follow their ijtihād.

---

115 https://www.okaz.com.sa/news/local/2106523 [last access: 16 January 2023].

Conclusion

This book has investigated the Saudi jurists' understanding of an Islamic judiciary and how this understanding is reflected in the Saudi legal system, its institutions, and the courts' practice.

I have argued that there has been a significant shift in the understanding and application of Islamic law in the Saudi judiciary over recent decades, largely without any interference from the state. Despite the Saudi government's claims of comprehensive reform in the legal sector, I have demonstrated that many of these initiatives, including the codification of Islamic law, are a continuation of past efforts by Islamic jurists to adapt the idea of an Islamic legal system to the changing social and economic conditions in the kingdom.

By adopting the viewpoint of the ʿulamāʾ, I have attempted to overcome commonly held dichotomies such as "exceptional" vs. "normal," "progressive" vs. "traditional," and "liberal" vs. "conservative," which are frequently used to describe the Saudi judiciary. From the perspective of the ʿulamāʾ, the ideal Islamic judiciary addresses the conflicts that arise in court today through a re-evaluation of the Islamic legal tradition. Two main aspects guide the jurists' approach to Islamic jurisprudence, the first being the influence of the Salafī tradition, which demands a critical attitude towards established opinions in fiqh. Second, the ʿulamāʾ view themselves as serving the needs of a society, which, they acknowledge, is changing with time and the introduction of new customs and technologies. As a result, contemporary Saudi jurists incorporate opinions from various schools and traditions, resulting in a distinct approach to Islamic law.

I also questioned the (still) widespread narrative that the codification of Islamic law leads to a rupture in the way Islamic law is understood. The recent codification in Saudi Arabia is not considered a break with the Islamic legal tradition by the ʿulamāʾ themselves, nor is it introducing new rulings. Instead, codification in Saudi Arabia should be viewed as the next step in a long-standing debate among Saudi jurists over standardizing Islamic law.

1 Tradition and Reform: Reinterpreting the Islamic Legal Tradition

Three main aspects result from the jurists' re-evaluation of the Islamic legal tradition: First, Saudi ʿulamāʾ have deviated from the teachings of the Ḥanbalī school, with which they are usually associated, and in some aspects also from rulings shared by all schools of Islamic jurisprudence. This is not only visible in their daily practice at court but also in their understanding of an Islamic judiciary. Before the codification of Islamic law, Saudi judges included opinions from all schools of Islamic jurisprudence in their decisions. While the Ḥanbalī school still played an essential role – most references were made to books written by Ḥanbalī jurists – the analysis of Saudi court practice showed that the application of non-Ḥanbalī opinions was a reality. The ʿulamāʾ recognize the schools as necessary vehicles to structure legal knowledge but reject their binding authority, which in their eyes constitutes a forbidden innovation in Islam. Although the Saudi critique of the schools' authority dates back to the eighteenth century with the teachings of Muḥammad bin ʿAbd al-Wahhāb, the widespread use of non-Hanbali opinions is a relatively recent phenomenon. The ʿulamāʾ use the possibility to deviate from the schools' teachings to adapt Islamic law to modern life. They do not understand these changes as a break with the tradition but rather as a sign of the tradition's vitality. However, the Salafī ideal of legal reasoning as an individual journey, in which the judge determines the correct ruling on a case-to-case basis through the interpretation of the revelation, was only partly visible in court practice even before the codification. Yet, the focus on the circumstances of the individual case remains an important ideal, which from the perspective of the ʿulamāʾ distinguishes Islamic law from contemporary Western law.

Second, the jurists' desire to establish a functioning legal system led to the introduction of two institutions that ensured the consistent application of Islamic law in the courts: the concept of prevailing practice and an extensive appeal court system. Leading Saudi ʿulamāʾ reinterpreted the premodern idea of a prevailing practice of the courts and obliged the judges at the first instance level to follow the opinions of high-ranking scholars and judges in most legal questions. At the same time, the appeal court system was gradually expanded and guaranteed the judges' compliance with the prevailing practice. While premodern ʿulamāʾ largely rejected the concept of judicial appeal (as it is generally understood today), appeal courts have become an integral part of the Saudi jurists' conception of an Islamic legal system. These reforms had significant implications for the balance of power between the Saudi government and the judiciary: by appointing appeal court judges and promoting certain Islamic scholars, the Saudi government increasingly gained control over the judiciary.

Thirdly, the jurists have included codified law in their conception of an Islamic legal system. This has resulted in the general acceptance of the king's codes (*anẓima*) that were meant to supplement Islamic law. However, the question of a binding codification of Islamic law was long disputed. The main reason for the jurists' refusal of a binding codification was their fear that it would make Islamic law inflexible. Like many European legal theorists in the past, the ʿulamāʾ believed that abstract rulings could not deliver justice. Instead, the law must always be adapted to individual cases. These concerns, however, are increasingly swept away by the practical demands of twenty-first-century capitalism and a society that demands a transparent and predictable judiciary.

Hence, the Saudi judiciary is not the last surviving premodern Islamic legal system as it is often portrayed. While the ʿulamāʾ's extensive references to premodern books suggest that they are stuck in the past, this impression is misleading. Research on premodern Islamic law can thus only insufficiently explain contemporary phenomena in the Saudi judiciary.

2 The Continuing Hegemony of Islamic Jurisprudence

Is the Saudi judiciary therefore on its way to becoming "normal"? Chibli Mallat has recently argued that the Saudi judiciary is undergoing a process of "normalisation."[1] He claims that the Saudi legal system was long an exception among legal systems in the Middle East but has now lost its uniqueness and become similar to other legal systems. Mallat is right when we look at the publication of court cases, the introduction of codified law, and the establishment of an appeal court system. However, as long as the ʿulamāʾ control the judiciary, their unique understanding of Islamic law will continue to shape the Saudi legal system, and most of the unique characteristics of Saudi legal thought will persist in the foreseeable future.

It is important to keep in mind that the codification of Islamic law does not abolish siyāsa sharʿiyya but rather represents the next step in the evolution of the doctrine, as Islamic law is still following the ʿulamāʾ's interpretation, as illustrated by the codification of family and inheritance law in 2022. Unlike in many other Arab countries, where the introduction of codification limited the role of Islamic law to family and inheritance law, no such development is expected to take place in Saudi Arabia. Moreover, the ongoing codification of Islamic law will not diminish the dominant role Islamic jurisprudence plays in the Saudi legal system. The hegemony of Islamic jurisprudence over codified law is today already visible in the way Saudi judges approach the king's codes, as we have seen in Chapter 6. The judges consider them texts that have to be interpreted based on Islamic jurisprudence alone. It is more than likely that judges will approach future codifications in the same way.

---

1 Chibli Mallat, *The Normalization of Saudi Law* (Oxford: Oxford University Press, 2022).

As discussed in Chapter 3, codification is usually connected to a certain legal epistemology. For the ʿulamāʾ, codification means something very different than for a German or British lawyer.[2] Hence, as long as the ʿulamāʾ occupy their position in the legal system, the codification of Islamic law alone will not change the dominant way of legal thinking. Although there are rumors that judges who are not trained in Islamic jurisprudence may be appointed in some courts, replacing the ʿulamāʾ will be difficult. Not only are they specialists in adjudication, but they (still) play a crucial role in providing religious legitimacy to the Saudi king.

3 The Global Dimension of the Saudi Legal Discourse

As the birthplace of Islam, Saudi Arabia occupies a unique symbolic place in the Muslim world. The kingdom's jurists have successfully used this symbolic capital to establish themselves as the guardians of Islamic orthodoxy in the contemporary world. Whereas Saudi scholars stood at the margins of the Muslim intellectual world at the beginning of the twentieth century, their ideas today dominate Islamic discourses in many countries inside and outside of the Arab world. Saudi understandings of Islamic law are increasingly becoming a reference point for Muslims all around the globe, especially for younger generations.

The support of the Saudi kings is an important factor in the jurists' growing influence. Siyāsa sharʿiyya obliges the kings not only to follow Islamic law in their actions but also to help propagate Saudi views on sharīʿa. Financed by the king, Saudi organizations have in the last decades distributed writings by Saudi ʿulamāʾ to mosques and Islamic cultural centers worldwide. Moreover, Islamic universities in the kingdom attract thousands of international students from all over the Muslim world, who, once returned to their home countries, apply Saudi understandings of Islamic law in their teaching or judging.[3]

However, it was the internet that put Saudi views at the center of contemporary discourses on Islam and Islamic law. A quick search in English or Arabic

---

2 See Dominik Krell, "Codification and the Legacy of Islamic Jurisprudence," *Oriente Moderno* (forthcoming).

3 In early 2024, I had the chance to interview a large number of Islamic judges (*cadis*) in the Gambia. Many of the cadis had been educated in Saudi Arabia. Although they were not simply imitating Saudi scholars, their education in the kingdom undoubtedly influences their approach to Islamic law. This is most visible in their approach to the schools of jurisprudence. While the cadis still respect the authority of the Mālikī school, which prevails in the Gambia, they also regularly apply opinions from other schools.

on a random question of Islamic jurisprudence most likely leads to the website of a Saudi scholar. A younger generation of Saudi ʿulamāʾ, like Muḥammad bin ʿAbd al-Raḥmān al-ʿArīfī or Ṣāliḥ bin ʿAwād al-Maghāmsī, have managed to gain a massive social media following that is not anymore limited to the kingdom.[4]

The world will thus closely look at how and whether Saudi efforts to combine Islamic orthodoxy with twenty-first-century capitalism, the digital revolution, and other challenges of our times will succeed. The development of the Saudi judiciary will show if and how Islamic jurisprudence can survive as a living tradition.

---

4 In 2023, more than 19.2 million users followed al-ʿArīfī's personal twitter account (now X), which made it the most followed Arab-speaking account on the platform. He has more followers than the Dalai Lama (in English, 19.1 million) and the pope (in English, 18.9 million) and almost as many followers as Al Jazeera (in Arabic, 19.9 million).

Bibliography

ʿAlī, Muḥammad Kurd. *Rasāʾil al-bulaghāʾ*. Cairo: Dār al-Kutub al-ʿArabiyya al-Kubrā, 1331/1913.

ʿAṭwa, ʿAbd al-ʿĀl bin Aḥmad. *Al-Mudkhal ilā al-siyāsa al-sharʿiyya*. Riyadh: Jāmiʿat al-Imām Muḥammad bin Saʿūd al-Islāmiyya, 1414/1993.

Abdel Haleem, Muhammad. *The Qur'an*. Oxford: Oxford University Press, 2008.

Abou El Fadl, Khaled. *Speaking in God's Name: Islamic Law, Authority, and Women*. London: Oneworld Publications, 2001.

Abou El Fadl, Khaled. *Rebellion and Violence in Islamic Law*. Cambridge: Cambridge University Press, 2001.

Abū Dāwūd. *Sunan Abī Dāwūd*. Damascus: Dār al-Risāla al-ʿĀlamiyya, 1430/2009.

Abū Zayd, Bakr bin ʿAbd Allāh. *Fiqh al-nawāzil*. Riyadh: Muʾassasat al-Risāla, 1416/1996.

Abū Zayd, Bakr bin ʿAbd Allāh. *Muʿjam al-manāhī al-lafẓiyya*. Riyadh: Dār al-ʿĀṣima, 1417/1996.

Agrama, Hussein Ali. *Questioning Secularism*. Chicago: University of Chicago Press, 2012.

Al-ʿAbd al-Laṭīf, ʿAbd Allāh bin Muḥammad. *Daʿāwā al-munāwiʾīn li-daʿwat al-shaykh Muḥammad bin ʿAbd al-Wahhāb: ʿArḍ wa-naqḍ*. Riyadh: Dār Ṭayba li-l-Nashr wa-l-Tawzīʿ, 1409/1989.

Al-Atawneh, Muhammad. "Is Saudi Arabia a Theocracy? Religion and Governance in Contemporary Saudi Arabia." *Middle Eastern Studies* 45, no. 5 (2009): 721–37.

Al-Atawneh, Muhammad. *Wahhabi Islam Facing the Challenges of Modernity: Dār al-Iftā in the Modern Saudi State*. Leiden: Brill, 2010.

Al-ʿAṭṭiya, ʿĀlī bin Sulaymān. *Al-Siyāsa al-sharʿiyya fī al-niẓām al-asāsī li-l-ḥukm*. Riyadh: N.p, 1432/2011.

Al-ʿUthaymīn, ʿAbd Allāh bin Ṣāliḥ. *Al-Shaykh Muḥammad bin ʿAbd al-Wahhāb: ḥayātuhu wa-fikruhu*. Riyadh: Dār al-ʿUlūm, 1406/1986.

Al-ʿUṣaymī, Ṣāliḥ bin Muqbal. *Bidaʿ al-qubūr: Anwāʿuha wa-aḥkāmuha*. Riyadh: Dār al-Faḍīla, 1426/2005.

Āl al-Shaykh, ʿAbd al-Malik bin Aḥmad. *Taṭawwur idārat al-qaḍāʾ fī al-Mamlaka al-ʿArabiyya al-Saʿūdiyya*. Riyadh: N.p, 1431/2010.

Al-Albānī, Muḥammad Nāṣir al-Dīn. *Silsilat al-aḥādīth al-ḍaʿīfa wa-al-mawduʿa*. Riyadh: Maktabat al-Maʿārif, 1412/1992.

Al-Albānī, Muḥammad Nāṣir al-Dīn. *Ṣaḥīḥ sunan al-Nasāʾī*. Maktabat al-Maʿārif li-l-Nashr wa-l-Tawzīʿ, 1419/1998.

Al-Amāna al-ʿĀmma li-Hayʾat Kibār al-ʿUlamāʾ, ed. *Abḥāth Hayʾat Kibār al-ʿUlamāʾ*. Riyadh: Hayʾat Kibār al-ʿUlamāʾ, 1434/2013.

Al-Bahūtī. *Kashshāf al-qināʿ ʿan matn al-iqnāʿ*. Beirut: ʿĀlam al-Kutub, 1403/1983.

Al-Bahūtī. *Al-Rawḍ al-murbiʿ sharḥ zād al-mustaqniʿ*. Cairo: Dār al-Ḥadīth, 1425/2004.

Al-Bukhārī. *Ṣaḥīḥ al-Bukhārī*. Damascus: Dār Ibn Kathīr, 1423/2002.

Al-Būṭī, Muḥammad Saʿīd Ramaḍān. *Al-Lāmadhhabiyya: Akhṭar bidʿa tuhaddidu al-sharīʿa al-islāmiyya*. Damascus: Dār al-Fārābī, 1426/2005.

Al-Dardīr. *Al-Sharḥ al-ṣaghīr ʿalā aqrab al-masālik ilā madhhab al-Imām Mālik*. Cairo: Dār al-Maʿārif, 1392/1972.

Al-Dawīsh, Aḥmad bin ʿAbd al-Rāziq. *Fatāwā al-Lajna al-Dāʾima li-l-Buḥūth al-ʿIlmiyya wa-l-Iftāʾ*. Riyadh: Riʾāsat Idārat al-Buḥūth al-ʿIlmiyya wa-l-Iftāʾ, n.d.

Al-Dughayther, ʿAbd al-ʿAzīz bin Saʿd. "Ḥujjiyyat al-sawābiq al-qaḍāʾiyya." *Majallat al-ʿAdl* 34 (1428/2007): 174–200.

Al-Daqaylān, ʿAdnān bin Muḥammad. "Nasab walad al-zinā." *Majallat al-ʿAdl* 22 (1425/2004): 123–39.

Al-Dusūqī. *Ḥāshiyat al-Dusūqī ʿalā al-sharḥ al-kabīr*. Beirut: Dār al-Fikr, 1437/2016.

Al-Dhahabī. *Siyar aʿlām al-nubalāʾ*. Beirut: Muʾassasat al-Risāla, 1409/1988.

Al-Fahad, Abdulaziz. "Ornamental Constitutionalism: The Saudi Basic Law of Governance." *Yale Journal of International Law* 39, no. 2 (2005): 376–96.

Al-Fawzān, Muḥammad bin Barrāk. *Al-Tanẓīm al-qaḍāʾī al-jadīd fī al-Mamlaka al-ʿArabiyya al-Saʿūdiyya*. Riyadh: Maktabat al-Qānūn al-Iqtiṣād, 1431/2010.

Al-Fawzān, Ṣāliḥ bin Fawzān. *Mulakhkhaṣ al-fiqhī*. Riyadh: Dār al-ʿĀṣima, 1423/2002.

Al-Fāyiz, Muḥammad bin ʿAbd al-ʿAzīz. *Taqnīn al-aḥkām al-qaḍāʾiyya*. N.p, 1431/2010.

Al-Ghāmdī, ʿAbd al-ʿAzīz bin ʿAlī. "Aqall muddat al-ḥaml wa-aktharuha bayna al-fiqh wa-l-ṭibb." *Majallat al-ʿAdl* 43 (1430/2009): 200–224.

Al-Ghashīmī, Ḥamūd bin Muḥammad. "Mabādiʾ al-siyāsa al-sharʿiyya wa-athāruhā fī al-niẓām al-asāsī li-l-ḥukm fī al-Mamlaka al-ʿArabiyya al-Saʿūdiyya." *Majallat al-Jāmiʿa al-Islāmiyya li-l-ʿUlūm al-Sharʿiyya* 185, no. 1 (1439/2017): 325–88.

Al-Ḥajjāwī. *Al-Iqnāʿ*. Beirut: Dār al-Maʿrifa, n.d.

Al-Ḥamd, Nāyif bin Aḥmad. "Working paper for the conference 'Intiqāl Ḥaqq al-Ḥaḍāna fī Ḍawʾ Mutaghayyirāt al-ʿAṣr (Transferring the Right to Custody in the Light of the Changes of the Century)' at the Imām Muḥammad bin Saʿūd Islamic University in Riyadh on the 23.10.1433/10.9.2012."

Al-Ḥaqīl, Yāsir bin Ḥamd. "Al-Siyāsa al-sharʿiyya fī mukāfaḥat al-fasād wa-l-wiqāya minhu." *Majallat al-Qaḍāʾiyya* 3 (1433/2011): 132–200.

Al-Ḥaydarī, Manṣūr bin ʿAbd al-Raḥmān. "Al-Taṭwīr fī al-jānib al-ijrāʾī." In *Al-Niẓām al-ʿadl fī al-Saʿūdiyya*, edited by Markaz al-Fikr al-ʿĀlamī ʿan al-Saʿūdiyya, 218–31. Riyadh: Markaz al-Fikr al-ʿĀlamī ʿan al-Saʿūdiyya.

Al-Ḥaydarī, Manṣūr bin ʿAbd al-Raḥmān. "Muʾassasat al-qaḍāʾ al-ʿāmm." In *Al-Niẓām al-ʿadl fī al-Saʿūdiyya*, edited by Markaz al-Fikr al-ʿĀlamī ʿan al-Saʿūdiyya, 128–57. Riyadh: Markaz al-Fikr al-ʿĀlamī ʿan al-Saʿūdiyya.

Al-Jarīsī, Khālid bin ʿAbd al-Raḥmān. *Al-Fatāwā al-sharʿiyya fī al-masāʾil al-ʿaṣriyya min fatāwā ʿulamāʾ al-balad al-ḥarām*. Riyadh: Muʾassasat al-Jarīsī, 1420/1999.

Al-Khaṭṭābī. *Maʿālim al-sunan*. Vol. 3. Aleppo: Al-Maṭbaʿa al-ʿIlmiyya, 1352/1933.

Al-Khazail, Lauan, and Dominik Krell. "Die Wirksamkeit von Minderjährigen- und Zwangsehen nach syrischem und irakischem Familienrecht." *Das Standesamt* 73, no. 1 (2020.): 10–16.

Al-Khuḍayrī, Ḥamd bin ʿAbd al-ʿAzīz. "Al-Ijrāʾāt al-qaḍāʾiyya fī al-mushkilāt al-zawjiyya." *Majallat al-ʿAdl* 45 (1431/2010): 123–68.

Al-Khuḍayrī, Ḥamd bin ʿAbd al-ʿAzīz. *Al-Ijrāʾāt al-qaḍāʾiyya*. N.p, n.d.

Āl Khunayn, ʿAbd Allāh bin Muḥammad. "Muqābila maʿ ṣāḥib al-faḍīla al-shaykh ʿAbd Allāh bin Muḥammad bin Saʿd Āl Khunayn." *Al-Majalla* 1086 (1421/2000).

Āl Khunayn, ʿAbd Allāh bin Muḥammad. *Al-Khulʿ bi-ṭalab al-zawja*. Riyadh: Dār Ibn Farḥūn, 1421/2001.

Āl Khunayn, ʿAbd Allāh bin Muḥammad. "Marjaʿiyyat al-aḥkām al-qaḍāʾiyya." *Majallat al-ʿAdl* 22 (1425/2004): 224–25.

Āl Khunayn, ʿAbd Allāh bin Muḥammad. *Al-Madkhal ilā fiqh al-murāfaʿāt*. Riyadh: Dār Ibn Farḥūn, 1431/2010.

Āl Khunayn, ʿAbd Allāh bin Muḥammad. *Al-Kāshif fī sharḥ niẓām al-murāfaʿāt al-sharʿiyya al-saʿūdī*. Riyadh: Dār Ibn Farḥūn, 1433/2012.

Āl Khunayn, ʿAbd Allāh bin Muḥammad. "Working paper for the conference ʻAl-Sawābiq al-Qaḍāʾiyya wa-l-Iʿtimād ʿalyha fī al-Qaḍā" (Legal precedents and the reliance on them in the judiciary)" at the Imām Muḥammad bin Saʿūd Islamic University in Riyadh on the 20.11.1434/25.9.2013."

Āl Khunayn, ʿAbd Allāh bin Muḥammad. *Tawṣīf al-aqḍiya fī al-sharīʿa al-islāmiyya*. Riyadh: Dār Ibn Farḥūn, 1434/2014.

Āl Khunayn, ʿAbd Allāh bin Muḥammad. "Ḥaqīqat taghayyur al-fatwā wa-asbābuhu." *Majallat al-Buḥūth al-Islāmiyya* 117 (1440/2019): 17–104.

Al-Kubaysī, Aḥmad. *Al-Wajīz fī sharḥ qānūn al-aḥwāl al-shakhṣiyya wa-taʿdīlātuhu*. Baghdad: Maktabat al-Sanhūrī, 2015.

Al-Majdhūn, Muḥammad. *ʿUlamāʾ wa mufakkirūn ʿarraftuhum*. Riyadh: Dār al-Shawāf, 1992.

Al-Mardāwī. *Al-Inṣāf fī maʿrifat al-rājiḥ fī al-khilāf*. N.p, 1375/1956.

Al-Mawārdī. *Al-Ḥāwī al-kabīr fī fiqh madhhab al-Imām al-Shāfiʿī*. Beirut: Dār al-Kutub al-ʿIlmiyya, 1414/1994.

Al-Mashʿal, ʿAbd al-ʿAzīz bin ʿAbd al-Raḥmān. "Sharṭ al-ijtihād fī man yalī al-qaḍāʾ." *Majallat al-ʿAdl* 34 (1430/2009): 100–28.

Al-Matroudi, Abdul Hakim. *The Ḥanbalī School of Law and Ibn Taymiyyah*. London: Routledge, 2006.

Al-Maymān, Nāṣir bin ʿAbd Allāh. *Al-Nawāzil al-sharʿiyya*. Dammam: Dār Ibn Jawzī, 1430/2009.

Āl Mubārak, Qays bin Muḥammad. "Al-Madhhab al-qaḍāʾī fī al-Saʿūdiyya." In *Al-Niẓām al-ʿadl fī al-Saʿūdiyya*, edited by Muḥammad bin Saʿūd al-Bashr and Manṣūr bin ʿAbd al-Raḥmān al-Ḥaydarī, 278–84. Riyadh: Markaz al-Fikr al-ʿĀlamī, 1436/2010.

Al-Muḥammādī, ʿAbd Allāh bin Aḥmad "Al-Kafāʾa bayna al-zawjayn fī al-nasab wa-taṭbiqātuhu al-qaḍāʾiyya." *Majallat al-ʿAdl* 8 (1422/2001): 20–66.

Al-Mutawwaʿ, ʿĀṣim bin ʿAbd Allāh. *Al-ʿUdūl ʿalā al-qawl al-rājiḥ fī al-futyā wa-l-qaḍāʾ*. Riyadh: Dār al-Maymān, 1439/2018.

Al-Musnad, Muḥammad bin ʿAbd al-ʿAzīz, ed. *Fatāwā islāmiyya*. Riyadh: Dār al-Waṭan, n.d.

Al-Nasāʾī. *Sunan al-Nasāʾī*. Beirut: Maktabat al-Maʿārif li-l-Nashr wa-l-Tawzīʿ, 1421/2001.

Al-Nasafī. *Kanz al-daqāʾiq*. Beirut: Dār al-Bashāʾir, 1432/2011.

Al-Nāṭūr, Khālida Ribḥī, and Muḥammad Aḥmad al-Quḍāh. "Jarīmat al-mutājara bi-l-mukhadirāt min ṣuwar jarīmat al-ifsād fī al-arḍ." *Al-ʿUlūm al-Sharīʿa wa-l-Qānūn* 41, no. 1 (2014): 268–89.

Al-Nawawī. *Rawḍat al-ṭālibīn*. Beirut: Maktab al-Islāmī, 1412/1991.

Al-Qaraḍāwī, Yūsuf. *Madkhal li-dirāsat al-sharīʿa al-islāmiyya*. Beirut: Muʾassasat al-Risāla, 1414/1993.

Al-Qarāfī. *Al-Iḥkām fī tamyīz al-fatāwā ʿan al-aḥkām*. Beirut: Dār al-Bashāʾir al-Islāmiyya, 1416/1995.

Al-Qarāfī. *Al-Furūq: Anwār al-burūq fī anwāʾ al-furūq*. Beirut: Dār al-Kutub al-ʿIlmiyya, 1418/1998.

Al-Qārī, Aḥmad bin ʿAbd Allāh. *Majallat al-aḥkām al-sharʿiyya*. Jeddah: Tiḥāma, 1401/1981.

Al-Qāsim, ʿAbd al-Raḥmān bin ʿAbd al-ʿAzīz. *Al-Islām wa-taqnīn al-aḥkām*. Riyadh: Dār al-Maʾārifa al-Saʿūdiyya, 1977.

Al-Qāsim, ʿAbd al-Raḥmān bin Muḥammad. *Ḥāshiyat al-rawḍ al-murbiʿ sharḥ zād al-mustaqniʿ*. N.p, 1397/1977.

Al-Qāsim, Muḥammad bin ʿAbd al-Raḥmān, ed. *Fatāwā wa-rasāʾil samāḥat al-shaykh Muḥammad bin Ibrāhīm bin ʿAbd al-Laṭīf Āl al-Shaykh*. Mecca: Maṭbaʿat al-Ḥukūma bi-Makka Mukarrama, 1399/1979.

Al-Qudūrī. *Mukhtaṣar al-Qudūrī fī fiqh al-ḥanafī*. Beirut: Dār al-Kutub al-ʿIlmiyya, 1418/1997.

Al-Ramlī. *Nihāyat al-muḥtāj*. Beirut: Dār al-Kutub al-ʿIlmiyya, 1424/2003.

Al-Raṣāʿ. *Sharḥ ḥudūd Ibn ʿArafa*. Beirut: Dār al-Gharab al-Islāmī, 1993.

Al-Saʿdī, ʿAbd al-Raḥmān bin Nāṣir. *Al-Fatāwā al-saʿdiyya*. Riyadh: Maktabat al-Maʿārif, 1402/1982.

Al-Saʿīdī, Muḥammad bin Ibrāhīm. "Ishkāliyat al-taqnīn wa-l-tadwīn." In *Al-Niẓām al-ʿadl fī al-Saʿūdiyya*, edited by Muḥammad bin Saʿūd al-Bashr and Manṣūr bin ʿAbd al-Raḥmān al-Ḥaydarī, 298–311. Riyadh: Markaz al-Fikr al-ʿĀlamī, 1436/2010.

Al-Ṣaghīr, Ṣaghīr bin Muḥammad. "Maʿālim min al-siyāsa al-sharʿiyya ʿand al-ʿalāma Ibn Saʿdī." In *Al-Sijll al-ʿilmī li-muʾtamar al-shaykh al-ʿalāma ʿAbd al-Raḥmān bin Nāṣir al-Saʿdī*, edited by Jāmiʿat al-Qaṣīm, 1938–73. ʿUnayza: Jāmiʿat al-Qaṣīm, 1441/2019.

Al-Ṣanʿānī, Muhammad bin Ismāʿīl. *Subul al-salām sharḥ bulūgh al-marām*. Riyadh: Maktabat al-Maʿārif, 1427/2006.

Al-Sarakhsī. *Al-Mabsūṭ*. Beirut: Dār al-Maʿrifa, 1409/1989.

Al-Shaqafa, Muḥammad bin Bashīr. *Al-Fiqh al-mālikī fī thawbihi al-jadīd*. Damascus: Dār al-Qalam, 1432/2011.

Al-Shinqīṭī. *Nashr al-bunūd ʿalā marāqī al-saʿūd*. UAE: Ṣundūq Iḥyāʾ al-Turāth al-Islāmī, n.d.

Al-Shīrāzī. *Al-Muhadhdhab fī fiqh al-Imām al-Shāfiʿī*. Damascus: Dār al-Qalam, 1413/1996.

Al-Shirbīnī. *Mughnī al-muḥtāj ilā maʿrifat maʿānī alfāẓ al-minhāj*. Beirut: Dār al-al-Kutub al-ʿIlmiyya, 1421/2000.

Al-Shithrī, ʿAbd al-Raḥmān bin Saʿd. *Ḥukm taqnīn al-sharīʿa al-islāmiyya*. Riyadh: Dār al-Ṣamīʿī li-l-Nashr wa-l-Tawzīʿ, 1428/2007.

Al-Shithrī, ʿAbd al-Raḥmān bin Saʿd. *Taqnīn al-aḥkām al-sharīʿa: Tārīkhuhu wa-ḥukmuhu*. Riyadh: Dār al-Tawḥīd li-l-Nashr, 1435/2014.

Al-Shithrī, Muḥammad bin Nāṣir. *Āl al-Shithrī: ʿUlamāʾuhum wa-tārīkhuhum*. Riyadh: Dār al-Ḥabīb, 1430/2009.

Al-Shithrī, Saʿd bin Nāṣir. *Sharḥ al-waraqāt fī uṣūl al-fiqh*. Riyadh: Dār Kunūz Ishbīliyā, 1425/2004.

Al-Tirmidhī. *Jāmiʿ al-Tirmidhī*. Riyadh: Bayt al-Afkār al-Dawliyya, 1424/2003.

Al-ʿUtaybī, Saʿd bin Maṭar. *Maqālāt fī al-siyāsa al-sharʿiyya*. Riyadh: Al-Bayān, 1434/2012.

Al-ʿUtaybī, Saʿd bin Maṭar. *Aḍwāʾ ʿalā al-siyāsa al-sharʿiyya*. Riyadh: Dār al-Alūka, 1434/2013.

Al-ʿUtaybī, Saʿd bin Maṭar. "Khaṣāʾiṣ al-anẓima fī al-Mamlaka al-ʿArabiyya al-Saʿūdiyya." In *Al-Niẓām al-ʿadl fī al-Saʿūdiyya*, edited by Markaz al-Fikr al-ʿĀlamī ʿan al-Saʿūdiyya, 74–101. Riyadh: Markaz al-Fikr al-ʿĀlamī ʿan al-Saʿūdiyya, 1436/2015.

Al-Zayd, Zayd bin ʿAbd al-Karīm. "Maṣādir istimdād al-anẓima al-ʿadliyya." In *Al-Niẓām al-ʿadl fī al-Saʿūdiyya*, edited by Muḥammad bin Saʿūd al-Bashr and Manṣūr bin ʿAbd al-Raḥmān al-Ḥaydarī, 18–39. Riyadh: Markaz al-Fikr al-ʿĀlamī, 1436/2010.

Al-Zuḥaylī, Muḥammad bin Muṣṭafā. *Al-Tanẓīm al-qaḍāʾī fī fiqh al-islāmī wa-taṭbīquhu fī al-mamlaka al-ʿarabiyya al-Saʿūdiyya*. Damascus: Dār al-Fikr, 1402/1982.

Al-Zuḥaylī, Muḥammad bin Muṣṭafā. *Al-Qawāʿid al-fiqhiyya wa-taṭbiqātuhu fī al-madhāhib al-arbaʿa*. Damascus: Dār al-Fikr, 1427/2006.

Al-Zuḥaylī, Wahba. *Juhūd taqnīn al-fiqh al-islāmī*. Beirut: Muʾassasat al-Risāla, 1408/1987.

Al-Zuḥaylī, Wahba. *Al-Fiqh al-islāmī wa-adillatuhu*. Damascus: Dār al-Fikr, 1418/1997.

Ali-Karamali, Shaista, and Fiona Dunne. The Ijtihad Controversy. *Arab Law Quarterly* 9, no. 3 (1994): 238–57.

Amīn, Qāsim. *Taḥrīr al-marʾa*. Cairo: Muʾassasat al-Ḥindāwī, 2016.

Amitai, Reuven. "The Mongol Occupation of Damascus in 1300: A Study of Mamluk Loyalties." In *The Mamluks in Egyptian and Syrian Politics and Society*, edited by Michael Winter and Amalia Levanoni, 21–41. Leiden: Brill, 2004.

Amnesty International. *Amnesty International Global Report: Death Sentences and Executions 2019*. London: Amnesty International, 2020.

Anderson, J.N.D. "Codification in the Muslim World: Some Reflections." *RabelsZ* 30, no. 2 (1966): 241–53.

Anjum, Ovamir. "Islam as a Discursive Tradition: Talal Asad and His Interlocutors." *Comparative Studies of South Asia, Africa and the Middle East* 27, no. 3 (2007): 656–72.

Anjum, Ovamir. *Politics, Law and Community in Islamic Thought: The Taymiyyan Moment*. Cambridge: Cambridge University Press, 2012.

Asad, Talal. *Formations of the Secular*. Stanford: Stanford University Press, 2003.

Asad, Talal. "The Idea of an Anthropology of Islam." *Qui Parle* 17, no. 2 (2009): 1–30.

Bälz, Kilian. "The Secular Reconstruction of Islamic Law: The Egyptian Supreme Constitutional Court and the "Battle over the Veil" in State-Run Schools." In *Legal Pluralism in the Arab World*, edited by Baudouin Dupret, Maurits Berger, and Laila al-Zwaini. The Hague: Kluwer Law International, 1999.

Barakāt, ʿAlī bin Ramaḍān. *Al-Wasīṭ fī sharḥ niẓām al-qaḍāʾ al-saʿūdī al-jadīd*. Riyadh: Maktabat al-Qānūn wa-l-Iqtiṣād, 1433/2012.

Baugh, Carolyn 2013. "Ibn Taymiyya's Feminism?: Imprisonment and the Divorce Fatwās." In *Muslima Theology: The Voices of Muslim Women Theologians*, edited by Ednan Aslan, Marcia Hermansen, and Elif Medeni, Elif. Berlin: Peter Lang, 181–96.

Beccaria, Cesare. *An Essay on Crimes and Punishments*. Albany: W. O. Little & Co, 1872.

Belhaj, Abdessamad. "Law and Order According to Ibn Taymiyya and Ibn Qayyim al-Jawziyya: A Re-Examination of siyāsa sharʿiyya." In *Islamic Theology, Philosophy and Law: Debating Ibn Taymiyya and Ibn Qayyim al-Jawziyya*, edited by Birgit Krawietz and Georges Tamer. Berlin: De Gruyter, 2012.

Berger, Maurits, and Nadia Sonneveld. "Sharia and National Law in Egypt." In *Sharia Incorporated: A Comparative Overview of the Legal Systems of Twelve Muslim Countries in Past and Present*, edited by Jan Michiel Otto. Leiden: Leiden University Press, 2010.

Bernard-Maugiron, Nathalie. "The Judicial Construction of the Facts and the Law: The Egyptian Supreme Constitutional Court and the Constitutionality of the Law on the khulʿ." In *Narratives of Truth in Islamic Law*, edited by Baudouin Dupret, Barbara Drieskens, and Annelies Moors, 241–64. London: I.B. Tauris, 2008.

Bori, Caterina, and Livnat Holtzman. "A Scholar in the Shadow." *Oriente Moderno* 90, no. 1 (2010): 13–44.

Bori, Caterina. "Ibn Taymiyya (14th to 17th Century): Transregional Spaces of Reading and Reception." *Muslim World* 108, no. 1 (2018): 87–123.

Burak, Guy 2019. "Codification, Legal Borrowing and the Localization of 'Islamic law.'" In *Routledge Handbook of Islamic Law*, edited by Khaled Abou El Fadl, Ahmad Atif Ahmad, and Said Fares Hassan, 389–99. London: Routledge.

Calder, Norman. "Al-Nawawī's Typology of Muftīs and Its Significance for a General Theory of Islamic Law." *Islamic Law and Society* 3, no. 2 (1996): 137–64.

Canale, Damiano. "The Many Faces of the Codification of Law in Modern Continental Europe." In *A History of the Philosophy of Law in the Civil Law World, 1600–1900*, edited by Damiano Canale, Paolo Grossi, and Hasso Hofmann, 135–83. New York: Springer, 2009.

Caroni, Pio. *Gesetz und Gesetzbuch: Beiträge zu einer Kodifikationsgeschichte*. Basel: Helbing & Lichtenhahn, 2003.

Charlow, Andrea. "Awarding Custody: The Best Interests of the Child and Other Fictions." *Yale Law & Policy Review* 5 (1986): 267–90.

Clarke, Morgan. "The Judge as Tragic Hero." *American Ethnologist* 39, no. 1 (2012): 106–21.

Commins, David. *The Wahhabi Mission and Saudi Arabia*. London: I.B. Tauris, 2006.

Cook, Michael. *Forbidding Wrong in Islam: An Introduction*. Cambridge: Cambridge University Press, 2003.

Denker, Hendrik. "Die Wiedereinführung des ḫulʿ und die Stärkung der Frauenrechte." In *Leipziger Beiträge zum Islamischen Recht IV*, edited by Silvia Tellenbach and Thoralf Hanstein, 125–209. Frankfurt am Main: Lang, 2004.

Derrida, Jacques. "The 'Mystical Foundation of Authority.'" In *Deconstruction and the Possibility of Justice*, edited by Drucilla Cornell, Michel Rosenfeld, and David Carlson, 3–67. New York: Routledge, 1992.

Encyclopedia of Islam, Second Edition. Article "Al-Bahūtī." Available online: dx.doi.org/10.1163/1573-3912_islam_SIM_1079.

Encyclopedia of Islam, Second Edition. Article "Kānūn." Available online: dx.doi.org/10.1163/1573-3912_islam_COM_0439.

Encyclopedia of Islam, Second Edition. Article "Siyāsa." Available online: dx.doi.org/10.1163/1573-3912_islam_COM_1096.

Ebert, Hans-Georg. *Die Qadrî-Pâshâ-Kodifikation*. Frankfurt am Main: Peter Lang, 2010.

El-Alami, Dawoud. "Remedy or Device? The System of Khul' and the Effects of its Incorporation into Egyptian Personal Status Law." *Yearbook of Islamic and Middle Eastern Law* 6 (1999): 134–39.

El-Rouayheb, Khaled. "From Ibn Hajar al-Haytami (d. 1566) to Khayr al-Din al-Alusi (d. 1899): Changing Views of Ibn Taymiyya amongst Sunni Islamic Scholars." In *Ibn Taymiyya & His Times*, edited by Shahab Ahmed and Yossef Rapoport, 269–318. Karachi: Oxford University Press, 2010.

Ellethy, Yaser. *Islam, Context, Pluralism and Democracy: Classical and Modern Interpretations*. London: Routledge, 2015.

Elrod, Linda, and Milfred Dale. "Paradigm Shifts and Pendulum Swings in Child Custody: The Interests of Children in the Balance." *Family Law Quarterly* 42, no. 3 (2008): 381–418.

Emon, Anver. "Codification and Islamic Law: The Ideology Behind a Tragic Narrative." *Middle East Law and Governance* 8 (2016): 275–309.

Engelcke, Dörthe, Dominik Krell, and Nadjma Yassari. "Underage Marriage: Legal and Social Practice in Muslim Jurisdictions." *Arab Law Quarterly* (forthcoming).

Fadel, Mohammad. "The Social Logic of Taqlīd and the Rise of the Mukhtaṣar." *Islamic Law and Society* 3, no. 2 (1996): 193–233.

Fadel, Mohammad. "Reinterpreting the Guardian's Role in the Islamic Contract of Marriage: The Case of the Maliki School." *Journal of Islamic Law* 3, no. 1 (1998): 1–26.

Fawzy, Essam. "Muslim Personal Status Law in Egypt: The Current Situation and Possibilities of Reform through Internal Initiatives." In *Women's Rights and Islamic Family Law: Perspectives on Reform*, edited by Lynn Welchman, 30–45. London: Zed Books, 2004.

Fuchs, Ernst. *Was will die Freirechtsschule*. Rudolstadt: Greifenverlag, 1929.

Gläser, Mathias. *Lehre und Rechtsprechung im französischen Zivilrecht des 19. Jahrhunderts*. Frankfurt am Main: Vittorio Klostermann, 1996.

Griffel, Frank. "What Do We Mean by 'Salafī'? Connecting Muḥammad ʿAbduh with Egypt's Nūr Party in Islam's Contemporary Intellectual History." *Die Welt des Islams* 55, no. 2 (2015): 186–220.

Griffiths, John. "What is Legal Pluralism?" *Journal of Legal Pluralism* 24 (1986): 1–55.

Haj, Samira. "Reordering Islamic Orthodoxy: Muḥammad ibn ʿAbdul Wahhāb." *Muslim World* 92, no. 3–4 (2002): 333–70.

Hallaq, Wael. "Was the Gate of Ijtihad Closed?" *International Journal of Middle East Studies* 16, no. 1 (1984): 3–41.

Hallaq, Wael. "Can the Shariʿa Be Restored?" In *Islamic Law and the Challenges of Modernity*, edited by Yvonne Yazbeck Haddad and Barbara Freyer Stowasser, 21–53. New York: AltaMira, 2004.

Hallaq, Wael. *An Introduction to Islamic Law*. Cambridge: Cambridge University Press, 2009.

Hallaq, Wael. *Sharīʿa: Theory, Practice, Transformations*. Cambridge: Cambridge University Press, 2009.

Ḥamdī, Muḥammad bin Muḥammad. *Al-Mutūn al-fiqhiyya wa-ṣilatuha bi-taqnīn al-fiqh*. Jeddah: Dār al-Bilād li-l-Ṭabāʿa wa-l-Nashr, 1421/2000.

Ḥamza, Fuʾād. *Al-Bilād al-ʿarabiyya al-saʿūdiyya*. Riyadh: Maktabat al-Naṣr al-Ḥadītha, 1355/1968.

Hourani, Albert. *Arabic Thought in the Liberal Age, 1798–1939*. Cambridge: Cambridge University Press, 1983.

Ibn ʿĀbidīn. *Radd al-muḥtār ʿalā al-darr al-mukhtār*. Beirut: Dār ʿĀlam al-Kutub, 1423/2003.

Ibn ʿAbd al-Barr. *Al-Intiqāʾ fī faḍāʾil al-thalātha al-aʾimma al-fuqahāʾ*. Cairo: Maktabat al-Quds, 1350/1931.

Ibn ʿUthaymīn, Muḥammad bin Ṣāliḥ. *Izālat al-sitār ʿan al-jawāb al-mukhtār li-hadāyat al-muḥtār*. N.p., n.d.

Ibn ʿUthaymīn, Muḥammad bin Ṣāliḥ. *Tashīl al-Farāʾiḍ*. Riyadh: Dār al-Ṭayba, 1404/1983.

Ibn ʿUthaymīn, Muḥammad bin Ṣāliḥ. *Sharḥ al-arbaʿīn al-nabawiyya*. Dār al-Thurayyā, 1425/2004.

Ibn ʿUthaymīn, Muḥammad bin Ṣāliḥ. *Sharḥ kitāb al-siyāsa al-sharʿiyya li-shaykh al-islām Ibn Taymiyya*. Beirut: Dār Ibn Ḥazm, 1425/2004.

Ibn ʿUthaymīn, Muḥammad bin Ṣāliḥ. *Al-Taʿlīq ʿalā al-siyāsa al-sharʿiyya fī iṣlāḥ al-rāʿī wa-l-raʿiyya*. ʿUnayza: Madār al-Waṭan, 1427/2006.

Ibn ʿUthaymīn, Muḥammad bin Ṣāliḥ. *Al-Sharḥ al-mumtiʿ ʿalā zād al-mustaqniʿ*. Dammam: Dār Ibn al-Jawzī, 1428/2007.

Ibn al-ʿArabī. *Aḥkām al-Qurʾān*. Beirut: Dār al-Kutub al-ʿIlmiyya, n.d.

Ibn Qāsim, ʿAbd al-Raḥmān bin Muḥammad. *Al-Durar al-saniyya fī al-ajwiba al-najdiyya*. N.p., 1417/1996.

Ibn al-Qayyim. *Al-Ṭuruq al-ḥukmiyya fī al-siyāsa al-sharʿiyya*. Beirut: Dār al-Kutub al-ʿIlmiyya, 1415/1995.

Ibn al-Qayyim. *Iʿlām al-muwaqqiʿīn ʿan rabb al-ʿālamīn*. Beirut: Dār al-Kutub al-ʿIlmiyya, 1425/2004.

Ibn al-Qayyim. *Zād al-maʿād fī hadī khayr al-ʿibād*. Cairo: Dār al-Āfāq al-ʿArabiyya, 1428/2007.

Ibn Bāz, ʿAbd al-ʿAzīz bin ʿAbd Allāh. *Al-Adilla al-naqliyya wa-l-ḥissiyya ʿalā imkān al-ṣuʿūd ilā al-kawākib wa-ʿalā jarayān al-shams wa-l-qamr wa-sukūn al-arḍ*. Riyadh: Maktabat al-Riyāḍ al-Ḥadītha, 1982.

Ibn Bāz, ʿAbd al-ʿAzīz bin ʿAbd Allāh. *Majmūʿ fatāwā wa-maqālāt mutanawwiʿa*. Riyadh: Dār al-Qāsim, 1420/1999.

Ibn Ḥajāj. *Ṣaḥīḥ Muslim*. Riyadh: Dār Ṭayba li-l-Nashr wa-l-Tawzīʿ, 1427/2006.

Ibn Ḥamdān. *Ṣifat al-fatwā wa-l-muftī wa-l-mustaftī*. Damascus: Al-Maktab al-Islāmī, 1380/1960.

Ibn Ḥazm. *Al-Muḥallā bi-l-athār*. Beirut: Dār al-Kutub al-ʿIlmiyya, 1425/2003.

Ibn Mājah. *Sunan Ibn Mājah*. Cairo: Dār Iḥyāʾ al-Kutub al-ʿArabiyya, n.d.

Ibn Manṣūr. *Kitāb al-sunan*. Mumbai: Al-Dār al-Salafiyya, 1403/1982.

Ibn Mufliḥ/Al-Mardāwī/Al-Baʿlī. *Kitāb al-furūʿ wa-maʿhu taṣḥīḥ al-furūʿ wa-ḥāshiyyat Ibn Qaldas*. Beirut: Muʾassasat al-Risāla, 1424/2003.

Ibn al-Mundhir. *Al-Ijmāʿ*. Ajmān: Maktabat al-Furqān, 1420/1999.

Ibn Nujaym. *Al-Baḥr al-rāʾiq sharḥ kanz al-daqāʾiq*. Beirut: Dār al-Kutub al-ʿIlmiyya, 1434/2013.

Ibn Qudāma. *Al-Mughnī*. Beirut: Dār ʿĀlam al-Kutub, 1417/1997.

Ibn Rushd. *Bidāyat al-mujtahid wa-nihāyat al-muqtaṣid*. Cairo: Maktabat Ibn Taymiyya, 1415/1994.

Ibn Taymiyya. *Al-Siyāsa al-sharʿiyya fī iṣlāḥ al-rāʿī wa-l-raʿiyya*. Riyadh: Wizārat al-Shuʾūn al-Islāmiyya, 1419/1998.

Ibn Taymiyya. *Majmūʿat al-fatāwā*, 1432/2011. Beirut: Dār Ibn Ḥazm.

Ibrahim, Ahmed Fekry. *Pragmatism in Islamic Law: A Social and Intellectual History*. Syracuse: Syracuse University Press, 2015.

Ibrahim, Ahmed Fekry. *Child Custody in Islamic Law: The Best Interests of the Child in Theory and Practice: Egypt 1517–2014*. Cambridge: Cambridge University Press, 2018.

Jackson, Sherman. *Islamic Law and the State: The Constitutional Jurisprudence of Shihāb al-Dīn al-Qarāfī*. Leiden: Brill, 1996.

Jackson, Sherman. "Domestic Terrorism in the Islamic Legal Tradition." *Muslim World* 91 (2001): 293–310.

Jacobs, Struan. "Edward Shils' Theory of Tradition." *Philosophy of the Social Sciences* 37, no. 2 (2007): 139–62.

Jawfān, Nāṣir bin Muḥammad. "Istiqlāl al-qaḍāʾ fī al-Mamlaka al-ʿArabiyya al-Saʿūdiyya." *Majallat al-ʿAdl* 1 (1420/1999): 143–65.

Johansen, Baber. *Contingency in a Sacred Law: Legal and Ethical Norms in the Muslim Fiqh*. Leiden: Brill, 1999.

Johansen, Baber. "Signs as Evidence: The Doctrine of Ibn Taymiyya (1263–1328) and Ibn Qayyim al-Jawziyya (d. 1351) on Proof." *Islamic Law and Society* 9, no. 2 (2002): 168–93.

Johansen, Baber. "A Perfect Law in an Imperfect Society: Ibn Taymiyya's Concept of 'Governance in the Name of the Sacred Law.'" In *The Law Applied: Contextualizing the Islamic Shariʿa*, edited by Peri Bearman, Wolfhart Heinrichs, and Bernard Weiss, 259–94. London: I.B. Tauris, 2008.

Jokisch, Benjamin. "Ijtihād in Ibn Taymiyya's Fatāwā." In *Islamic Law: Theory and Practice*, edited by Robert Gleave and Eugenia Kermeli, 119–37. London: I.B. Tauris, 1997.

Jokisch, Benjamin. *Islamic Imperial Law: Harun Al-Rashid's Codification Project*. Berlin: Walter de Gruyter, 2007.

Kéchichian, Joseph. *Legal and Political Reforms in Saʿudi Arabia*. London: Routledge, 2013.

Krell, Dominik. "Saudi Arabia." In *Filiation and the Protection of Parentless Children: Towards a Social Definition of the Family in Muslim Jurisdictions*, edited by Nadjma Yassari, Lena-Maria Möller, and Marie-Claude Najm, 299–323. The Hague: T.M.C. Asser, 2019.

Krell, Dominik. "Die Reform der Loskaufscheidung (*ḫulʿ*): Lehren aus Saudi-Arabien." *Die Welt des Islams* 60, no. 4 (2020): 408–32.

Krell, Dominik. “Was kann man von Saudi-Arabien für die Entwicklung des islamischen Familienrechts in Europa lernen?” In *Migration und Heimatrecht*, edited by Irene Schneider, Hatem Elliesie, and Silvia Tellenbach, 93–118. Wiesbaden: Harrassowitz, 2022.

Krell, Dominik. “The Role of Jurists in Contemporary Islamic Family Law.” *Arab Law Quarterly* (forthcoming).

Krell, Dominik. “Codification and the Legacy of Islamic Jurisprudence.” *Oriente Moderno* (forthcoming).

Krygier, Martin. “Law as Tradition.” *Law and Philosophy* 5, no. 2 (1986): 237–62.

Lacroix, Stephane. “Al-Albani’s Revolutionary Approach to Hadith.” *ISIM Review* 21 (2008): 6–7.

Lahusen, Benjamin. *Alles Recht geht vom Volksgeist aus*. Berlin: Nicolai, 2013.

Lanci, Michael. “The Child’s Best Interests? Rethinking Consideration of Physical Disability in Child Custody Disputes.” *Columbia Law Review* 118, no. 3 (2018): 875–914.

Lambton, Ann. *State and Government in Medieval Islam*. London: Routledge, 1981.

Laoust, Henri. *Le Traité de Droit Public d’Ibn Taymiyya*. Beirut: Institut Français de Damas, 1948.

Lauzière, Henri. “The Construction of Salafiyya: Reconsidering Salafism from the Perspective of Conceptual History.” *International Journal of Middle East Studies* 42, no. 3 (2010): 369–89.

Lauzière, Henri. *The Making of Salafism: Islamic Reform in the Twentieth Century*. New York: Columbia University Press, 2015.

Layish, Aharon. “The Transformation of the Sharīʿa from Jurists’ Law to Statutory Law in the Contemporary Muslim World.” *Die Welt des Islams* 44, no. 1 (2004): 85–113.

Lewis, Bernard. *Political Words and Ideas in Islam*. Princeton: Markus Wiener, 2008.

Little, Donald. “Did Ibn Taymiyya Have a Screw Loose?” *Studia Islamica* 41 (1975): 93–111.

Lombardi, Clark. *State Law as Islamic Law in Modern Egypt: The Incorporation of the Sharīʿa into Egyptian Constitutional Law*. Leiden: Brill, 2006.

Lombardi, Clark. “The Constitution as Agreement to Agree: The Social and Political Foundations (and Effects) of the 1971 Egyptian Constitution.” In *Social and Political Foundations of Constitutions*, edited by Denis Galligan and Mila Versteeg, 398–431. Cambridge: Cambridge University Press, 2013.

Luhmann, Niklas. *Law as a Social System*. Oxford: Oxford University Press, 2004.

Mahmood, Saba. *Politics of Piety: The Islamic Revival and the Feminist Subject*. Princeton: Princeton University Press, 2005.

Maimanī, Wajnāt bin ʿAbd al-Raḥīm. “Li-man al-ḥaḍāna?” *Majallat Jāmiʿa ʾUmm al-Qurā* 14, no. 27 (1424/2003): 369–97.

Maisel, Sebastian. “The New Rise of Tribalism in Saudi Arabia.” *Nomadic Peoples* 18, 2 (2014): 100–22.

Mallat, Chibli. "The Normalization of Saudi Family Law." *EJIMEL* 5 (2017): 1–27.

Mallat, Chibli. *The Normalization of Saudi Law*. Oxford: Oxford University Press, 2022.

Masud, Muhammad Khalid, Rudolph Peters, and David Powers. "Qāḍīs and Their Courts: An Historical Survey." In *Dispensing Justice in Islam: Qadis and their Judgments*, edited by Muhammad Khalid Masud, Rudolph Peters, and David Powers, 1–44. Leiden: Brill, 2006.

Markaz al-Buḥūth. *Majmūʿat al-aḥkām al-qaḍāʾiyya li-ʿām 1434*. Riyadh: Markaz al-Buḥūth, 1436/2015.

Markaz al-Buḥūth. *Majmūʿat al-aḥkām al-qaḍāʾiyya li-ʿām 1435*. Riyadh: Markaz al-Buḥūth, 1438/2017.

Markaz al-Buḥūth. *Al-Mabādiʾ wa-l-qarārāt al-ṣādira min al-hayʾa al-qaḍāʾiyya al-ʿulyā wa-l-hayʾa al-dāʾima wa-l-ʿāmma bi-majlis al-qaḍāʾ al-ʿālā wa-l-maḥkama al-ʿulyā min ʿām 1391 ilā ʿām 1437*. Riyadh: Markaz al-Buḥūth, 1438/2017.

Melchert, Christopher. *The Formation of the Sunni Schools of Law, 9th–10th Centuries C.E.* Leiden: Brill, 1997.

Melchert, Christopher. *Ahmad ibn Hanbal*. Oxford: Oneworld Publications, 2006.

Messick, Brinkley. *The Calligraphic State: Textual Domination and History in a Muslim Society*. Berkeley: University of California Press, 1996.

Messick, Brinkley. *Sharīʿa Scripts: A Historical Anthropology*. New York: Columbia University Press, 2018.

Möller, Lena-Maria. *Die Golfstaaten auf dem Weg zu einem modernen Recht für die Familie*. Tübingen: Mohr Siebeck, 2015.

Mollnau, Karl. "The Contributions of Savigny to the Theory of Legislation." *American Journal of Comparative Law* 37, no. 1 (1989): 81–93.

Mouline, Nabil. *The Clerics of Islam: Religious Authority and Political Power in Saudi Arabia*. Yale: Yale University Press, 2014.

Moussa, Jasmine. *Competing Fundamentalisms and Egyptian Women's Family Rights: International Law and the Reform of Sharīʿa-Derived Legislation*. Leiden: Brill, 2011.

Moussa, Jasmine. "Egypt." In *Parental Care and the Best Interests of the Child in Muslim Countries*, edited by Yassari, Möller, and Gallala-Arndt, 1–28. The Hague: T.M.C. Asser, 2017.

Munir, Muhammad. "Triple Ṭalāq in One Session: An Analysis of the Opinions of Classical Medieval and Modern Muslim Jurists under Islamic Law." *Arab Law Quarterly* 27 (2013): 29–49.

Nakissa, Aria. "An Epistemic Shift in Islamic Law: Educational Reform at al-Azhar and Dār al-ʿUlūm." *Islamic Law and Society* 21 (2014): 209–51.

Naseem, Sana, and Kamini Dhruva. "Issues and Challenges of Saudi Female Labor Force and the Role of Vision 2030: A Working Paper." *International Journal of Economics and Financial Issues* 7, no. 4 (2017): 23–27.

Oberauer, Norbert. *Religiöse Verpflichtung im Islam: Ein ethischer Grundbegriff und seine theologische, rechtliche und sozialgeschichtliche Dimension*. Würzburg: Ergon, 2004.

Oberauer, Norbert. *Islamisches Wirtschafts- und Vertragsrecht: Eine Einführung*. Würzburg: Ergon, 2017.

Oberauer, Norbert. "Wahrheitssuche und 'Mut zur Hölle': Zum Problem juristischen Entscheidens im Islam." In *Religion und Entscheiden: Historische und kulturwissenschaftliche Perspektiven*, edited by Wolfram Drews, Ulrich Pfister, and Martina Wagner-Egelhaaf, 142–62. Baden-Baden: Ergon, 2018.

Opwis, Felicitas. *Maṣlaḥa and the Purpose of the Law: Islamic Discourse on Legal Change from the 4th/10th to 8th/14th Century*. Leiden: Brill, 2010.

Ogorek, Regina. *Richterkönig oder Subsumtionsautomat? Zur Justiztheorie im 19. Jahrhundert*. Frankfurt am Main: Vittorio Klostermann, 1986.

Ostrorog, Count Léon. *The Angora Reform: Three Lectures Delivered at the Centenary Celebrations of University College*. London: University of London Press, 1927.

Peters, Rudolph. *Crime and Punishment in Islamic Law: Theory and Practice from the Sixteenth to the Twenty-first Century*. Cambridge: Cambridge University, 2005.

Peters, Rudolph. "From Jurists' Law to Statute Law or What Happens When the Shari'a is Codified." *Mediterranean Politics* 7, no. 3 (2007): 82–95.

Powers, David. "On Judicial Review in Islamic Law." *Law & Society Review* 25, no. 2 (1992): 315–42.

Powers, David. "Kadijustiz or Qāḍī-Justice? A Paternity Dispute from Fourteenth-Century Morocco." *Islamic Law and Society* 1, no. 3 (1994): 332–66.

Rapoport, Yossef. *Marriage, Money, and Divorce in Medieval Islamic Society*. Cambridge: Cambridge University Press, 2005.

Rehman, Javaid. "The Sharia, Islamic Family Laws and International Human Rights Law: Examining the Theory and Practice of Polygamy and Talaq." *International Journal of Law, Policy and the Family* 21, no. 1 (2007): 108–27.

Rohe, Mathias. *Das islamische Recht: Geschichte und Gegenwart*. München: Beck, 2009.

Rosenthal, Franz. *The Herb: Hashish versus Medieval Muslim Society*. Leiden: Brill, 1971.

Rückert, Joachim, and Thomas Duve. *Savigny international*. Frankfurt am Main: Klostermann, 2015.

Rubin, Avi. "Modernity as a Code: The Ottoman Empire and the Global Movement of Codification." *Journal of the Economic and Social History of the Orient* 59 (2016): 828–56.

Safar, Ḥasan bin Muḥammad. "Taqnīn aḥkām al-sharīʿa fī al-tajruba al-islāmiyya." *Majallat al-Qaḍāʾiyya* 3 (1433/2012): 88–114.

Samin, Nadav. "Kafāʾa fī l-Nasab in Saudi Arabia: Islamic Law, Tribal Custom, and Social Change." *Journal of Arabian Studies* 2, no. 2 (2012): 109–26.

Samin, Nadav. *Of Sand or Soil: Genealogy and Tribal Belonging in Saudi Arabia.* Princeton: Princeton University Press, 2015.

Schacht, Joseph. *An Introduction to Islamic Law.* Oxford: Clarendon, 1982.

Schneewind, Jerome. "MacIntyre and the Indispensability of Tradition." *Philosophy and Phenomological Research* 51, no. 1 (1991): 165–68.

Schweitzer, Elisa. "Zum Straftatbestand der Kindesmisshandlung: Ein Blick auf die Rechtspraxis in Saudi-Arabien." *Zeitschrift für Recht & Islam* 11 (2019): 113–44.

Schwoerer, Julius. "Die Rechtsprechung des BGH zu § 74 EheG." *JuristenZeitung* 8, no. 1/2 (1953): 15–19.

Shaʿīshaʿ, Fādī bin Muḥammad. *Al-Tanẓīm al-qaḍāʾī al-jadīd fī al-Mamlaka al-ʿArabiyya al-Saʿūdiyya.* Riyadh: Maktabat al-Rushd, 1435/2014.

Shaltūt, Maḥmūd. *Al-Islām: ʿAqīda wa-sharīʿa.* Cairo: Dār al-Shurūf, 2001.

Shams, Maḥmūd Zakī. *Ijtihādāt al-hayʾa al-ʿāmma li-maḥkamat al-naqḍ.* Damascus: Maṭbaʿat al-Dāwūdī, 2008.

Shapiro, Martin. *Islam and Appeal. California Law Review* 68, no. 2 (1980): 350–81.

Sheikh, Mustapha, and Tajul Islam. "Islam, Alcohol, and Identity: Towards a Critical Muslim Studies Approach." *ReOrient* 3, no. 2 (2018): 185–211.

Sonneveld, Nadia. *Khulʿ Divorce in Egypt: Public Debates, Judicial Practices, and Everyday Life.* Cairo: American University in Cairo Press, 2012.

Steinberg, Guido. *Religion und Staat in Saudi-Arabien: Die wahhabitischen Gelehrten 1902–1953.* Würzburg: Egon Verlag, 2002.

Syed, Mairaj. "Ijmāʿ." In *The Oxford Handbook of Islamic Law*, edited by Anver Emon and Ahmed Rumee, 271–98. Oxford: Oxford University Press, 2018.

Traboulsi, Samer. "An Early Refutation of Muḥammad ibn ʿAbd al-Wahhāb's Reformist Views." *Die Welt des Islams* 42, no. 3 (2002): 373–415.

Trubek, David. *Max Weber on Law and the Rise of Capitalism.* Wisconsin Law Review 720 (1972): 720–53.

Turner, Bryan. *Weber and Islam.* London: Routledge, 1998.

Von Savigny, Friedrich Carl. *Of the Vocation of Our Age for Legislation and Jurisprudence.* London: Littlewood, 1831.

Vogel, Frank. "The Complementarity of Iftaʿ and Qaḍa: Three Saudi Fatwas on Divorce." In *Islamic Legal Interpretation: Muftis and Their Fatwas*, edited by Muhammad Khalid Masud, Brinkley Messick, and David Powers, 262–69. Harvard: Harvard University Press, 1996.

Vogel, Frank. *Islamic Law and Legal System: Studies of Saudi Arabia.* Leiden: Brill, 2000.

Vogel, Frank. *Saudi Business Law in Practice: Laws and Regulations as Applied in the Courts and Judicial Committees of Saudi Arabia.* Oxford: Hart, 2019.

Wāfī, Maḥmūd bin ʿAlī. *Al-Qaḍāʾ al-ʿāmm fī al-Mamlaka al-ʿArabiyya al-Saʿūdiyya.* Riyadh: Maktabat al-Rushd, 1436/2015.

Wapler, Friederike. *Kinderrechte und Kindeswohl.* Tübingen: Mohr Siebeck, 2015.

Warshak, Richard. "Parenting by the Clock: The Best-Interest-of-the-Child Standard, Judicial Discretion, and the American Law Institute's 'Approximation Rule.'" *University of Baltimore Law Review* 41, no. 1 (2011): 83–164.

Watt, Montgomery. "The Closing of the Door of Iǧtihād." *Orientalia Hispanica* 1 (1974): 675–78.

Weber, Max. *Economy and Society*. Berkeley: University of California Press, 1978.

Weber, Max. *Wirtschaft und Gesellschaft*. Tübingen: Mohr Siebeck, 2010.

Weiss, Bernard. "Interpretation in Islamic Law: The Theory of Ijtihad." *American Journal of Comparative Law* 26, no. 2 (1978): 199–212.

Welchman, Lynn. *Women and Muslim Family Laws in Arab States: A Comparative Overview of Textual Development and Advocacy*. Amsterdam: Amsterdam University Press, 2007.

Wiktorowicz, Quintan. "Anatomy of the Salafi Movement." *Studies in Conflict & Terrorism* 29 (2006): 207–39.

Wizārat al-Awqāf wa-l-Shu'ūn al-Islāmiyya al-Kuwaitiyya. *Al-Mawsūʿa al-fiqhiyya al-kuwaitiyya*. Kuwait City: Wizārat al-Awqāf wa-l-Shu'ūn al-Islāmiyya al-Kuwaitiyya, 1404/1983.

Wood, Leonard. *Islamic Legal Revival: Reception of European Law and Transformations in Islamic Legal Thought in Egypt, 1875–1952*. Oxford: Oxford University Press, 2016.

Yassari, Nadjma, Lena-Maria Möller, and Imen Gallala-Arndt, eds. *Parental Care and the Best Interests of the Child in Muslim Countries*. The Hague: T.M.C. Asser, 2017.

Yassari, Nadjma. *Die Brautgabe im Familienvermögensrecht: Innerislamischer Rechtsvergleich und Integration in das deutsche Recht*. Tübingen: Mohr Siebeck, 2014.

Zakariyah, Luqman. *Legal Maxims in Islamic Criminal Law: Theory and Applications*. Leiden: Brill, 2015.

Zakī, ʿĀbd al-Barr. *Taqnīn al-fiqh al-islāmī: Al-Mabdaʾ wa-l-manhaj wa-al-taṭbīq*. Qatar: Idārat Iḥyāʾ al-Turāth al-Islāmī, 1407/1986.

Zaman, Muhammad Qasim. "Evolving Conceptions of Ijtihād in Modern South Asia." *Islamic Studies* 49, no. 1 (2010): 5–36.

Zimmermann, Reinhard. "Codification: The Civilian Experience Reconsidered on the Eve of a Common European Sales Law." *European Review of Contract Law* 8, no. 4 (2012): 367–99.

Interviews

Interview with Ibn Khunayn in his house in Riyadh, 1 August 2018 & 24 May 2018.

Interview with Muḥammad Jār Allāh in his office at the Riyadh Court of Appeal, 31 July 2018.

Interview with Ḥamd al-Khuḍayrī in his office at the Riyadh Court of Appeal, 25 July 2018.

Interview with Manṣūr al-Ḥaydarī and Bashār al-Mufadda in the Ministry of Justice in Riyadh, 8 May 2018.

Interview with various lawyers of Manṣūr al-Dhufayrī law firm at the law firm's offices in Riyadh, 13 May 2018.

Interview with Salmān al-Muhaynī in his law firm in Riyadh, 15 May 2018.

Interview with ʿAbd Allāh al-ʿAsaylān in a hotel in Riyadh, 23 July 2018.

Interview with Usāma al-Qaḥṭānī in his office in Riyadh, 15 May 2018.

Interview with Salmān al-Muhaynī in his law firm in Riyadh, 15 May 2018.

Index

Printed in the United States
by Baker & Taylor Publisher Services